Contemporary Analysis in Education Series

Humanities in the Primary School

Edited by
Jim Campbell and Vivienne Little

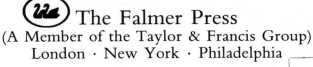 The Falmer Press
(A Member of the Taylor & Francis Group)
London · New York · Philadelphia

UK   The Falmer Press, Falmer House, Barcombe, Lewes, East Sussex, BN8 5DL

USA   The Falmer Press, Taylor & Francis Inc., 1900 Frost Road, Suite 101, Bristol, PA 19007

First published 1989

British Library Cataloguing in Publication Data

Humanities in the primary school. — (Contemporary analysis in education series)
1. England. Schools. Curriculum subjects : Humanities. Curriculum. Development
I. Campbell, Jim II. Little, Vivienne III. Series 001.3'07'1042
ISBN 1–85000–544–3

Jacket design by Leonard Williams

Typeset in 11/13 Bembo by
Bramley Typesetting Limited, 12 Campbell Court, Bramley, Basingstoke, Hants. RG26 5EG

Printed in Great Britain by Taylor & Francis (Printers) Ltd, Basingstoke

Contents

Contents

Dedication

To Alan Blyth, whose work has helped shape the way we think about both primary education and the role of the humanities in it.

General Editor's Preface

Humanities:

A term used to distinguish literature, languages, philosophy, art, theology and music from the Social Sciences and the Natural Sciences. The term originated in Renaissance times, when *Litterae humaniores* signified the humane 'letters of the revived Latin and Greek authors . . .'

Fontana Dictionary of Modern Thought★

The *idea* of the humanities was born in Renaissance Europe and in the nineteenth century became an intrinsic part of the concept of Education. When toward the last third of that century elementary schooling began to be established aspects of the humanities were expected to play their part in the social and moral upbringing of the young and by the turn of the century they were.

It is to achieve goals in the social and moral sphere that is the concern of the humanities though not without those special intellectual capabilities that give meaning to social and moral thought. Without a grounding in the humanities in the primary school the development of the young child would be little more than basic technical training. It is the humanities that provide the meaningful context for much that is taught and learned.

It is in this sense that this reader: *Humanities in the Primary School*, so ably edited by Jim Campbell and Vivienne Little, is to be welcomed. It brings together much current thought about, and makes available examples of, the teaching of the humanities as they seek and find footholds in the changes that are taking place in primary education. The teaching of the humanities is not, perhaps has never been, able to take itself for granted. It has from time to time been under pressure to reassess itself

★*Fontana Dictionary of Modern Thought*, Bullock, A. and Stallybrass, O. (Eds)

and its values. It is the virtue of the many contributors to this book that they have recognized this need and have risen to the challenge.

Philip H. Taylor
University of Birmingham
1989

Editors' Preface

In commissioning articles for this book, we decided on three organizing rules for ourselves and for contributors. First, we wanted the book to examine the principles on which a curriculum in primary school humanities might be based. We were aware of a considerable amount of advice about what to teach in the humanities, and how to organize children's learning in the field. We also know that more advice will be forthcoming from the working groups in history and geography set up by the Secretary of State to develop attainment targets and programmes of study for the National Curriculum. Such advice only makes sense when teachers and other educationalists have clarified to themselves why they want children to learn aspects of the humanities. We hope, therefore, that this book makes a contribution to the discussion about the basic purposes and principles of primary school humanities. It is a discussion that ought not to be sidestepped in the rush to produce specifications of pupil attainment targets and levels for the National Curriculum.

Second, we wanted to use the work of people we knew to have been recently, or to be currently, engaged in research of a kind where theoretical considerations were closely connected to practice in classrooms, and disciplined by consideration of children's responses to curricular demands in the humanities field.

Our third rule was that we should not avoid the political and cultural context of curriculum development in the humanities. For this reason, many of the contributions to this book deal with children's encounters with controversial issues. These include ethnic and gender identities; global and economic awareness; and religious and cultural differences.

A final point should be made explicit, though it is obvious to anyone glancing at the contents page. We have not have attempted comprehensive or balanced coverage of all aspects of humanities, partly because it would not have been feasible in the space, and partly because to attempt it, would have conflicted with our other three rules.

Jim Campbell
Vivienne Little
Department of Education
University of Warwick

Part One
Introduction

Chapter 1

The Humanities in Primary Schools: Principles, Issues and Justifications

Jim Campbell

Introduction

To secure agreement over definitions of humanities is a difficult and normally unproductive task. When the term is applied to the primary school curriculum – and it does not as a term settle easily into primary school discourse – it can lead to arid discussions of what to leave in or out. History and social geography are in, English literature is probably out, but religious education in some aspects is in. Social studies, and topic work, may be included, but only after inspection of what is actually involved in practice. Aspects of sociology, anthropology, archaeology, economics and politics have also been contenders in England and Wales since the late nineteen sixties, (Rogers, 1968; Lawton *et al.*, 1971) and in the United States, (Senesh, 1964) earlier than that.

I would want to argue that the titles of subjects are relatively unimportant, even though they may be signals of symbolic claims to curriculum territory. More important for me are the distinguishing principles of children's learning in the broad field which we call humanities.

The Cognitive and the Affective Dimensions

Learning in the humanities has been associated with two characteristics, one cognitive, the other affective. First, it distinctively focuses upon children's relationship to society, using 'society' to include past societies and societies culturally different from those in which the children live. It was perhaps this feature that encouraged HM Inspectorate (DES, 1978) to designate the field 'the social subjects.' It is from this characteristic that most considerations of content and methods arise.

A second characteristic of the humanities is that they have always been associated with values. In the past, people were urged to study the humanities not merely because thereby they would come to understand their relationship to society, but also because the study involved learning values, being concerned with, according to the Oxford English Dictionary, those 'branches of literature which tend to humanize'. This ancient feature of humanities in university curricula has been retained in most of the forms of humanities that have emerged in the curricula of contemporary primary schools. In its modern forms, the value stance is often procedural, towards evidence, sometimes referred to as 'critical awareness', sometimes 'respect for evidence'. In other forms substantive values such as 'respect for other people', 'co-operation', and 'democratic decision making' emerge as the value orientation. We can see this from a brief consideration of three projects that have been concerned with the field.

The Inner London Education Authority (ILEA, 1980) produced, as part of its overall curriculum guidelines, a booklet, *Social Studies in the Primary School*. It identified the concepts skills and attitudes that should be the basis for this aspect of the curriculum, which, 'is about people and their relationships in society . . . it aims to encourage children's natural curiosity about the social life they experience . . . it is concerned to develop children's critical awareness and understanding. It does this by using their everyday experiences of social life as a starting point, and then . . . the understandings that children have of their immediate world are explored and extended in wider studies.'

It listed as aims:

1 to recognize and value various sources of knowledge about society;
2 to recognize and take into consideration the variety of social life and organization;
3 to develop an enquiring attitude towards how society works;
4 to come to an understanding of other people's views of society.

Like several projects, the ILEA guidelines identified a basic structure of social concepts. They included such sociological ideas as The Distribution of Power and Authority, Division of Labour, Social Control, Conflict and Co-operation; and they stressed the importance of enquiry-based approaches to learning such concepts, calling up drama and role play, discussion groups, interviewing, and quoting an explicit value position:

We educate children in order to change their behaviour by changing their view of the world . . . not so that they will carry out our purposes, but so that they can formulate their own purposes and estimate their value. (Barnes, 1976)

The curriculum project associated with the psychologist Bruner, MACOS, *Man: a Course of Study*, represented the implementation of a particular 'theory of instruction' (Bruner, 1974). It incorporated Bruner's ideas on a spiral curriculum – the idea that children should have recurring encounters with the same concepts and skills, but in increasingly more complex versions. The ideas in the project were largely ideas about society, and it used specially commissioned and visually dramatic material on salmon, herring gulls, baboons, and the Netsilik Eskimo, to provide the curriculum encounters.

This project too, mixed the cognitive and the value dimensions. Bruner argued that the project was not only concerned to help children understand what was distinctive about humans but also about improving society. In his, now unfashionably sexist, terms, the project was about, 'What makes man human? and how can he become more so?'

The third project was the Schools Council Time Place and Society project, developed from a feasibility study (Lawton, *et al.*, 1971) on the possibility of teaching social science-based social studies in the middle years of schooling. *The Place Time and Society, 8-13* project, directed by Blyth at Liverpool, also worked with a collection of social concepts. (Blyth, *et al.*, 1976). Blyth, (1984) in an extension of the work of the project, developing his idea of an 'enabling curriculum', has argued that the four concepts identified by the project – communication, power, values and beliefs, conflict/consensus – are organizing key ideas which overarch lower order concepts such as the family, tribe, peninsula, etc. Their main function is to give direction to curriculum planning, and it is on this basis that their usefulness is to be judged:

> The choice of such concepts is itself problematic, but if they are borne in mind when actual subject matter is chosen and organized, then purpose is imparted to the curriculum process.

In respect of attitudes and values, Blyth notes two that particularly relate to time place and society for young children. One is to do with evidence – 'caution about taking up any rigid point of view or adopting any rigid interpretation'; the other concerns empathy – 'the cognitive and emotional capacity to identify with somebody else and to understand their position as it were from the inside, without adopting or supporting their point of view.'

Transmission and Transformation

There is a third characteristic, which is implicit in most approaches to humanities, and is derived from a combination of the cognitive and affective dimensions, though it is primarily a value position. It is captured in the polarization of two models of teaching and learning about society – 'transmission' and 'transformation.' In the transmission model, the task of the teachers is to identify the important knowledge, skills and understandings about society that children need to learn, and to find ways of transmitting such understandings to them. Assessment in this model would be the relatively simple matter of finding out how well the children could reproduce what had been previously identified as important for them to learn.

In the transformation model the task of the teacher would be to provide learning experiences, evidence, materials, which help the children reconstruct or interpret (transform) them in the light of their own experience, judgments and discussion. In this model the social worlds about which the children are learning are seen as changeable, made by humans, as orderings that might have been, or might be, different. A purpose of the humanities curriculum in this respect is to enable children to envisage such alternative orderings, and even if only by implication, to develop a kind of mental set towards society in which alternative orderings are always on the agenda. Assessment in this model would need to include issues such as the extent to which pupils treated evidence critically, and could develop interpretations in which other possibilities were embodied.

Two points, however, need to be made about the above distinction. First it really is a false polarization. You cannot engage in the second model without being disciplined by the first. Any random or ill-informed alternative invention, which encourages children to ignore evidence, facts, and the discipline of learning what was really the case, in so far as it can be determined, is to trivialize the endeavour. Equally, restricting learning to the first model, other than restrictions consequent upon children's developmental stages, is to work upon the assumption that reproducing received ideas about society is the only purpose for the curriculum in humanities. The two models need to be interdependent. As Rosen (1984) put it, 'Telling what happens demands that some transformation should be imposed upon experience.'

The second point is that it is very important to maintain both models for the National Curriculum. To limit our notions of purpose to the former model, is not merely unnecessarily restricting upon children's potential but is also politically dangerous. If the general framework of learning about society is defined by the State, in terms of programmes of study and attainment targets, the transmission model alone renders all pupils vulnerable to indoctrination. I shall return to this issue below.

Transmission and Transformation in one School

We can see the value of using both models in a topic that was developed with a class of 8–9 year olds in a primary school in the Midlands in 1988. The children had been using the TV series, *How We Used to Live*, as a basis for some work on the Second World War. The classroom was full of realia from the Second World War, much of it lent by grandparents and other relatives of the children; ration books, newspapers, gasmasks, photos, and a range of evidence about particular episodes, for example, the bombing of nearby Coventry. The children's work included writing, drawing and sketching, cooking with recipes of the period, as well as some simple investigations based on oral accounts from people in the school's catchment area.

In addition, and towards the end of the topic, the class produced a presentation for an assembly. Instead of the conventional reporting of their work, the children were asked to produce a simple drama in which the class formed three invented groups, the Mritizis, the Flogmonites, and the Ogglas. The essence of the drama was that the three groups lived near to one another but with different values, styles of organization, methods of food production and economies. They could co-exist happily until there was a shortage of resources.

Thus the Mritizis lived in a dry area, grew lots of turnips, had a leader who was authoritarian, who 'demands that you salute him before you speak to him and anyone who doesn't obey him is locked away in a cage in the village', were short of land, had their own national dance, and chant. The Flogmonites lived in a wet part of the country, grew cabbages, had two leaders, who both had to agree on decisions before any action was taken, and they too had a national dance, and chant. The Ogglas had a lot of land, and were wealthy enough to be able to buy food from the other groups. They had one leader, who had to follow majority votes. They too had a national dance and chant. The drama in the assembly comprised the children miming their various social values and life styles to a commentary by a pupil acting as narrator, and doing their dances and chants. The critical moment comes when the pupils face the audience with choice and dilemma over a dispute, following on from a drought, and the refusal of the Mritizis to sell water to the Flogmonites, and the embryonic emergence of an alliance between the Flogmonites and the Ogglas in order to obtain food and water from the Mritizis:

Narrator: And so the Flogmonites didn't have any water or cabbages, *(point at fields, looking dismayed)* and the Ogglas didn't have any food *(rub tummies)* and the Mritizis didn't have any money *(empty pockets)*

5

This country was not a very nice place to live in. What should they all do?

Katy: In our class we came up with lots of different plans. The problem isn't over yet. Will it end peacefully or will it end up with *War*?

For very young children of course, the concepts and issues are exceedingly complex, perhaps too complex to be resolved in a way that relates to reality as they know it. Thus when I talked to Jane about what she had learned she said of the work that it didn't relate to real disputes:

It was more like a game. You don't have time with your friends – say when you quarrel with your friends, you don't try to sort it out like we did in this. So it's more like a game really.

For Sean, however, the possibility of trying solutions was of considerable interest, both because the solutions could be flexible and change in unplanned ways, and because they gave some pointers to real life conflict resolution. He too acknowledged that in real life things were different from the school work, but made the distinction between solutions when people were already committed to war, and the period beforehand:

But we, like before the assembly, we were rehearsing and we found a way of everyone coming together, not just the Flogmonites and the Ogglas. We saw a way of getting everyone to have what they wanted, but in the assembly we had to say that we (the Mritizis) were still not joining with the others . . . I think that it's the government that wants war but if everyone found, well if everyone said that they wouldn't fight the government would not be able to go to war . . . it would be different if you were at war, like with Hitler, when the war was on I don't think that anything could be done then to change it. You would still have to go war, because he just hated the British and wanted to kill them.

It would be rash to claim too much for one project with one group of children. And it is probable that for most of the class the open–ended drama was somewhat separated from the mainstream part of the topic, which they saw as, and referred to as, history. But the teacher's purpose was important, irrespective of the extent to which it was achieved, perhaps. She was attempting to incorporate into the project the possibility for transformational learning as well as the learning of historical information and historical skills. If there is consistency of purpose in her school as the children progress, they will be learning both about actual social orders and about their potential re-ordering.

rofessional Issues

of humanities outlined above raises five problematic which is sufficiently complex to deserve a chapter to itself. at this stage is to identify them and to sketch in the problematic elements, referring to the ways in which they are taken up in the rest of the book. In the form they are presented here, they may be thought of as an agenda for primary teachers to experiment with, since they are genuinely open to empirical investigation.

This kind of attitude – seeing the curriculum as experimental – will be increasingly important as the National Curriculum comes in, since teachers will be the main source of evidence about whether the attainment targets are appropriate to their children, whether the levels are set appropriately, whether the programmes of study are workable and so on. In addition, the National Curriculum Council has a statutory brief to engage in consultation to keep the curriculum under review, and to make recommendations for its revision where necessary. For all these reasons if for no others it will be important for teachers to have an agenda of problematic issues in respect of every curriculum area.

An agenda for humanities might be as follows and is elaborated below:

1 how children's cognitive linguistic and affective development relates to their ability to manipulate the complex social concepts involved;
2 how, or if, indoctrination can be avoided;
3 how the multi-ethnic dimensions of society can be appropriately incorporated;
4 how far the organization of learning in classrooms needs to be subject specific;
5 how the values represented in the overt humanities curriculum are reflected in the covert curriculum of the school and classroom.

1 Development and Understanding

The first issue is in many ways the most uncertain. The history of the postwar humanities curriculum is a history of a puzzling but persistent mismatch; between the undemanding levels of what teachers in general have thought appropriate to expect of children and the grand ambitions of curriculum projects and semi-official policy. The problem was particularly clearly illustrated in a case study analysis (Skilbeck, 1969) of a BBC radio series, called *Man*. The series was a year-long programme covering evolution, the cultures of Ancient Egypt and the Bushmen of the Kalahari, and life in a contemporary Indian village.

The conceptual framework was demanding; it included cognitive aspects such as the understanding of religious ritual and experience, the extension of mind and muscle through tools and technology, social interdependence, the division of labour, art and language, and child care. On the affective side the programme was intended to evoke sympathetic appreciation of cultural diversity, open-mindedness, empathy and so on. Skilbeck concluded that the eleven year olds that he taught did not reach a stage that he would describe as 'understanding' these concepts, though they became very interested in the topics of the programmes. 'Children very readily became immersed in the foreground and only partly comprehended, where they saw it at all, the background that could help to explain.' (Skilbeck, quoted in Lawton, *et al.*, 1971)

The conclusion to be drawn from such analyses is not that difficult conceptual frameworks should be abandoned in favour of a pragmatic commitment to expecting only what you believe children can cope with; but that such frameworks should be systematically examined by teachers reflecting on children's responses to them. A working hypothesis in this respect is that, on balance, under-expectation has been normal, and the task of teachers is to find better ways of enabling children to achieve depth and quality in the humanities, as they are doing in other areas of the curriculum.

A related issue is the ability of children to 'transform' their understandings, in the sense outlined above. Here too we may have underestimated children' capacities. It is a sub-text to several of the contributors to this volume. Blyth (Chapter 13) points to the relatively sophisticated 'metacognitive self awareness' in social understandings of young children, while Ross (Chapter 7) refers to their ability to 'organize and re-construct' their knowledge. The role of language in this process is of particular concern, both to Campbell (Chapter 10) and to Steedman (Chapter 9) who stresses the importance of children playing around with ideas in writing. As she puts it, 'the script is there, but the children re-write it.'

2 Indoctrination

The issue of indoctrination is especially of interest in the humanities field given that the focus of curriculum content is upon the nature of the social order. To this special interest is added special concern given the age of primary school children, and their general readiness to trust and respond to the authority of the teacher. The conventional analysis of indoctrination, (Snook, 1974) requires that content, teaching method, teacher intentions, and the actual consequences for the children's beliefs, should all be taken into account in attempting to determine whether or not a teacher is engaged in indoctrination.

Useful as this analysis is, however, it has two weaknesses. First, by concentrating upon the activities, intentions and curriculum selections of teachers, it removes the State from the frame of analysis. But in a situation where the ideas about society which children should learn are prescribed by the State, it is important to ask questions about the role of the teacher as a servant of the State. Second, certain kinds of teaching about society have been made illegal by the 1986 Education Act, which prohibits political indoctrination and requires balanced presentation of opposing views. Thus what was previously an interesting but somewhat academic exercise in conceptual analysis has been turned into a professional imperative for teachers in England and Wales. The potentially explosive nature of this professional issue has been demonstrated in the debate on World Studies (Scruton, 1985; Fisher and Hicks, 1985; Hicks, 1982; Hicks, 1985 and Hicks, in this volume). The adoption of a neutral chairman role (Stenhouse, 1971) at primary school level has been advocated to teach children about political conflict (Harwood, 1987). But, given the difficulty secondary teachers and pupils found in adopting the neutral role, it is difficult to see this as a generalized solution, especially with younger primary school children. Marsden (Chapter 6) makes the point about indoctrination extremely sharply in his discussion of the catechitical teaching of geography in the last century, which legitimated the teaching of adverse views of foreign peoples, especially in the colonies. It reflected 'an early politicization of the curriculum, the prime objective being to inculcate prescribed values. The twin thrusts are fundamentalism and nationalism.' His historical analysis of geography teaching serves to remind us that the State has used the curriculum for its own purposes in the past, and alerts us to the easy possibility that it continues to do so in the contemporary situation.

3 Multi-ethnic Dimensions

The multi-ethnic curriculum for a multi-ethnic society has become an officially sponsored ideal in the 1980s in England and Wales. This has happened not only through the suggestions of HM Inspectorate (DES, 1978 and DES, 1985b), but also through the proposals from some of the National Curriculum subject working groups (DES, 1988a and DES, 1988b). The consequence has been to some extent that the debate has become focused upon what kind of values and attitudes such a curriculum should attempt to foster, with distinctions being made between multi-culturalism and anti-racism.

In the humanities field, the issue is twofold. The first concerns the content of the curriculum itself, and is a thread running clearly through most contributions to this book, explicitly in respect of language (Campbell, Chapter 10), cultural studies (Arkell, Chapter 12 and Hicks, Chapter 8), of religious education (Jackson, Chapter 11) and of history and geography (Sylvester, Chapter 2 and Marsden, Chapter 6). The second concerns the cultural backgrounds of the children in any particular school. The most advantaged schools in this sense are those with children from different cultural backgrounds in them, since it is easier to justify multi-ethnic dimensions to the curriculum, and to implement them, through the contributions that children and their parents can make from their experience and cultural histories.

In schools without such advantages the challenges are greater for primary school teachers, whose backgrounds and cultural experiences make the task of curriculum development extremely difficult, unless they are provided with expertise and resources from a specially created support service (David and Campbell, 1988). Without such support, and especially without staff development initiatives, multi-ethnic perspectives risk being confined to saris, samosas and steel bands (Troyna, 1987), and may lead to the reinforcement of stereotyping.

4 Subjects and Integration

The National Curriculum is being established on the basis of a model that uses the term 'subject' as a basic category in its framework. In the humanities field, the most germane subjects are history and geography, in both of which the Secretary of State has established subject working groups to make proposals for attainment targets, and programmes of study. The position however is not as simple as the overall model would suggest. In practice, the working groups have been given a brief to consider cross-curricular themes and links. Moreover, in practice the idea of a 'subject' has turned out to be elastic and elusive. Thus the science working group identified material within its proposals that would conventionally be thought of as health education, home economics and environmental studies, as well as the ubiquitous concern for 'communication'. The English working group included consideration of drama, media studies and information technology. For history or geography groups to define their subjects in a narrowly exclusive manner, would make them out of line with the other groups, as well as out of line with what is commonly thought of as good practice.

Whatever the final proposals from the working groups, the legal position deriving from the 1988 Education Reform Act is that how a school organizes its curriculum is the responsibility of the governing body and the Head. However the practicalities of the situation must push schools towards considering some form of integration. These practicalities include, most forcefully, the time available after the core subjects of mathematics, science and English, which are expected to take just over 50 per cent of time, has been delivered. The remaining time is, for junior pupils, just over twelve hours per week at maximum, assuming quite unrealistically that none of what one local authority (ILEA, 1989) has referred to as 'evaporated time' is counted in. This is for religious education, the other foundation subjects (history, geography, art, PE, music and technology), other non-foundation subjects, and time for non-subject activities like assemblies, registration, and seasonal activities. If a school develops a subject specific approach to each foundation subject, each will be left with the equivalent of around two forty-five minute periods weekly. A sustained approach to work of depth and quality is unlikely to result from such a degree of specialization.

The alternative is not necessarily an all embracing integration, with a series of topics in which a false balance across all subjects has to be created in each topic. A more helpful way forward might be to identify a programme of topics in which only appropriate linking across the curriculum is created, with each topic having a particular emphasis on history, or geography, or environmental science or some other subject. The balance would then be achieved over a period of time – it would have to be at most over the period of a key stage of the National Curriculum – through a whole school agreement about the nature and ordering of the topic programme.

There is no overall evidence that humanities are learned more effectively if the learning is organized in separate subject forms, or that integration is in itself more effective (DES, 1978 and DES, 1985a), and the contributors to this book do not take a common line on this point. What seems commonsense, and has some backing from research into other subjects, is that teachers need to develop the organization that they believe suits their purposes best (Burstall, 1974).

5 The Overt and Covert Curriculum

The fifth issue concerns the degree of harmony between the ideas and values experienced in a study of the humanities, and the ideas and values experienced in the everyday school life of a primary school pupil. The humanities curriculum will typically be concerned with the ways people have related to one another, whether in the family, the locality, or on the larger stage of the nation and the world. It will also be concerned with the ways in which power has been exercised in society, with freedom of expression, the importance of critical alternatives, and with the development of democracy.

For example, children investigating a road widening scheme in their locality might well interview some of the council officials from the Planning Department, and some objectors, and find out both how the objectors were able to express their opposition, and the extent to which the decision-making was democratic. The National Curriculum History Working Group has had as part of its brief to recommend ways of encouraging children to understand how 'a free and democratic society has developed over the centuries.' Moreover, through all the work in humanities, the process requires commitment to being disciplined by evidence, as Blyth argues (Chapter 13).

Thus the field implies not merely that children should learn about democracy, about freedom of expression, about decision making, about respect for evidence; but that the context in which they learn should itself encourage democratic treatment of pupils and staff, develop freedom of expression, involve participation in decision-making, and embody respect for evidence. The idea that there is a common mismatch in primary schools arising from expectations that children should, but that staff need not, work collaboratively, (Alexander, 1985), has been elaborated on by a study of 'reflective teaching' in primary schools, showing the interconnectedness of the overt and covert curriculum most directly (Pollard and Tann, 1987). The authors argue:

> Concepts associated with human rights can, and should, be acquired from an early stage. For example, non-violent resolution of conflict and respect for other people can already be experienced within the life of a pre-school or primary class . . . The study of human rights in schools should lead to an understanding of, and sympathy for, concepts of justice, equality, freedom, peace, dignity, rights and democracy . . . Democracy is best learned in a democratic setting, where participation is encouraged, where views can be expressed openly and discussed, and where there is freedom of expression for teachers and pupils, and where there

is fairness and justice. An appropriate climate is therefore an essential complement to effective learning about human rights.

The issue for teachers here is a twofold one. First that the climate of the school as a whole is not directly in their control, even if the climate of learning in their classroom is. There is a limit upon what they can be expected to be held responsible for. If children in their classrooms learn to work in groups, to listen to one another's opinions, and to value taking turns in discussion and group activity, that is enough to expect. They and their pupils may simply have to live with any mismatch in treatment outside their classroom. Secondly, all teachers do not find the notion of a democratic classroom – an 'incorporative' classroom in Pollard and Tann's terminology – equally attractive or workable. This may be as much to do with what they perceive as the needs of their children as any intrinsic desire to be authoritarian. Whatever the reasons, such teachers are faced with the dilemma that their classroom practice may not match the precepts of their curriculum, and may be seen by pupils as not doing so. As a recent aphorism puts it: 'Democracy is dead unless children learn to take turns' (Thomas, 1989).

Humanities in the National Curriculum: Sources of Justification

The curricula of a nation's schools embody the knowledge that is regarded as too important a selection from culture to be left to chance, or too crucial for power élites to lose control over (Lawton, 1983 and Bernstein, 1975). Those engaged in constructing national curricula in the humanities are in a particularly significant position in this respect since they are creating for the nation a framework of images of the nation itself, (whether of the nation as it was, or as it might be). More eloquently, Inglis (1987) has expressed this view thus:

> The curriculum should be understood as an ensemble of stories told by one generation to the next about what the possibilities are for the future and what it may be going to be like to attempt to live well at the time.

There is a tendency in discussions of curriculum matters to attribute to the curriculum greater potency than the evidence might bear (Musgrove, 1973). Inglis *(op. cit.)* makes the point precisely: 'The most virtuous curriculum in this world would not prevent of itself our being blown into the next one, if those in power had a mind to it.' Even so, the justification of the humanities in the National Curriculum is inescapably tangled up in aspects of political socialization – in deciding on images of the desirable social order that young children should encounter.

From this perspective, the humanities curriculum is dangerous; it can be used on the one hand to promote a state-approved view of the social order, or on the other to subvert such a view through the development of critical awareness. There is nothing intrinsically virtuous about a National Curriculum (White, 1988), or about its constituent parts. The virtue or vice resides in the purposes it serves. In most industrialized societies it has been used to contribute to political socialization. In the Soviet Union it has been used to help in the formation of an approved citizen personality (Avis, 1987); in the United States of America it has been used to help create cultural conformity in a culturally diverse population (Carlson, 1987). The basis for the curriculum in humanities is thus more problematic than in most other curriculum areas.

Three sources of justification have been hinted at in the opening section of this chapter. They are complementary sources and to some extent overlap. They require that we take a position on the following:

1 the nature of the knowledge defined as facts, understandings and skills distinctive to the humanities;
2 the nature of the society and its need for shared, socially cohesive, values and understandings amongst its citizens;
3 the nature of children's development, and their ability to transform their experiences.

The contributors to this book have made explicit the positions that might be held in respect to some or all of these three sources of justification.

First that the knowledge selected for inclusion in the curriculum must be intrinsically worthwhile for its purpose – to help children learn like historians (Sylvester and Little, Chapters 2 and 3), or geographers (Marsden, Chapter 6) or like children in a different religious tradition (Jackson, Chapter 11) and not because it suits some more overtly instrumental purpose of the state.

Second that the society our children are growing up into is linguistically and culturally diverse (Campbell, Chapter 10, Arkell, Chapter 12 and Jackson, Chapter 11) and global in its manifestations (Hicks, Chapter 8) as much as socially and economically differentiated (Ross, Chapter 7 and Steedman, Chapter 9). The images of such a society offered to children through the curriculum in humanities must reflect and respect its variety, not pretend to unreal aspirations for uniformity, British or otherwise. Telling stories of the 'good life' must not come to mean telling lies about it.

Thirdly, and most importantly, the humanities should be justified by the extent to which they enable children to reconstruct the stories we tell them into meanings of their own. The potential here for information technology is only now coming to be realized, as a means of enabling children quite literally to manipulate information and ideas (Wagstaff, Chapter 4). It is in this respect that the processes we encourage become critical and these in turn reflect what counts as worthwhile aspects for assessment (Blyth, Chapter 13).

A National Curriculum in humanities that is designed to serve the alleged or perceived interests of the State at the expense of the interests of the children, outlined above, is thus not only educationally unattractive; it is in the end a contradiction in terms. It will contribute little to children's understanding in the humanities, it will erode commitment to a pluralist society, and in the long run will discourage the development in its youngest members of the critical awareness that will enable it to respond to change. Short-sighted governments may wish for such outcomes from the curriculum, but when or if they do, teachers and other educationists have a moral imperative to re-define its purposes differently. Such re-definition must include the aim of helping children envisage for themselves, to the extent of their developmental abilities, their own social purposes and values. This cannot be done without encountering important skills, facts and knowledge about society; but equally it cannot be done without experiencing a regular sense of their tractability. It is the tractability that may humanize society and the curriculum in which it is reflected.

References

ALEXANDER, R. (1985) *Primary Teaching*, London, Holt Rinehart and Winston.

AVIS, G. (1987) *The Making of the Soviet Citizen*, London, Routledge.

BARNES, D. (1976) *From Communication to Curriculum*, London, Penguin.

BERNSTEIN, B. (1975) *Class Codes and Control, Vol. 3*, London, Routledge & Kegan Paul.

BLYTH, W.A.L. (1984) *Development, Experience and Curriculum in Primary Education*, London, Croom Helm.

BLYTH, W.A.L. *et al.* (1976) *Place, Time and Society 8–13*, Bristol, Collins/ESC.

BRUNER, J. (1974) *Towards a Theory of Instruction*, Harvard, Harvard University Press.

BURSTALL, C. (1974) *Primary French in the Balance*, Windsor, National Foundation for Educational Research.

CARLSON, R.A. (1987) *The Americanization Syndrome*, London, Routledge.

DAVID, P. and CAMPBELL, R.J. (1988a) *Inter-cultural Support Service: an interim report*, University of Warwick, Department of Education.

DES (1978) *Primary Education in England: a survey by HMI*, London, HMSO.
DES (1985a) *Education 8 to 12 in Combined and Middle Schools. An HMI Survey*, London, HMSO.
DES (1985b) *Curriculum Matters 2: The Curriculum from 5–16*, London, HMSO.
DES (1988a) *The National Curriculum: Science for Ages 5 to 16*, London, HMSO.
DES (1988b) *The National Curriculum: English for Ages 5 to 11*, London, HMSO.
FISHER, S. and HICKS, D. (1985) *World Studies 8–13: a teacher's handbook*, Edinburgh, Oliver and Boyd.
HARWOOD, D. (1985) 'We need political not Political Education for 5–13 year olds', *Education 3–13*, 13, 1, 12–17.
HICKS, D. (1982) *Teaching World Studies: an introduction to Global perspectives in the curriculum*, London, Longman.
HICKS, D. (1987) 'World Studies 8–13: Practice and Principles', *Education 3–13*, 15, 2, 51–56.
INGLIS, F. (1985) *The Management of Ignorance*, London, Blackwell.
INNER LONDON EDUCATION AUTHORITY (1980) *Social Studies in the Primary School*, London, ILEA.
INNER LONDON EDUCATION AUTHORITY (1989) 'The National Curriculum: a planning guide for primary schools', London, ILEA.
LAWTON, D. (1983) *Curriculum Studies and Educational Planning*, London, Hodder and Stoughton.
LAWTON, D., CAMPBELL, J. and BURKITT, V. (1971) *Social Studies 8–13*, London, Schools Council, Evans/Methuen.
MUSGROVE, F. (1973) 'Power and the Integrated Curriculum', *Journal of Curriculum Studies*, 5, 1, 3–13.
POLLARD, A. and TANN, S. *Reflective Teaching in the Primary School*, London, Cassell.
ROGERS, V. (1968) *The Social Studies in English Education*, London, Heinemann.
ROSEN, H. (1984) *Stories and Meanings: NATE Papers in English*, London, National Association for the Teaching of English.
SCRUTON, R. (1985) *World Studies: Education or Indoctrination*, London, Institute for European Defence and Strategic Studies.
SENESH, L. (1964) *Our Working World*, Chicago, Science Research Associates.
SKILBECK, M. (1969) 'Man: an enquiry-centred broadcast series for primary school children', Mimeo, University of Bristol, School of Education.
SNOOK, A. (1974) *Indoctrination and Education*, London, Routledge & Kegan Paul.
STENHOUSE, L. (1971) 'The Humanities Project: the Rationale', *Theory into Practice*, X, 3, 154–162.
THOMAS, N. (1989) 'Personally Speaking, *Junior Education*, March.
TROYNA, B. (1987) 'Beyond multiculturalism: towards the enactment of anti-racist education in policy, provision and pedagogy', *Oxford Review of Education*, 13, 307–320.
WHITE, J. (1988) 'Two national curricula – Baker's and Stalin's', *British Journal of Educational Studies*, XXXVI, 3, 218–231.

Part Two
Investigating The Past

Chapter 2

Children as Historians

David Sylvester

Children in groups in a classroom reading extracts from Pepys' diary and marking in on copies of contemporary seventeenth-century maps how the Great Fire sped through London in 1666. Nine-year-old girls dressed as parlour maids in the house and boys dressed as farm labourers in the yard re-enacting the past by working for a day at Cogges Farm, Witney. Children listening to a teacher telling the story of what happened to Charles I. Children in the National Army Museum wearing uniforms and finding out how heavy a rifle is by holding it. Children building in their classroom the houses of North American Indians. Top infants walking round their village of Bloxham, in Oxfordshire and then making a large age-of-buildings map of their visit for display in the school.

This recall of cameos of children as historians could be continued but not infinitely. Though in some schools children enjoy doing history there is a reluctance in many to ensure that children do history even for some of their time in the primary years. History has not figured as a priority for primary teachers.[1]

The reasons schools give for this lack of history seem, on first hearing, plausible enough. 'Children cannot understand time'. 'History is about adults and beyond the minds of children'. 'History is about the past and children live in the present'. 'Children learn holistically and separate studies in history or geography are inappropriate'. 'Why should children do history when anthropology, archaeology, economics, psychology and sociology have equal claims for consideration'?

More considered reflection will show that such reasons will not do. Children cannot understand time in the abstract but they can learn how to handle chronology and by the age of eleven too. Whether adults, let alone children, can understand time in the abstract remains questionable. History is about adults but not wholly so. There were children in the past even as there are adults in the present world which the child inhabits. Children are interested in adults and know that they themselves will grow to be adults. It is true that the present presses its claims for attention on children, as indeed it does on adults, in urgent ways, but this does not mean that children have no interest in the past. Children may learn holistically some but not all of the time and indeed like adults they need to focus on one thing before they can fit it into a wider context.[2] Children need structures to learn and subjects are one way in which such structures may be appropriately and effectively provided. Further, given that time to provide children with a wide range of educational experiences in school is limited, arguments have to be made why some subjects seem more important in the context of the younger school child than others. The question cannot be avoided by contending that children should, of course, do everything. That is not a possibility.

This chapter will try to give good reasons why schools should give children opportunities to do history and be historians. It will deal with the skills and ideas children need to develop to do history and which they will develop as a consequence of doing history. It will also suggest ways in which children need to be taught history if they are to develop these skills and ideas and acquire some historical knowledge and understanding.

Why History?

The case for history must rest on a reasoned consideration of the purposes of schooling and the particular role that history can contribute to their achievement. Though there is not space to argue it here, it would seem reasonable to suggest that the purposes of school are to further children's physical, moral and emotional development, to educate their minds into a breadth of knowledge and to socialize them, that is to introduce them to the ways of life of a society while avoiding indoctrination, (Barrow, 1981). It is in this context that the following reasons for history in school may be recognized as good reasons rather than arbitrary assertions. Young children often display a natural curiosity about where they were born. They are concerned to satisfy a human need to establish their identity, not only in relation to others, but also to time. Such questions may lead to others about the family; where were we living then? what did daddy do? was grandma there? With help it will lead to larger questions but these initial questions are significant pointers.

The reason why schools should enable children to do history is because the past is important to the development of human beings and human societies in ways which are not true for other animal or insect species. History is an essential part of what makes us human. Other creatures cannot consciously discover their past, remember it or use it to build different futures. Humans can and should. In helping children to be historians schools are engaged in a central task of human education. If they fail to do this their products will be less than human as they were in Aldous Huxley's *Brave New World* or Orwell's *1984*. This curiosity which children have about the past is evidenced in other ways. Children aged five to nine are interested in historical things and they have a love of detailed observation. These empirical facts are further reasons why schools should help children to be historians. It is starting where children are.

Secondly, and never to be forgotten, history can be enjoyable. Its main vehicle is story and children respond to stories. History has them all; stories of adventures, mystery, travel, intrigue, villainy, self–sacrifice, pathos and saints and sinners. But, by exposing children to such stories history helps children in their personal development. Young children, as they grow, need to learn to distinguish between people in fact and people in fantasy or literature. The point can be made most poignantly by reference to Father Christmas. To come to realize that he is not a real figure is a shattering experience for many children but it is a necessary stage in human development. It is in this context that talk about a whole range of people, mythical, legendary or historical can help young children develop their perceptions of reality and aid their development as people.

Because it aims to tell the truth about human affairs children doing history learn how this kind of knowledge is acquired and how it differs from knowledge in the sciences. They learn to collect evidence, to sort it and analyze it and to use it to give an account of what humans have done, (Hexter, 1971). In this way they are doing more than history. They are also involved in part of an education for citizenship which is particularly necessary in an age where multi–media present accounts of human affairs in which the truth needs some teasing out.

Doing history can also help children to understand their own present and how it is made from the past. The historical roots, whether of family, locality or nation, help to explain present situations and identities by giving a perspective without which any understanding of the present can at best be only partial. Children need to know what their society is like and what it expects of them, how its culture arose and the cultural differences both within it and without in other contrasting societies. Cultures, religions, institutions and landscapes differ because they are an inheritance from the past and, whether or not the heritage is valued or shared, to understand this is part of what it means to be educated, (Reeves, 1980).

Further, since history aims to identify and understand the thought patterns, assumptions and motivations of other societies in different times and places, doing history contributes to the multi-ethnic education of children.

Again, since it is the only subject in the school curriculum which deals with the *long term* effects of people's decisions, actions and accidents it is a major means of children's political education. On the one hand, it prevents them from being prisoners of their present, of thinking that what is, must be; or that current values are the only ones. On the other hand, it gives some understanding of how change occurs in human societies, revealing that the causes of change in human affairs are never simple or singular but always complex and plural and that the future is for the making.

Doing history also helps in the moral education of the young. Because it is wholly about people, what they have done and why, it raises questions about human intentions, and about the consequences of human action, and the extent to which they were good or evil. History is essentially about man's humanity — or inhumanity — to others. It cannot avoid discussion of moral issues and though it cannot dictate moral judgments it should put children in a position to make their own.

Children doing history cannot escape developing their language skills. Because its method is essentially that of inquiry and because there are few completely right answers, (this is not to suggest that we do not know the dates of events and their main features) history is a matter of talk and discussion. Reading, talking, listening and writing are the methods of history. To deny children this subject in school is, apart from anything else, to limit their opportunities for language development.

In the same way, far from constraining the curriculum, doing history can provide immense opportunities for work with fiction, poetry, art, craft, drama, music and holistic approaches to children's learning in topic work.

Finally, if children become historians they may develop life-long interests in history which will inform and engage both their working and leisure life as adults.

The reasons why children should do history have been rehearsed at length because many teachers are either unaware of them, or indifferent to them. Not all of the reasons given will operate all of the time. Nevertheless taken together they make a convincing case for a subject about which many primary headteachers and teachers have lacked, and still do lack, conviction. There will still be differences of opinion about the priority which should be given to history but there is no longer excuse for not knowing the great potential which there is educationally if children are encouraged to be historians.

What is History?

There is no great mystique about history which makes it difficult to teach or inaccessible to children. It has no jargon: like Wordsworth's poetry it uses 'the language really spoken by men'.[3]

Most teachers, whatever their original main subject, are, with a few moments thought, easily able to say what the main characteristics of history are and what it is about.[4] For example, they quickly agree that it is about people, about change, about causes and about different sources of evidence. The characteristic most often omitted is, surprisingly enough, that of time past and chronology.

It will be useful to gather together common perceptions and to summarize what history is.

1 It is about human events and affairs from the past, as far back in time as we can know it and up to the present. For ease of understanding these events are sequenced chronologically from past to present using various chronological terms, which have been used now for so long that they have become conventions, such as, for example, centuries.

2 Historians commonly ask questions about these human events in terms of their causes and their effects, the extent to which they made for change and development or preserved continuities and consequently, by implication, the ways in which past and present show similarities or differences.

3 In finding out about the past and in trying to reconstruct and understand it, historians have two basic methods. First, they use various sources from the past (artefacts, pictures, maps or documents) as evidence. Secondly, keeping in mind the evidence, they try to empathize with people in the past, using their imagination to enter as far as is possible into the minds, the mentalities, of past people.

Whatever the school timetable may call the activity and whatever the title of the topic, boys and girls are doing history, say as opposed to science or English, when the following characteristics may be observed.

1 When it is about people and what they did — and not about dinosaurs, or transport without the people who used it.

2 When it is set in chronological sequence and related to other events which children have experienced or studied.

3 When it tries to explain how and why *change* occurred.

4 When it asks the question 'How do we know?'

5 When it provides opportunities for children to study historical evidence which includes primary source material (e.g. artefacts, pictures, buildings, documents) as well as secondary source material (e.g. topic books, text books, artists' impressions).

6 When it asks children to imagine what it was like to be people in the past but ensures that imagination is disciplined by evidence so that children become aware of (a) anachronisms, (b) the difference between fantasy and history.

Doing History

What sort of learning environment are children going to need if they are to become enthusiastic about being historians? No special equipment is required; no laboratory has to be built. The ordinary classroom will do but it will need to have some basic historical aids, such as historical topic and reference books and access to a library for others. It will need a visible time-line to which the children can refer, to help them sequence their historical enquiries and findings. It need not always be to scale and certainly it should be about human and historic time and not try to include geological time. As we have seen history is about people and it is confusing to draw time-lines which give more space to geological than human historic time. Time-lines work best when they are produced in school, relate to the children's own experience and historical enquiries and can be added to with pictures and dates as the children's historical work proceeds, (West, 1986).

It will need maps and atlases, and space for display. At some time in the school year, every classroom should also have a museum table, as so often it has a nature table or music corner. Here artefacts, either borrowed from a local museum loan service or brought in by children and teachers, can be used to stimulate historical talk and enquiries. In the same way, there is a need for space to show documents whether original, copied or in facsimile, and a school often has its own log-books as a first point of entry to this process.

If children are to do history they will obviously need to know the chronological conventions which historians use to sequence historical events, the sorts of questions they ask, and the skills needed to sort out sources of evidence and to enable them to gain some measure of empathy with people in the past.

Chronology is basic to history. If a girl turns to a book, reference or otherwise, which says 'In the middle ages' and she has no idea what the term denotes it will hinder her historical enquiries. Or if in a local environmental study, a guide book says 'this is a Georgian house', or in 'Victorian times' or a church guide refers to a Norman doorway or, more confusing still, to a Jacobean pulpit, then it helps to know what these commonly used historical, chronological terms mean. There is no point in trying to teach or learn all these terms at one go, but if children are exposed to them and the terms are explained and used in time–lines, most children can acquire all the basic terms needed by the age of 11 or 12. If they do not become familiar with them, then their historical explorations will be the poorer.

Although children may sometimes ask the question 'why?' without tuition, it is not natural for them to know intuitively those other questions which lead to the most enjoyable and interesting historical enquiries. They can be listed succinctly and used to guide children doing history whatever their age, and whatever the event or topic.

> What happened and when?
> What was the consequence or result, if any?
> How do we know?

These are general questions which children need to get into the habit of asking. If they do so their work will immediately take on more historical focus. It is also useful to equip children with a list of some more specific questions which they can try out in turn to illuminate any historical enquiry, whether of a single picture postcard or of a whole series of books and sources on some past period. Sometimes some of the questions will not work for a particular postcard, source or topic, but the act of trying to ask these questions, even if the response is negative, will help children to be historians. Here is a list of them, (DES, 1985).

> Where and how did people live? (settlements and housing)
> How did the people of the time feed and clothe themselves? (agriculture, clothes, trade)
> How did people keep themselves alive and well? (health and medicine)
> What power and technology were available at the time? (power, industry, transport, weapons, communications)
> What were the different social and gender groups and their life styles? (social classes and groups, male and female)
> What did people worship and what values did they try to live by? (ideas and beliefs)
> What was their sport, art, music, literature and entertainment? (leisure life)

Who governed and how and with what results? (government and
politics)

What differences are there between then and now or between
different civilizations of the same period?

Imagine a class where children are doing their own choice of topic for
historical enquiry. One might have chosen 'Arsenal Football Club',
another 'The Roman Army', a third 'Life on a Jamaican Plantation'. If
the children refer to their lists of questions and ask them of their particular
topics the resulting work will never be a mere copying from reference
books, as so often it is, but some real historical enquiry.

Using sources as evidence from which to learn about the past is also
basic. Whether it is an artefact, a document, picture or some other written
source, children need to learn to ask what it tells them about life in the
past, which time in the past it comes from, which time in the past it tells
about (they may not be the same) and whether they can trust it as evidence.
More specifically for written sources they need to tease out what is fact
and what is opinion and the extent to which bias may colour those
opinions.

It is less easy to suggest how children may learn the other main
method which historians use in approaching the past, that of empathy.
It is acquired gradually, it depends upon *and is not separate from* the
chronological, evidence-analyzing and question-asking skills already
described. One thing seems certain. To discuss with children what
historical empathy is and what it is not is a necessary beginning. Empathy
is the ability to stand metaphorically in someone else's shoes in a different
time and place in an attempt to understand how they thought about things.
It is not sympathy: it is not necessarily agreeing with the thoughts and
actions of someone else. A single, if stark, example may make the point.
We might expect historians, even young ones, to empathize with
nineteenth-century factory owners who made young children work long
hours but not sympathize with them. Two other things are certain about
empathy. One is that to be carried out successfully, we have to rid
ourselves of anachronisms and this is where a knowledge of chronological
sequencing gradually acquired is enormously helpful. The other is that
historical empathy while it employs the imagination, can never be wholly
creative. It is not creative writing: it must always take into account the
historical evidence it has from sources other than the imagination and
it must never go unreasonably beyond them in its imaginative
reconstructions of the past.

The following example of a seven-year-old girl's writing shows how
knowledge based on the evidence of some pictorial source, is interwoven
with imagination to make a good historical story:

How I Lived Through the Bubonic Plague and the Fire

One day as I was playing with my friend, I heard a cry it was 'Quick put a red cross on the door.' I said 'What does that mean.' My friend said 'it means someone's got the bubonic plague.' At night when I went to bed, I heard a bell ringing. This is what I heard. 'Ding aling. Bring out your dead ding aling bring out your dead ding aling aling ding.' I got out of bed and went to the window. I looked out, I could see a man with a cart piled with dead. I went back to bed. A few months later on September 2nd 1666 I heard this, 'Fire! Fire! Fire! Fire! Fire! Fire!' I saw my mother and father on the other side of the bridge. I crossed the bridge. Then I saw a sailor coming, he was followed by lots of other sailors. Suddenly I heard a 'Bang' our house was blown up. Lots of the other houses were blown up. Soon the fire stopped. My mother and father and I lived in a house the king gave us.

The next example is an extract from a twelve-year-old boy in a middle school. It shows a very skilful use of sources in making a reconstruction of the past. Entitled *A Day in the life of a Victorian Boy, 20 February, 1888* it is based on directories, building plans and school log books and includes notes indicating the sources which the boy had used:

Hello, my name is Edward Sawyer, I live at 5, Western Road, Grandpont, Oxford. It is a brand new house.[*1] We moved to Oxford from Leafield because of my father's job, you see, he's a clerk at the Gasworks and he is called George Sawyer.[*2]
I have two brothers and one sister. My two brothers are 6 months and four years old and my sister is ten. I am the oldest at twelve years old.
I like living in Grandpont because there are lots of new houses. All the houses in our street were built in the last two years,[*3] so everybody is very friendly.
My best friend is John England, aged twelve, his dad built our house; he also built 1, 7, 9, 14, 16, 20, 22, 24, 26, 28, 30, and 32 Western Road,[*4] so you see he is very rich. My Mum and Dad pay him five shillings a week rent for our house.[*5] Altogether there are ten builders in our street,[*6] at the moment they are building some houses opposite us.[*7]
Today is my first day back at school after the great snow of 1888. You see, in late winter on February 18th we had more snow in one day than since 1826.[*8] It was incredible, our basement area had five or six feet of snow, which drifted into it, and the

pavement had two feet of snow, so they closed our school. Hoorah!

I go to St Aldates School. There are 269 children in our school.*⁹ My school is just over Folly Bridge*¹⁰ so it is very close.

I go to school with John, when he goes, but he's always playing Charlie Wag — truant really or making excuses.*¹¹

Today at school our headmaster, Mr Cole*¹², welcomed us back to school and hoped we had enjoyed our extra holiday but said we'd have to work even harder than usual to make the work up. We are learning about the red deer, and thunder and lightning. We had to say our multiplication tables and do lots of sums on our slates.

When I arrived home for dinner, my mum sent me over the road to Mrs Pusey, the butcher,*¹³ to buy some sausages. Mrs Pusey also gave me a bone for the dog. My mum also sent me to Mr Crapper*¹⁴ᵃ to get some coal. His shop is at 59 Western Road.*¹⁴ᵇ I had to push my sister's old pram and buy a sack of coal. My mum can't do the shopping very well because of my baby brother.

When I went back to school after dinner we had to do Geography. I like learning about other countries especially America because my aunt and uncle went to live there in 1881 with lots of other immigrants.*¹⁵

Bibliography and References

1 1880–90 Kelly's Directory
2 1880–90 Kelly's Directory
3 Building plans Western Rd, local history dept Central Library
4 As above 3
5 Butler (1912) feels that five room houses built in Oxford during 1890s would be let for between 4/6 and 5/6 per week
6 Oxford city engineers' dept plans of building application
7 Nos 2–12 built by Jarvis and Son
8 Daily Mail 1888
9 School log book ST ALDATES SCHOOL
10 Plans of Oxford, local history dept Central Library
11 John and Mary England were taken before school board for non-attendance in 1892
12 Kelly's 1890 Directory

13 1888 Valter's Directory
14 1888 Valter's Directory
15 Emigration from England to USA reached a peak in 1888: *Peoples'
    Chronology* by James Traiger

Teaching Approaches

The following suggestions about what children of different ages might
do as young historians are meant to indicate some of the possibilities and
are in no sense exhaustive, (Blyth, 1982 and 1988).

Work with, and observation of, children aged five to eight, shows
that they can be excited by historical stories, become keen about historical
things, can ask questions about artefacts and photographs and pictures
from the past, can sequence them, can begin to ask particular historical
questions, such as 'what does this tell us about?' and 'is it true?' and collect
oral evidence. They can engage in historical enquiries into their own
history, as for example: 'Do you remember your first day at school?' They
can find out about family and local history, write about it and sequence
it in time-lines. For example a topic on 'Wash Days: Now and Then'
can involve young children in finding out from parents and grandparents,
books and pictures, in talking, writing, drawing and painting about what
happened and in dressing up and even having an Edwardian wash-day
in the classroom. Through stories they can also put themselves in the
position of other people in the past. It is unsophisticated but they can
do it and it is the beginning of that historical method which has been
described as empathy.

Between the ages of eight and eleven children should acquire a
growing vocabulary of terms used in history such as king, ruler, knight,
bishop, government. They can also gain a knowledge of how historians
in the West date in centuries, of the terms BC and AD and the sequence
of terms which apply to much British national and local history, such
as Saxon, Viking, Norman, Elizabethan, etc. They might be expected
to have used some small pieces of documentary sources as well as artefacts,
maps and pictures, and practised some ways of analyzing them as historical
evidence. They can also begin to ask a wide range of historical questions.
Again through stories and the use of historical fiction both of which
remain enjoyable and fruitful approaches, children of this age can widen
their interests in the past. In particular doing a 'patch' or period of history,
as for example, Ancient Egypt, the Aztecs or Mughal India in some detail
and breadth can be a stimulating experience. Following some topic
through time such as Buildings or Agriculture and noting how changes

occurred can also provide opportunities for interesting historical enquiry.

Inevitably we have come to content. Much of this chapter has been about teaching historical skills within historical content, but it cannot be said too often or too loud, that skills cannot be taught in a vacuum. They are taught through historical content and every teacher has to choose some content. How then to choose? Reference back to the reasons given for teaching history is logical and productive.

One of the reasons for teaching history is to satisfy curiosity about local and national roots or heritage. This implies that some local and some national history should be taught. Another is to know how contemporary society came from the past and this implies some twentieth-century history. A third is to learn to understand other societies and this suggests both world history and some remote periods of history. A fourth is the need to understand the long term effects of actions in the past and this suggests some study, over a long term, of political history in some aspect and its effect on social and economic life. Another reason was to give opportunities for holistic approaches to learning and this suggests that a period of history might be chosen which is helpful in terms of the experience it gives of using a variety of sources as well as opportunities to respond through art, craft, drama and music and in spoken and written language. The example of Pepys' England given above is especially good in this respecct but many other periods would also be fruitful.

Returning to the reasons for having history in the education of the younger child provides a range of criteria for choosing content, without being prescriptive. It leaves freedom for teachers and children to be their own historians. However, I have always found the following remark challenging and helpful and hard to dismiss: 'Have we really educated children if they know nothing of Greek and Roman civilization, medieval and modern Islam, the Reformation and Renaissance and the French and Russian Revolutions?'[5] This is not to imply that children should have studied these particular topics by the age of eleven but it does suggest that in choosing content teachers should consider the claims of major events which have changed the world.

It remains finally to indicate how we will not turn children into historians. Dictated notes, copied reference works, one-word answer worksheets, always local history on the one hand or always twentieth century social and economic history on the other, all these help to create that miracle of pedagogy, dull history.

If time has gone into teaching children to be historians it is worth trying to assess their progress. It will give children themselves the satisfaction of knowing that they can now do things which they could not do before.

Reference back to the section on what history is will suggest what might be assessed:

1 Can children use the language of chronology and use time-lines to sequence their historical knowledge?
2 Can they so ask questions about pictures, artefacts or documents that they make these sources give up their evidence about the past?
3 To what extent are children remembering to ask the historical questions listed on pages 25 and 26 when they discuss or write about the past?
4 How well are children understanding the attitudes, beliefs and conditions of people in the past without intruding present day or other anachronisms?

These four main areas can be sub-divided into more specific items so that a check list or grid of the ideas and skills which we might expect children to develop can be made.

Actually assessing children's progress may be done both formally and informally. By talking to children or by noting whether they can use historical ideas and skills in their written work is one way. Devising specific tests of particular historical skills is another. Whatever the method used the results can be recorded on simple record cards.

If children have been turned into historians they will enjoy history, revelling in tackling its questions and marvelling at their discoveries. They will have the confidence to do it, knowing that they have the skills and knowledge of terms which they need. They will not mind being wrong because they will know that there are no completely right answers, but they will have respect for facts and be able to distinguish between fact and opinion. They will also be on the way to developing one of the main tools of an educated person, namely an ability to detect lies and nonsense, particularly in utterings about human affairs.

Notes

1 In a survey of teachers of the age groups of 5, 7, 9 and 11 all the teachers said that they made little or no contribution to furthering the aim that 'the child should have *ordered subject knowledge* in, for example, history and geography'; Taylor, P.H. and Holley, B.J. (1975) *A Study of the Emphasis given by Teachers of Different Age Groups to Aims in Primary Education*, London, Schools Council; In 1978 HM Inspectors of Schools reported that while history was given some attention in 60 per cent of the 7-year-old-classes, in 90 per cent of the 9-year-old-classes and in almost all 11-year-old-classes, 'taken as a whole in four out of five of all classes which studies history, the work was superficial'; DES, (1978) *Primary Education in England*, London, HMSO.

2 See Entwhistle, N.Z. (1987) *Understanding Classroom Learning*, London, Hodder and Stoughton for a useful account of the research knowledge about how children learn and the differences between *holist* and *serialist* styles of learning. In summary, it suggests that while less is known about how children of primary age learn than about older students, in general two distinctive styles are used. For example a holist style sets the task in broad perspectives and uses analogies, visual images and personal experience to build up understanding. A serialist style takes a step-by-step approach, interpreting facts and evidence cautiously and with logical analysis.

3 Wordsworth's Preface to the *Lyrical Ballads*, 1805.

4 This has been demonstrated many times in meetings on courses with primary and middle school teachers.

5 By the late John Jennings, one of Her Majesty's Inspectors for Schools.

References

BARROW, R. (1981) *The Philosophy of Schooling*, London, Wheatsheaf Books.

BLYTH, J. (1982) *History in Primary Schools*, New York, McGraw Hill.

BLYTH, J. (1988) *History 5–9*, London, Hodder and Stoughton.

DES (1985) *History in the Primary & Secondary Years: an HMI view*, London, HMSO.

HEXTER, O.H. (1971) *The History Primer*, Harmondsworth, Penguin.

LOW BEER, A. and BLYTH, J. (1983) 'Teaching History to Younger Children', *Teaching of History Series, No. 52*, Historical Association.

REEVES, M. (1980) *Why History?*, London, Longman.

WEST, J. (1986) *Time Line: History Pack*, Walton-on-Thames, Nelson.

Chapter 3

Imagination and History

Vivienne Little

Introduction

Imagination and history are at first sight strange bedfellows, but there is an intimate relationship between them, which needs to be understood if children's learning about the past is to be effective. The plastic and performing arts are readily associated with imagination. Geography, history, and religious studies, are in contrast, bodies of knowledge-facts and competing interpretations – to be understood, memorized and reproduced as accurately as possible. Imaginative activities in primary classrooms where they are the subject of study, are viewed with suspicion by those who do not understand children's minds and undertaken with feelings of guilt by some of those whose pedagogical instincts are superior. It is the contention of this chapter that, in respect of history, such doubts betray a misconception of the discipline and of the needs of children attempting to learn about the past. Imaginative activity is an inescapable part of history and should be included in the study of the subject at school level. Approaches via imagination are indispensable to the task of rendering intelligible to immature minds knowledge otherwise excessively difficulty to access.

Historical Imagination

A girl is missing, a body is found, a murder is reported. The hunt is on. Soon, TV screens show a young look-alike following the presumed route of the victim. A policeman turned actor, wearing clothes like those of someone seen in the vicinity at the time simulates a knife attack. The reconstruction stems from bits and pieces abandoned by chance or carelessness, incomplete information and deduction. In this instance it represents actual events so accurately that it triggers recall in witnesses and ultimately a confesssion. The murderer is apprehended.

Analogies linking historians and detectives are familiar, even overworked, and can be misleading as models for curriculum building, (Arkell, 1986), but exploring the device of reconstruction can elucidate the nature of the historical record and illuminate its dependence upon imagination. A process of representation or image-making is central to our perception of the world as psychologists and philosophers demonstrate (Warnock, 1976). The same activity is involved when we perceive an object as signifying something beyond itself. A detective on a murder hunt sees a fragment of cloth, a wound, as clues to the explanation of a mysterious death. The historian sees a piece of clay, an arrangement of wattle and daub, ink marks on parchment not only as a kitchen utensil, a house, a document, but also as evidence of the past. On the basis of clues the detective guides the participants in the reconstruction. What they enact is *not* the murder itself, but it is neither fictitious nor fanciful. It is a rational construction of known facts and accumulated experience. In the same way history, the historian's picture of the past, is imaginary. Men and women of the past cannot be brought back to life. Their experiences cannot occur again. The physical and mental elements of past events can only be reconstructed in imagination by the operation of the historian's mind upon what he takes to be evidence of the past. Nevertheless, though their subject-matter is a past world whose living reality they can never recover, historians claim that their statements about it are valid, just as a fruitful reconstruction depends upon verisimilitude. Sources, like clues, afford mute and ambiguous testimony, but existing historical knowledge, analogue of the sense impressions which enable recognition of physical objects and of the accumulated experience of a detective, helps the historian to see them not only as indicative of the past, but of particular past people and events. The deeper his knowledge the more the traces yield to his scrutiny. What his spoken or written works convey is not a flight of fancy, but a work of imaginative reconstruction, grounded in evidence, and valid to the extent that he clearly infers and faithfully encodes the messages with which evidence is charged. The detective can sometimes discover that his reconstruction was correct, the historian never.

Structural Imagination

Not only is the historian's picture of the past 'imaginary in every detail', (Collingwood, 1946) once produced, but its making also involves, as does the detective's reconstruction, the exercise of imagination. Three types of imaginative activity are discernible in historical writing. The first is what Collingwood called 'a priori' or 'structural' imagination, the second is the now notorious empathy, and the third is part of the process of communication.

Structural imagination is that unavoidable gap-filling in which reporters of human events past or current must indulge to afford continuity to their narrative. Collingwood's own example, that sources indicating Caesar's presence first in Italy, later in Spain, justify the assumption that he made a journey from one to the other, entails no more than simple deduction, but Elton (1967) provides a better illustration of what is meant when he describes his doubts about the acceptability of a common explanation of changes in the composition and powers of the sixteenth-century Privy Council in terms of gradual transition. If, he says, one tries to imagine such a gradual transition, one cannot do it. The only sensible explanation is that the change must have been carried out upon some particular occasion of which there is no record. Loyn (1962) suggests misuse of the same process, when he shows the folly of projecting primitive democracy into Anglo-Saxon England upon the basis of existence of folkmoots, while ignoring the very evident authority of king over community and lord over dependant enshrined in the extant law-codes. One may fill gaps in the evidence imaginatively, but one may not leave out bits which spoil one's picture!

The capacity to envisage alternative constructions of the same evidence is a regular function of imagination in history. Its results can range from a new construing of a single phrase of a medieval document to the elaboration of an original explanatory thesis. Moreover, an essential element in historical explanation is the envisaging of possibilities other then those which occurred. To Carr's (1961) claim that history is the record of what people did, not what they failed to do, Trevor Roper opposes the contention that history is what happened in the context of what might have happened. The historian must discern the choices open to those involved in events in order to account for their actions and 'restoring to the past its lost certainties' (1980) is an exercise in historical imagination.

A further instance of imagination contributing to the structure of history occurs when historians tackle the common and tricky problem of generic statements about groups. Evidence concerning the thoughts and actions of common people, for example, occurs unsystematically in the archive. To make statements about them, historians have searched for details of as many different cases as possible, or 'formed in their minds a general impression on the matter and have allowed their imagination to supply what might be missing in the evidence and so have produced a coherent picture . . . the power of meditating upon a series of separate facts and forming a general opinion upon them is in fact one of the most valuable and mysterious which the human mind possesses . . . such power can reveal what the detailed process of research, however ingeniously its results may be manipulated by mathematics, can never reveal . . .' (Kitson-Clark, 1967).

> Alongside fear of the future, however there existed, when hunger was not actually on the doorstep, a propensity for almost frenetic gaiety, an obsessive urge to make the most of every moment of leisure and every occasion for celebrating. Family reunions for marriages above all but also deaths and births, fetedays, pardons, kermesses, public processions and fairs – all were occasions to bedeck oneself in whatever finery one possessed (and it might be little more than a clean kerchief, a less ragged shirt, a precious pair of inherited stays, a scrap of lace pinned on a bodice, a coiffe fabricated in snatched time, a crucifix, or a flower) to sally forth in search of enjoyment, determined to find diversion.

Here Hufton (1974), having wrung from the archives dozens of items of information, significant and apparently insignificant, relating to the inarticulate poor of eighteenth-century France, has skilfully woven them into a pattern revealing of their quality of life, so tellingly picked out with details – 'a scrap of lace', 'snatched time' – well-selected to reinforce its undeniable limitations. In a review article about books on popular culture in France, Beik (1977) argues that such matters can only be approached by means of imaginative constructs. Evidence concerning the thoughts and actions of common people comes in isolated descriptive passages and some selective and interpretive procedure must be used to forge a coherent framework. He discerns three in the books concerned – the 'slice of life' method which presents a series of individual life stories chosen as typical, the 'forms of association' method which tries to discover what the ways in which people grouped themselves can reveal about their affective life, political consciousness, etc., and the study of popular uprisings for the light they shed on *'mentalité'*. Such devices are as he admits, open to the charge of impressionism or even romanticism, but they are unavoidable and their limitations only overcome by fertility of imagination. Also as Fines (1977) points out, many commonly employed historical labels for groups of events are imaginative constructs. 'Renaissance' holds together many cultural aspects of the fourteenth to sixteenth centuries in Europe and also says something about their nature. The 'scramble for Africa' evocatively describes the behaviour of the great powers in the late nineteenth century, 'enlightened despotism' covers the policies of certain eighteenth-century monarchs, and attempts to show their behaviour as in some sense consistent and explicable. As all these examples show, one feature of structural imagination is the power to see things as a whole.

Thus historians are involved in an imaginative act when they perceive sources as indicative of the past and as evidence for particular aspects of it. In reconstructing and explaining it they constantly envisage men and rehearse events in their heads. Ruminating upon them, they frequently suppose that if this or that were the case then this or that must or might have followed; or try to select, with imagination, a comprehensive and effective organizing principle. In other words, their exercise of imagination helps to make possible and meaningful their learning and scholarship.

Empathy

Concern this far has been with historical imagination as a cognitive activity, a method of arriving at intellectual comprehension, of blending disparate information and creating a coherent world which has the ring of truth when tested against the criterion of evidence. Another type of imaginative activity which is frequently attributed to historians is:

> the art of making it (the past) fully intelligible to us by enabling us to enter, as it were, into the minds and passions of people who, in some ways, seem very different from us ... the function of historical imagination is to penetrate the minds, the strange and complicated minds, sometimes even the barbarous and repellent minds of remote centuries, in order not merely to retrace the routine of human behaviour, the old ruts and tracks of past events, but to understand the springs and compulsions, the dilemmas and predicaments, the genius and folly of the human decisions that made that behaviour (Roper, 1958).

This capacity for entering the minds of people of the past is often referred to as empathy. It is a concept easily misunderstood. Etymologically it is an affective concept – a rendering, via Greek, of the German *einfuhlung* – and it means 'in-feeling', or perhaps 'feeling with'. A person is said to behave empathetically when he or she feels the feelings of another. Some dictionary definitions and fairly common usage, in characterizing it as projecting oneself into another's personality or putting oneself into another's shoes, allow it to involve the sharing of another's thoughts as well as feelings, and since minds commonly contain both it is probably a justifiable extension. Most definitions, however, misrepresent the psychological processes denoted by empathy, and cause confusion, especially, but not only, in relation to history. It is simply *not possible* to think another's thoughts or feel another's feelings. What one does is to entertain or imagine the thoughts and feelings one supposes that person to have. The activity is therefore cognitive, though the impulse spurring one to it may be affective. In the present world empathy involves intuitive and inferential elements and relies on the sharing of a common form of life and some knowledge of particular experiences and circumstances. The more distant a person may be from me in habits of thought and patterns of response, the greater the imaginative effort I shall have to make in order to stimulate for myself his or her thoughts or feelings. Only on the level of what it means to be human do we share a common form of life and common experiences with people of the past, whose habits of thought and patterns of response may differ markedly from our own.

Historians' business is to discover the characteristics of that past form of life, to trace the internal connections between events so that they may fulfil their obligation to convey them to us as they actually were. To do this adequately they may sometimes need to put themselves in others' shoes. Wedgwood (1957) argues that 'without their capacity for entering into the fervour of our ancestors' beliefs we shall never gain real understanding of the Reformation' and 'we shall understand the Civil War and the Long Parliament better if we realize, not merely objectively as a quaint oddity, but with fully sympathy, how repugnant this idea of a divided Parliament was to the men of the time'. She provides a different instance where a failure of empathy blinded Gibbon to an insight about the behaviour of Sulplicianus. Had he imagined himself, as was Suplicianus, surrounded by the Praetorian Guard out for blood, he would have realized that plain fear rather than uncharacteristic ambition induced him to seize the imperial throne. Here Wedgwood, in the absence of evidence relies on common humanity and her own 'second record' to supply a convincing explanation of someone's behaviour. It is an explanation which fits the existing facts better than Gibbon's, which appeared to rely upon some general adage about universal ambition, but, as she admits, it might still be wrong. In history this type of empathy can result in no more than what Hexter (1971) calls a hypothetical subjunctive.

> But the victory was not crowned by further successes. Perhaps
> Vercingetorix let the change in his fortunes go to his head. Perhaps
> the arrival of reinforcements from a number of cities gave him
> a false idea of his army's power in attack. Perhaps rumours that

Caesar was pulling out from independent Gaul encouraged him to abandon his strategy of caution and stake everything on one throw. We cannot be sure; but Caesar and his staff seem to have realized that Vercingetorix's usual coolness and caution were deserting him (Latouche, 1986).

More trustworthy is the effort historians make, on the basis of evidence, to think of themselves as people who thought the earth was flat, the better to explain unfamiliar responses; or to look at the same situation through the eyes of a number of different participants in it. Most constant and significant of all historians' empathizing activities is the effort they must often make to forget what they know about subsequent events. Just as they must try hard not to impose their own second record upon the past, though they may sometimes fruitfully draw from it, so must they sometimes set aside the outcome of events in order, like the men who lived through them, to confront them in uncertainty.

Thus historians use empathy, an imaginative activity, in order to make sense of the past. They must take account of past feelings as well as of past thoughts because human activity is motivated at least as often as feelings as by thought, normally by a mixture of both. Unless the dimension of feeling is attended to, understanding in the fullest sense will not be obtained. But historians do not normally use empathy affectively. Only rarely can they feel their way into the shoes of another. They must know a great deal about the exact size, shape, fit and constituting material of those shoes. They do not think past thoughts or feel past feelings, they *imagine* them; and when they write about the past so imagined they do not try to persuade their readers to think past thoughts or feel past feelings or even, very often, to imagine them. Empathy is an heuristic device which historians abandon when it has done its work, just as builders remove scaffolding. Its work is to aid the faithful reconstruction of the past, which is presented for the reader to contemplate and thus come to know what happened and what it was like.

Ornamental Imagination

Historians, having arrived, by a thoughtful and imaginative approach to evidence, at an understanding of the past have further to go. They must communicate their findings and unless they write effectively their readers will fail to appreciate the fruits of their labours. To this task again the historian must bring imagination, this time in a form a shade dismissively but aptly described by Collingwood (1946) as 'ornamental'.

Like novelists, they must set the scene, delineate the characters, organize the narrative, point judgments. Moreover they must do this without the freedom of the creative artist. They 'cannot invent what went on in the mind of St Thomas of Canterbury ... cannot suppress inconvenient minor characters and invent others' (Wedgwood, 1960). They can only use simile, metaphor, analogy with the greatest possible care that they are truly representative of the facts. The greatness of the best historians has been evident in their style as well as in their learning – each in part the product of imaginative insight, each the result of thinking with imagination.

> The tempo of life in ancient regime France was not markedly faster than in the Middle Ages, and went at the pace of man, mule or plodding horse (Goubert, 1969).

How well this closing sentence of a description of the slowness of transport in the eighteenth century encapsulates the cumulative impression created by an earlier list of carefully selected typical journeys and how effectively the word 'plodding', reinforces the message. Selection of vivid and concrete detail, lively images, literary echoes and wit – these are some of the hallmarks of the ornamental imagination in the writings of historians.

The reader of history as well as the writer exercises historical imagination and does so to the extent that the historian engages his interest, and where appropriate his sympathetic understanding. Readers allow the words of the historian to create in their minds the picture of the past the researches have suggested and contemplate it 'in imagination'. As they do so they react according to their own structure of interests, knowledge and sentiments, use it to extend their existing conception of the past or evaluate it against that conception. They may do that 'with imagination'. Their success in both will depend partly upon the skill with which historians have employed their structural and ornamental imagination, and partly upon the richness and variety of their own 'second records' (Hexter, 1971).

History and Children

If historical imagination is an integral part of the process of producing history and of responding to it, then school history should develop the capacity for historical imagination in young minds. Enthusiasts for history among teachers are delighted by its status as a foundation subject in the

National Curriculum, but are wary of the guidelines given by the Secretary of State to the working group because they could result in syllabuses which confine children to memorizing those aspects of the historical record selected as suitable or edifying for them. Bruner, (1960), among many curriculum theorists, argued that knowledge involves understanding not only the content of a discipline, but also how it was produced. Society's need is not for people who can recite scientific facts, but for those who can do science, and the same is true for history. Children learning history must work with artefacts and documents as well as secondary sources and they must undertake tasks designed to promote historical imagination because such procedures are part of the nature of history.

An equally important and longer-standing[1] justification for the use of imaginative approaches in the teaching of history stems from the nature of children's learning. Amused exasperation at children's mistakes is a familiar, often redeeming, feature of staffroom life, but it is no accident that the most frequent and best-known howlers stem from school history, and inspired that most brilliant and sustained of howlers *1066 and All That*. In studying history, pupils are asked to learn and make judgments about a world of which they have no experience, involving adult interactions, responsibilities and formal relationships, or to which they cannot, without help, refer relevant experience they do possess. A large part of understanding concerns applying experience and knowledge to new situations. Howlers show children doing this, but failing because their 'second record', on which they depend to 'go beyond the information given' to make sense of it, is not effective or rich enough. If whatever history they learn is to have long-term value for pupils, we must try to enlarge the second record. We must find ways of translating and extending what they know through experience or observation of everyday life and sometimes provide simulated experience to help make personal sense of information about the past. If history is about what happened and why it happened, much explanation involves knowing what it was like.

Support for this argument can be found in Bruner's theory of cognitive growth (1960). A key element in his account of the process is the idea of representation. Knowing is a form of construction in which the knower plays an active part. On the basis of inchoate sense impressions, the mind generates models which correspond to external reality and are in turn instruments for transcending the momentary and making sense of the environment – for 'going beyond the information given'. In the case of the very young child, representation is achieved via action – a rattle is to shake and shaking continues after the rattle has been dropped. Later the child is able to replace actions with images – mental forms which stand for objects like maps stand for the locations to which they refer. Lastly the child acquires the ability to handle data symbolically, to deal in systems in which connections with reality are remote rather than direct.

These three modes of representation are labelled by Bruner enactive, iconic and symbolic. They progress separately and in association and the fuller their individual development, the more far-reaching their independent achievement. His theories suggest that imaginative work may have crucial importance for the emergence of symbolic thinking in history. They indicate that activity and the development of appropriate imagery are vital to genuine learning. They underline the importance of the teacher as the generator of intrinsic motivation and the agent of the culture of history – the knowledge and skills it enshrines. The literature of history pedagogy is over-preoccupied with formal thinking. Of course historians engage in formal thinking and the search for ways of promoting it is entirely justified. Paradoxically, the direct path is often the imaginative route.

Imaginative Approaches to History in Primary School Classrooms

Understanding of the nature of history and of children's minds suggest that in primary classrooms children should be engaging in role-play and simulation, watching dramatic reconstructions like those in Granada's *How we used to live* television series, reading historical fiction and undertaking imaginative writing about the past. Historians do not do these things in the course of their work. They exercise historical imagination 'in the head', as indicated above, in line with evidence and with the help of a well-stocked second record of knowledge and experience. Children need activity to spur them to research and historical imagination, to engage in gap-filling, seeing things as a whole, envisaging alternatives, putting themselves in others' shoes. They need to build a stock of images relating to the past to aid understanding and help retention. They need to write expressively in order to make personal sense of information with which they are confronted. Discussion of the imaginative approaches listed above is designed to show that they contribute to the development of a capacity for historical imagination in young minds *and* to that understanding of the past which is its foundation.

Drama

In recent years, there has been increasing interest in the use of stately homes and other historical sites as the locations for large-scale attempts at recreating the past or re-enacting events. The National Trust Youth Theatre has children fully costumed as Lords, Ladies or servants at the great house in a particular period. The English Heritage Association recently sponsored a number of Coventry schools to reconstruct at Kenilworth Castle the visit there in 1578 of Queen Elizabeth the First. Two lecturers at La Sainte Union College involved students and tutors at a meeting *in situ* of the Southampton Court Leet, the records and procedures of which, and the people involved, had been carefully studied at school beforehand (Chester Conference, 1988).

There is no doubt that such enterprises demonstrate that the past was real and is interesting, provide rich images vital to the sense of time and period and stimulate the learning of much history. Many museums now offer smaller scale activities of this kind. Victorian classrooms, where children and teachers role-play a very familiar situation in an earlier mode, are common. Education cuts and time-table disruption make even less ambitious outings from school increasingly difficult, however, and more regularly useful are simple informal classroom scale exercises which can equally stimulate interest and involvement, motivate to research, help the growth of understanding of past events and encourage historical imagination.

Role-play and simulation are the most useful tools. Simple drama exercises like mime can provide historical insight. Extending miming of repetitive movements such as digging or shovelling can often do as much as pages of description to convey to those carrying out the exercise and monotony and exhaustion of the life of peasant or labourer and attempts to suggest period costume, for instance, involve study and practice of movement and gesture, historically revealing in themselves, in terms of social attitudes and relationships. How could Victorian ladies of a certain class seem other than stiff and remote, boned and laced up as they were? Occupational mime is especially useful in doing history with the young or less able whose reading skills are limited. It is perfectly feasible in a normal classroom, and larger scale movement in groups to illustrate fear, triumph, menace, can, with careful organization, be undertaken where desks are pushed aside. These and similar short exercises are simple but valuable aids to finding out about, imagining and understanding the past.

For infants and younger juniors simple re-enactment of the past, using role-play to represent historical characters and events they have heard or read about, is important. More adventurous and productive in terms of historical thinking skills is the use of role-play to invent and represent 'typical' individuals or 'likely events' out of historical information children have discovered. Work with older juniors on the operation and effects of the Old Poor law using this method has been successful.

Simulation is variously defined. Participation in experiences which provoke a response or elucidate a concept is the most helpful for children learning history and probably only at age nine or over. In a simulation devised to represent feudalism, children were arranged in groups in the classroom and set to play a variety of board and card games. Communication with the teacher had to be through a child monitor. From time to time the monitor was sent to bring randomly selected children to the front of the room to perform copying tasks of no apparent relevance, depriving the team of a player and spoiling the game. This and the teacher's arbitrary decisions about the organization of the room and unsatisfactory or puzzling answers to children's reasonable requests via the monitor soon became irksome, and predictable reactions of boredom, resignation or rebellion began to appear. At that point the exercise was ended and discussion used to relate it to the pattern and frustrations of life as experienced by mediaeval villeins burdened with boon-work and ruled by the Lord of the manor and his bailiff. Thus relationships remote from modern society were translated into a more readily accessible mode in order, primarily, to get at the relevant feelings, which help to explain men's activities in events such as the Peasants' Revolt of 1381.

A class of nine year-olds found difficulty in comprehending the plight of a character from the Victorian series of *How We Used to Live* described as an 'orphan without expectations'. They needed to create a concept of a society in which inheritance was crucial to social position and the family was virtually the only welfare agency. A robe dating from 1840, in which the teacher had been christened, was the spring-board of a discussion about family heirlooms and the notion of the handing on of property through the generations. Then children were asked to consider how they might show, by making a shape using themselves and a set of rostra, the order of importance of people in their school. They demonstrated a grasp of the notion of hierarchy by giving the school secretary a prominent position, by the Head's admission a correct interpretation of her pivotal role in his organization. After establishing a shape to show their perception of hierarchy in their own families, children were asked to show what that implied in each of the three families featured in the TV programme. Finally they had to find a way, using shapes and different coloured lengths of ribbon, to show the creative status of the three families and the links of kinship and service within and between them. By this means the precarious position of the 'orphan without expectations' was graphically revealed and the class had a more secure understanding of some central characteristics of Victorian society. (Computer simulations relating to history are separately discussed in Chapter 4).

No formal evaluation of this type of work exists, but it seems reasonable to suppose, on the basis of theory and work in classrooms, that enactive representation is a worthwhile approach to the teaching of history. The subject, abstract in its very nature, presents special cognitive problems to children and acting out a story from the past can help to impose its reality, fix its details and clarify its meaning, while at the same time developing historical imagination. Children do this naturally in play – reiterating not only personal experiences, but the adventures of story-book characters and screen heroes, and it is clear that this activity is valuable to cognitive as well as to emotional development. Moreover, in the classroom they soon discover the limits of their knowledge, and, stimulated by the practical task, grow eager to find out more. They frame questions and seek information to answer them, thus exercising in an appropriate mode, the skills of an historian and even sometimes coming into meaningful contact with historical evidence. They live through sets of circumstances in imagination, suppose the outcomes of actions and the effects of occurrences on individuals and groups and exercise empathy. Drama, operating in the concrete mode, illuminates historical content for children, and by provoking questions and providing impetus to the search for answers, can afford initiation, by analogy, into history as a way of knowing.

Of course, there is a danger of over-generalization, of distorting history's concern with that time, those people, that place by drama's preoccupation with the universal, of history's record of change by drama's search for continuities and there is no suggestion that drama is a substitute for formal study of history. Rather it is a spur to it, for if events were entirely unique no-one could understand them and simulated experience is an aid to understanding where real experience is lacking, providing potent images to inform detailed investigation.

Historical Novels for Children

Contemplation of others' imaginative creations, argues Warnock (1976), is part of the process of individual imaginative development. Too much teacher talk in classrooms is frowned upon these days, but few can have done more to inspire a love of history and understanding of the past than those teachers of the subject who are born (or trained) raconteurs, persuading their listeners to participate imaginatively in the events they describe. Another model of historical imagination is provided by dramatic reconstructions of the past aimed at children such as the television series *How We Used To Live*. This 'soap-opera' approach, which takes a fictional family through the real events of a decade or so, is widely held by teachers to involve children and enhance through imaginative appeal their knowledge and understanding of the past, especially, perhaps, its physical characteristics.

Written history which displays the highest qualities of historical imagination is barely accessible to children. The best available substitute is historical fiction.[2] Since the 1950s a great variety of historical novels for children has been produced and many of them are well-researched, accurate without being didactic and, above all, a good read. They are invaluable and should be used in the classroom, not just referred to incidentally as an enjoyable but possibly suspect sideline.

Good children's historical fiction requires all the attributes of the good children's novel – the striking opening, the intriguing plot, the element of suspense, and characters who develop as the story unfolds and with some of whom children can identify. Moreover, it must take children back into an historical period whose way of life is unfamiliar, subtly supplying circumstantial detail of dress, buildings, goods, transport, tools, landscape and social organization without clogging the tale with mini-history lessons. It is, according to those who write it, fiction which exhibits 'the living changing elements linking the past to the present, without violating the essential character of the past' (Leeson, 1976) and creates through imaginative appeal a world into which children will willingly travel. It helps children to make that imaginative leap into the past which genuine understanding of history demands. It carries conviction of reality in relation to the past. It does both these things by putting historical information into three dimensions, by personalizing events and by making vivid the setting.

A history book for children may provide pictures and descriptions of the homes of people of differing status in the later fifteenth century, it may supply extracts from inventories and wills of the better off to indicate their contents, it may sketch clothing, list conveyances and the pace and hazards of travel, or refer to the importance of the printing press and the economic and social changes it wrought, but translating such information into recognition of the actuality of the past involves a greater effort of imagination than most children can manage. A story like *The Load of Unicorn* (Harnet, 1959), to take one of many possible examples, can help them to do this. A scrivener's son, and the story offers a vivid referent for this difficult word, cherishes his tiny attic room, minimal privacy and few possessions. He moves among the crowded and dirty streets between home and school. He encounters Caxton, a gentleman of higher status than his father, is excited by his first sight and study of a printing press, becomes apprenticed to Caxton and is involved in travelling to Warwickshire to secure for printing a manuscript of Malory's *Morte D'Arthur*. His own brothers, scriveners fearful of damage to their trade, have indulged in crime to prevent the printing of this manuscript. Thus a great deal of history can be absorbed effortlessly in the pursuit of a gripping adventure story.

But the benefits of putting history in the round are not confined to these. One of the more difficult concepts to grasp in history, particularly since it is learned bit by bit, one thing after another, is the simultaneity of events and the fact that some are connected and some are not. Novels like those centring on the Crusades, for instance, which involve happenings in different countries, can help prepare that horizontal perspective which is so often a vital ingredient of historical understanding. Even more significant perhaps, novels can help the development of the concept of historical time. Characters grow up during a tale which refers to a series of well-known events, developments dismissed in a line in a text-book are shown to have taken several years of someone's life. Family sagas like the Flambards reveal change and continuity over a considerable period.

Related to this are Rosemary Sutcliff's reflections (1967) upon the telescoping effects of the conventional periodization of English history and the distorted picture it can produce. Wanting to write about the late Roman era, she paused to realize that the familiar dates meant that the Romans were in occupation of Britain for 450 years, that is, as long a time as lies between us and the Tudors. Their withdrawal in the early fifth century after generations of inter-breeding cannot have been that simple, and the traditional picture of an easy Saxon victory over a people gone soft must be erroneous – after all the conquest took 250 years. Out of such musings grew *The Lantern Bearers* (1959), and out of such imaginative stopping of the historical clock can grow much insight.

Important insights of another kind can stem from the change of angle afforded by fiction writers. Characters involved in great events like the French Revolution, for example, unlike the history text-book writer, do not know how the story ends, just as the people who made them did not. Moreover events are viewed from the limited angle of single or groups of characters, who often see them differently, and apprehend their significance, if at all, differently from the all-wise, all-knowing view almost inevitably characteristic of the text book, if not of the best scholarly writing.

Historical fiction can help the history teacher by making clear the reality of the past, helping children to read between the lines of their history books and to know what they are saying when they say that some mediaeval people thought the world was flat, that before the nineteenth century it took a very long time to accomplish journeys which are now over in a few hours, or that it really mattered to individuals that the government introduced the Factory Acts. Discussing fiction read by and with their pupils, history teachers can help the development of horizontal and vertical perspectives on the past and sharpen perception of the complexity of past circumstances and happenings.

There remains the problem of the fictional element. The characters and stories in the novels are largely made up and great men and great events are presented in ways that are at once simpler and fuller than the historian's knowledge justifies – simpler because novels can rarely accommodate the qualifications and uncertainties of historians; fuller because narrative requires details unimportant or unknown to historians. Does this not confuse children and contaminate their historical imagination? And, if personalization is desirable, does that not merely imply that greater use should be made of historical biography and autobiography? There are some history teachers who will always feel that and they can make a strong case. Moreover it must be emphasized that there is no intention to suggest that children's historical experience should consist entirely of the reading of historical fiction. What such teachers ignore however is the age-old power of the story to teach as it entertains. Not for nothing are the myth, the parable and the fable universal devices of religious and moral education, and the same principle applies in other areas.

Imaginative stimulus is a powerful aid to learning, as it is to memory, and make-believe is a natural activity among children, who are, nevertheless, capable of distinguishing it from real experience. Many authors, Geoffrey Trease and C. Walter-Hodges for example, point out the elements of fact and fiction in their stories for children to consider and, if they do not, then teachers may. In distinguishing what is true from what is invented, children take early steps along the road to the critical appraisal of sources, explanations and interpretation characteristic of history. Biographies and autobiographies are useful but few are written at a level suitable for children and they do not range very widely among the different classes of society or reach very far into early times. There is plenty of historical fiction readily available. It is difficult for children to make the connections between the various biographies, which are made for them in a story about a number of characters fictitious or real. Jesting, Pilate asked 'What is truth?' Teachers who eschew historical fiction are guilty by implication of too hasty and simplistic an answer.

Imaginative Writing

Children are more often required to write imaginatively about the past than to engage in role-play or to read historical novels. This is arguably the most difficult of the three, however, and rarely yields convincing results in terms of history. The reason is that the tasks set make inappropriate demands.

It is impossible to imagine something about which one has little information. The attempt to do so results in fantasy or invention, neither of which is conducive to historical thinking. Imaginative activity not based on experience or full information is likely to rely on sterotyping. Many classroom requests for imaginative writing about the past fall into one or other of these traps. 'How did the Egyptians get the huge blocks of stone up to the top of the pyramids? No one knows in detail. Imagine you were the engineer in charge and explain in words and drawing exactly how you would plan this difficult operation. Incidentally the Egyptians had no pulleys.' Here children are expected to imagine what is not known and are given no more than a picture of the pyramids and the brief statements in the assignment to go on. It calls for problem-solving skills but is not an historical exercise because it calls for imaginative reconstruction from lack of evidence – the reverse of imaginative activity appropriate to history. Another common type of invitation to 'pretend you are an Athenian citizen and discuss whether the city should abolish slavery or not' based on a few lines in a text book, expects children to imagine situations about which they have too little or unsuitable knowledge. All they can do is refer to stereotypes which encourage unhistorical generalization and the importing of present-bound assumptions into the past, both of which the teachers of history should be concerned to prevent.

Often what is known about the personalities and exploits of the famous is sufficient to make them come alive to children. Imaginative effort is better directed to counteracting the anonymity of historians' categories, so that the slave, peasant, merchant becomes personalized and individual. But even here there are problems. It may be that children's experience of being under authority makes it easier to imagine the life of the common man and it is certainly easier to write imaginatively about circumstances which arouse one's sympathy; so imaginative writing is often set about subjects like the workhouse or children in the mines. Even the ship's boy adventuring with Drake scarcely relieves the saga of the oppressed. Historians, however, need just as frequently to empathize with the powerful and the unfamiliar, to entertain thoughts and feelings with which they are out of sympathy and to consider routine as well as colourful aspects of past life. Imaginative writing by children should therefore include, perhaps concentrate upon, these much harder tasks. Directed imagining about the past is not playing make-believe and it is useless for the development of historical imagination and understanding unless it is grounded in evidence and unless it presents cognitive as well as affective challenges.

There remains the thorny question of evaluation and assessment. The exercise of imagination limited by evidence may be characteristic of the production of history, but the picture of the past the historian presents is meant to be true. History is a record of facts and well-attested judgments. It is imaginary only in the strict sense defined earlier and in no sense fictitious. When children read and comment upon historical novels, take part in role-play or simulation or write imaginatively they deal in fiction, and many historians and some teachers of history are troubled by this, as is evident from the castigation in some quarters of the setting and marking of empathy questions for GCSE. For the reasons indicated, their misgivings and the difficulty of setting and evaluating valid tests of the capacity for historical imagination should not be allowed to drive imaginative exercises from the history classroom. Professor Blyth offers many effective methods of gauging historical understanding. That manifested in imaginative exercises could be validly assessed if the word 'empathy' were abandoned and the process properly understood as *imagining*, bound by evidence and knowledge. The fruits of imaginative work should be seen and judged not as history but as part of the process of learning history, as stages, and probably essential companions, on the route to mastery of the discipline and knowledge of some of the record. That differences of historical understanding and knowledge may clearly be discerned in such work is demonstrated by the following pieces of work by two ten-year-olds, following some work on Spain's conquest of the Inca:

My voyage to a new land.
The centre mast was 100 feet tall and the stern mast was 95 feet tall.

The eight sails were slowly rising, the ropes were cast off and we slowly sailed out of the harbour. There was a good head wind so we should make good time.

After two hours of sailing they had travelled about 25 miles. The wind dropped a great deal after this. We just drifted for about two days then a terrible storm blew up and the ship was tossed about all over the place. One of the crew was thrown to his death when he came out of his cabin.

The storm lasted for three hours. For one and a half months we kept a good course and with a good head-wind we sailed two hundred and fifty miles.

By this stage quite a few of the crew had scurvy. I hand't got it because I had kept to a regular diet of ship's meat, ship's biscuits and rum.

There was now about 225 miles to go. At the speed we're going it should take about one and a half to two months to reach our destination.

The good wind kept up for one month more then luck faded. There was another big storm and we were blown 50 miles off course. Ten of the crew lost there lives trying to fold the sails and save them from ripping. A sudden wave came from out of nowhere and picked up the men and clashed them on some nearby rocks.

After the storm we were all shaken up and none of us felt like carrying out our duties. In the end we went back to work.

It took a week to get back on our intended course. When we eventually got back on course we found the wind was very strong and we docked one and a half months later.

The crew stayed on board ship and waited. Pizzaro and his soldiers attacked the Incas and took the gold. He came back and shared the gold out. The journey back was similar to the journey here only nobody was killed.

An Early Civilization

At dawn I woke up as usual and had my breakfast. I walked to the fields after I had brushed my hair. When I got there I picked up my almost U-shaped implement which was used for preparing the ground for sowing the seeds. Most of the one-feathered people were there and a few two's and three's. The number of feathers you have got on your headress indicates what position you are in the Inca society. I have one feather – that means I am the lowest in the society. We all chanted the rhythm and started digging. After we had done half a day's work we all remembered it was Festival day. We were going to have a feast!

We all got in pairs. You had to be with someone with the same number of feathers as you. We stood behind each other in pairs forming a long procession. The people with five feathers were in front with the people with four feathers behind them etc. I was near the end.

When we reached the chief Inca the first pair bowed in Inca

style – first raising your hands in the air and bowing low, turning your palms upwards (as if praising the Gods) and pressing your hands to your lips and clicking your tongue. Then we sat down opposite the person you came in with. We were not allowed to speak to anyone except the person opposite you; that was why you came with someone with the same amount of feathers as you.

Atahualpa (our chief) had to be handed his food first by someone with five feathers. Then the first couple of people picked up their food, then the next couple and so on until we could pick up our food. I was glad when I could pick up mine for I was very hungry from working in the fields.

There are two reasons why we hold festivals – one: because it is harvest and we thank the Gods for a good harvest and two: to give the workers a rest. This one was to thank the Gods for a harvest. When the festival ended we all went home.

The first piece is well-written, if rather derivative, but could be a description of almost any sea voyage, almost any time before the twentieth century. Bits and pieces of knowledge about nautical terms and scurvy for instance are thrown in, but there is no sense of historical time, no detail about the physical conditions in the ship. Only right at the end, and again very generally, are we given any idea about place and time. The second piece, less well-written, gives much more of a sense that a foreign experience and a different way of life has been recognized and understood. There are accurate references to tools and to notions of hierarchy and ceremonial. Factual information has been absorbed and a grasp of its meaning revealed by its translation into imaginative reconstruction.

These are not cited as indications of the best that primary-age children can achieve in imaginative writing about the past but because they illustrate levels commonly attained within classes of children set this type of task. Sylvester's examples, (pp. 26–27) are a more appropriate guide to the quality of work that can be produced when close study of particular historical topics is undertaken by children. To deny opportunities for such concentration and to deny the validity of imaginative writing as a means of learning, because they take time and are hard to classify or quantify, is not only to misunderstand the nature of history and of children learning about the past, but to betray, with an improverished model, the proper study of mankind.

Notes

1 See for example, Caldwell-Cook, H. (1917) *The Play Way – an Essay in Educational Method*, London, Heineman.
2 Further information and comment about historical fiction for children and its uses in history teaching can be found in Little, V. and John, T. (1986) 'Historical Fiction in the Classroom', *Teaching of History Series*, No. 59, Historical Association.

References

ARKELL, T. (1986) 'History's role in the school curriculum', *Journal of Educational Policy*, 3, 1, 23–38.

BEIK, W. (1977) 'Searching for popular culture in eighteenth-century France', *Journal of Modern History*, 49.

BRUNER, J. (1960) *The Process of Education*, New York, Vintage.

CARR, E.H. (1961) *What is History*, Harmondsworth, Penguin.

COLLINGWOOD, R. (1946) *The Idea of History*, London, Fontana.

FINES, J. (1977) 'Imagination and the Historian', *Teaching History*, 18, Historical Association.

GOUBERT, P. (1969) *The Ancien Regime*, London, Weidenfield and Nicholson.

HARNET, C. (1959) *The Load of Unicorn*, London, Methuen.

HEXTER, J.H. (1971) *The History Primer*, Harmondsworth, Penguin.

HUFTON, O. (1974) *Poverty in Eighteenth Century France*, Oxford, Oxford University Press.

KITSON-CLARK, G. (1967) *The Critical Historian*, London, Heinemann.

LATOUCHE, R. (1968) *Caesar to Charlemagne*, London, Phoenix.

LEESON, R. (1976) 'The spirit of what age?' *Children's Literature in Education*, 23.

LOYN, H. (1962) *Anglo-Saxon England and the Norman Conquest*, London, Longman.

RYLE, G. (1979) *On thinking*, Oxford, Basil Blackwell.

SUTCLIFF, R. (1958) *The Lantern Bearers*, Oxford, Oxford University Press.

TREVOR-ROPER, H. (1980) 'History and Imagination', *Times Literary Supplement*, 25 July.

TREVOR-ROPER, H. (1958) 'Historical Imagination', *The Listener*, 27 February.

WARNOCK, M. (1976) *Imagination*, London, Fraser and Fraser.

WEDGEWOOD, C. (1957) *The Sense of the Past*, Cambridge, Cambridge University Press.

WEDGEWOOD, C. (1960) 'History and Imagination', *Truth and Opinion: Historical Essays*, London, Collins.

Chapter 4

Past Imperfect, Future Conditional

Andre Wagstaff

Personal memories, as all historians know, are imperfect. External experiences are not merely forgotten, they go through a period of internal renegotiation. Our past is not just another country, it is one whose roads are unreliable, they rarely lead one to the same destination twice. And yet how important our personal memories are. I still preserve the liveliest recollections of my PGCE year. It all seemed to prepare me perfectly for running a local education authority. Less lofty matters, like just how one sets about enthusing young minds with a love of learning, seemed to be taken for granted. There were consequently some areas of classroom practice in which I lacked both knowledge, experience and confidence when I started my first job. It was as a class teacher of some thirty-eight 8-year-olds. The school had a curriculum. All I had to do was follow it.

Unfortunately, the children had other ideas. Some time in the first term I decided that we really must get down to some history. I felt full of confidence as we began the first lesson on the Normans. After all, history was a subject I had always enjoyed, and the Norman period was an especial favourite. So I assumed that all would be well. Such misplaced confidence! Within five minutes I knew just how Harold might have felt when he was delivered into the hands of Duke William – deep unease with my present predicament and a sense that worse would follow. My children had no concept at all of how long ago all this was, no idea of why we might be studying these people, precious little interest in any of the resources I had scraped together; they did, however, have a lively suspicion that the lesson was going to wind up with them having to write all about it. We looked at some rather small illustrations of knights in hauberks and agreed that they were probably soldiers by profession. Towards the end of the lesson we managed a halting discussion about the ways in which people often keep things from the past. All the children said that they kept things. 'And my nan, she's got something the Normans left', came a comment from Jason at the back of the room. 'Wonderful',

I said, playing for time. 'I can bring it in tomorrow, if you like'. Now, I might have been a primary teacher for a matter of weeks, but I already knew that children often make offers which you're not meant to take too seriously. Imagine my surprise when Jason staggered in the next day with a duffle bag. Inside was a bundle of newspaper. 'There,' he said triumphantly. He unwrapped the bundle amidst a concentrated silence. There was a collective sigh of admiration. There, like some loathsome devil's fruit, lay a small incendiary bomb from the Second World War. That was the moment when questions began to form in my head about history, its niche in education, and the ways in which we teach it to young children. The questions have never ceased to come, perhaps they never will. One of the more recent questions concerns the use of information technology.

Educationists have always taken a delight in posing questions. Sometimes these are rhetorical, the predictable answers which follow may fill the page but our intellectual appetites remain unsatisfied. Sometimes the questions are much more awkward, they cause us to look searchingly at the very roots of the education process. These latter questions are often unanswerable or unanswered. They are, however, much more interesting – not because of any direct answers they produce, but because they cause us to stop and think for a moment.

This article revolves around one central question which is: has information technology a role to play in the study of history as part of the primary curriculum? It is tempting to plunge straight in with an answer, and as you might anticipate the answer is a qualified 'yes', but I should like to take a little time considering some of the underlying issues. Some of these relate to the primary curriculum, some to history as a subject of study. Is the primary curriculum actually discussable? Where does history fit in? What are the things – concepts, skills, attitudes – which a primary child can be expected to learn from history? How best should we teach history? How best do children learn? How do we arrive at a sensible content for the history syllabus?

In a sense the answers to some of these questions may seem self-evident. But there are at least two answers to the questions: why do giraffes have long necks? The two answers lead us to very different views of the world we live in. And so it is with any questions about primary education.

The primary curriculum has evolved over the past fifty or so years. There was a great deal of debate between the two World Wars as to the character of young children and how education should best service their needs. The consensus view was that the primary stage should be recognized as one deserving its own consideration and provision. And the nature of the primary curriculum is encapsulated in that timeless quote from the Hadow Report (1931):

> The curriculum is to be thought of more in terms of activity and experience rather than of knowledge to be acquired and facts to be stored.

But it took rather more than twenty years for these views to translate into the general establishment of primary schools. There was considerable experimentation in designs of building, in teaching and learning methods, and in the curriculum. A tradition of primary learning was engendered which springs from the ideas of theorists such as Montessori, Neale, Dewey, Piaget, and Froebel. The whole may be considered to have met with the seal of official approval when the Plowden Report (1967) observed:

> It lays special stress on individual discovery, on first hand experience and on opportunities for creative work. It insists that knowledge does not fall into separate compartments and that work and play are not opposite but complementary.

It would be nice if we could leave the primary curriculum at this point – a perfect example of optimistic history. Yet we cannot. Since 1967 the primary sector has been squeezed by financial constraints, pummelled by politicians of every political hue, belaboured by searching questions posed by academics and HMI. Perhaps this is as it should be but the inescapable conclusion is that the primary curriculum must not be thought of as something fixed, immutable, and reducible to a series of lists. Instead it is dynamic, subject to considerable change and external influences. In short, the primary curriculum relates more to the world of Ariel than Caliban.

Faced with a model of the primary curriculum in which change and re-interpretation are very much the order of the day, history must have some good reasons to offer if it is to maintain its place.

One main reason has been advanced by the recently published *History from 5 to 16* (DES, 1988):

> the school curriculum provides one of the fundamental ways in which society transmits its cultural heritage to new generations.

It is difficult to see any other subject than history being a suitable vehicle for the transmission of cultural heritage – their concerns lie elsewhere.

There are good psychological reasons to explain why very young children base their interpretations of events on how these directly affect them. They are, in a word, self-centred. Yet any workable model of society depends upon its individuals having some awareness of the needs and attitudes of others. So a second reason for the study of history might be that it leads to a realization of otherness, a growing awareness that the child is part of life, rather than at its centre.

Whatever else we may assume about the future which awaits our children, we are not entitled to assume that it will be like today. We should aim to equip our children with the mind–set which can make sense of a changing world. Thus, a third justification for the place of history might be that it can lead one to insights which help in the understanding of present and future social developments.

But where does information technology (IT) come into all this? *Curriculum matters: History from 5 to 16* devotes some nine lines to its consideration, four of which consist of a 'health' warning:

> Teachers should be on their guard against uses of IT which, while posing problems ostensibly set in past times, do not really stimulate pupils to ask historical questions or to think about historical issues.

Now it is true that IT like any other device can be beneficial or harmful according to the ways in which we use it. And of course IT should be subservient to the needs of historians rather than their masters, but its potential is so great that it surely demands further articulation.

First of all, IT covers all machines which process information. At its broadest it includes everything from telephones to washing machines, supermarket checkouts to calculators. But the most pervasive of all is the computer. It is pervasive because it is essentially a protean device, capable of assuming a myriad roles and guises. The computers that land a space shuttle or entertain at an amusement arcade are, like Kipling's Judy O'Grady and the colonel's lady, very much sisters under the skin.

Educationists have found that in the computer they too have a tool which can be used in very different ways to very different ends. As Turkle (1984) observes:

> The computer is evocative not only because of its holding power, but because holding power creates the condition for these different things to happen. An analogy captures the first of these: the computer, like a Rorschach inkblot test, is a powerful projective medium. Unlike stereotypes of a machine with which there is only one way of relating – stereotypes built from images of workers following the rhythm of a computer-controlled machine tool or children sitting at computers that administer maths problems for drill – we shall see the computer as a partner in a great diversity of relationships.

There has been a great deal of experimentation over the past six years since computers have been introduced into primary classrooms. We now seem to be reaching an agreement that computers are not there for their own sake. They are there to support and extend the existing curriculum, they are there so that children can learn to use them as tools which will help their learning, and they are there so that children can begin to appreciate the range of ways in which computers can be used and the likely effect of this on their lifestyles.

Some of the first computer programs to reach primary schools were of the type which offered support to the existing curriculum. They set out to offer practice in specific skills or convey specific information. The authors knew exactly what route the child would take through the program and the desired end. The content of such programs is usually fixed and they are very easy for teachers to use. Literally all that is required is the ability to load the program into the machine. At first, their quality was not of the highest. In the main they revolve around language and numbers. Perhaps fortunately, few of these lend themselves directly to use in a historical context. However, it is worth noting that a program such as CARTOON can be of indirect use to primary historians. In CARTOON children are set the task of constructing cartoons from a bank of pre-drawn, animated images. The order in which these images are shown, the time each will appear, and the explanatory commentary or sound track are left to the imagination of the children involved. Experience of using a program like CARTOON could help a child meet some of the objectives identified by HMI in *History from 5 to 16*:

- put objects or pictures with historical features in a sequence of 'before' or 'after' and to give reasons for doing so;
- use basic vocabulary related to time such as: 'now', 'long ago', 'before', 'after';

It was not long before people began to write programs which offered children experiences which enriched and extended the curriculum. They were written with a definite goal for the user but which left considerable latitude for the route taken to that goal. The content of such programs is often fixed, although some do allow for its variation through the creation of data files. Sometimes these programs have modest aims. SHIELDS allows children to design their own shield. They can choose from a limited selection of heraldic devices and so decide best where they should be placed. It is also possible to design new devices. Programs such as these are only of real worth if used as one of a wide range of activities. The teacher should not expect them to act as a central feature in any historical project.

Simulations offer more possibilities, but pose greater problems. Historical simulations appeared at an early stage. Some were simplistic: FLETCHER'S CASTLE casts children into the role of a knight trying to build a castle. Some were much more complex: MARY ROSE revolves around the raising of a sunken Tudor warship from the chilly waters of the Solent. Some teachers would wish to distinguish between simulations which are based on actual incidents – TITANIC is one such, or those which are more loosely based on the sort of thing that happened in a particular period of history. And there is obviously a fundamental difference between the two. But it is not likely that young children will perceive much of this difference – both will seem equally plausible. Both types are founded on the supposition that they offer the child an opportunity 'to set aside reality and, in his imagination, act within the created "world"' (Holmes, *et al.*, 1985) Both types hold to the idea that they are offering extensions to the existing curriculum. How do they do this?

Firstly, they give children access to experiences which would otherwise be denied them. Considerations of safety, time, expense and practicality militate against children actually building castles, salvaging warships or administering to a city stricken with plague. No simulation on any computer at present in our schools could pretend to offer perfect simulations of these phenomena, therefore they are in no way a subsitute for first hand experience. But they can offer an approximation of some of the main factors involved and allow children to experience events from the past. Experiences such as these can produce as indelible a mark in the mind as a well-written book, and we have yet to see literature condemned on the grounds of not offering first hand experience. It is the quality and educational value of an experience, not just its nature, which should be of concern to us.

Secondly, computer simulations can act as a focus or catalyst for other work in the classroom. A good historical simulation can kindle the enthusiasm of children and increase their enjoyment. Enthusiasm and enjoyment are not, of course, sufficient prerequisites for the study of history, but they are surely very necessary ones. An accurate simulation operates to extend the powers of the teacher, and to facilitate the setting up of circumstances in which equal appeal is made to children's imagination and to the skills and knowledge which they already possess. We should not see computer simulations as turning one's back on the real world, but as a window which offers a fresh vantage point. The views so gained should lead to children researching in books, conducting surveys, checking records, engaging in drama, dance, model making, creative writing, art, music and discussion. These are all activities which can be sparked off as a consequence of a class embarking on a simulation. These activities then echo back to the work on the micro, enhancing the educational value of the simulation.

Thirdly, simulations are worthwhile as a vehicle for the fostering of personal and social skills. They provide an opportunity for children to work in small groups under conditions which call for genuine co-operation. This makes a welcome change from the all too frequent pitting of one child against another. A good historical simulation will provide the opportunity for each child to feel that a valuable contribution has been made to the group's success. Simulations give a chance for children to engage in negotiation and purposeful debate with their peers. From this debate can come a respect for evidence and a toleration of a range of values. Many of these programs demand that the children engage in role-play and some do this to great effect. Empathy, or the ability to see things from a variety of viewpoints, is not something which develops easily in the young. The experience of arguing and decision-making whilst taking the role of another can be a strong mediating factor in the development of a child's ability to understand the distinct perspectives and preconceptions of another person who lived in the past. A program such as WAGGONS WEST can help children see that your view of the significance of events varies according to your place in society.

It would, of course, be a mistake to see simulations as being the only or even the main sort of program which can serve the needs of the primary historian. Simulations are not good in all circumstances; indeed not all simulations are good. FLETCHER'S CASTLE is a simulation which tries to approximate the problems of running a fief in Norman England. Decisions have to be made as to how best to employ scarce resources of labour. The relationship between actions taken and later effects are not always easy to explain or infer. Some groups of children succeed in building their castle, some don't. Success does not necessarily depend upon understanding of the consequences of the decisions taken. There are considerable doubts as to the historical accuracy of the content of the simulation. For example, desertion was a problem of a later age. And yet it would be equally hard to deny the great interest which this program initially generates. So we must be careful to look beyond the superficial appearance of a simulation. Other simulations are extremely well executed, yet have severe problems due to historical accuracy being sacrificed to other educational aims. Thus THE GREAT PLAGUE asks children to choose a character who will engage in the administration of the City of London as it reels under the impact of the plague. Many of the characters on offer are female. Perfectly understandable in a modern classroom context, but the plain fact is that few women held much executive administrative power in those days. A historical simulation should never sacrifice demonstrable historical evidence for contemporary convenience.

Finally, we should beware of equating the use of computers in primary history solely with the use of historical simulations. They necessarily attempt a crude model of a past reality. On their own, experiences such as those are no more sufficient than offering children a learning diet wholly made up of books. We should be encouraging children to use and understand first-hand evidence rather than second-hand, to be able to formulate their own hypotheses about the past and then to devise their own tests for them. It is very difficult to see how historical simulations on their own can achieve this. Perhaps we should look to them to provide the sort of experiences which will help children acquire the skills of researching, arranging and interpreting facts. These are all skills which are necessary if children are to think and reason well. Most historical tasks will require the setting of goals, the making of plans, and the carrying out and refining of those plans. An ability to do these things is one which we as teachers need to nurture and encourage. Simulations are a possible route to achieving this.

One final point on simulations concerns the role of the teacher. It is, as always, crucial. It is perfectly possible to use simulations in an extremely prescriptive and didactic fashion. The authors of a simulation package may have spent a lot of time and effort in trying to make it exciting, challenging, and thought provoking. But it will have none of these results unless the teacher encourages children to use their initiative, to consider the decisions which can be taken, and to reflect on their experience.

Besides simulations, primary historians have made use of the type of software which exists to be used as a tool. And these differ fundamentally from simulations. Simulations aim to provide questions; the children have to find answers. Tool software, on the other hand, will help provide answers, but it is up to children to determine the questions.

Writers of such software can envisage the broad purposes for which they may be used; they cannot pretend to know exactly what each user will have in mind. Into the tools category fall the word processors such as WRITER or FOLIO, information handling packages like GRASS, and computer languages such as PROLOG. These are not the easiest programs to use, since they impose a heavy burden on the teacher. The burden does not lie so much in the amount of effort needed to master the mechanics of how one drives the program, as in the need for a teacher to know where and when it is educationally appropriate to use it, and how best children should be taught to use it. Word processors are actually fairly easy for children and teachers to use – the hard bit is learning to use them profitably. Information retrieval packages pose greater problems. Firstly, it is much harder to see what it going on when you search a database. Secondly neither teachers nor young children have much in the way of pre-existing mental images to which they can attach their experience of using a computer to sort and classify information.

Teachers need to think hard before introducing information retrieval packages into the classroom. What sort of prior experiences should their children have had? How much previous practice should children have at sorting concrete objects into sets using a variety of sorting criteria? What experience of storing and sorting information on a conventional card index system do children need before being introduced to an information retrieval program? These questions demand an answer before a teacher embarks on the use of such powerful pieces of software. It is also important that teachers are aware of both the power and the limitations of such computer programs.

In view of the above, we might have expected primary historians to have made greater use of word processors than information retrieval packages. However, the reverse has been the case – perhaps because the latter seems to offer more. Thus Banks (1987) when head of Wadworth First and Middle School found CENSUS an invaluable aid in enabling his children to study census material for Wadworth from 1851 to 1881. The number of records involved total over 2500. Actually obtaining and then entering this information was not easy. Entries from the census could be compared with other data collected from other activities such as visiting local graveyards. His children were able to search through this comparatively large volume of data and use the results to support or rebut their differing hypotheses. Banks notes:

> All these activities gave the children an interesting insight into historical documents and a desire to unravel the mysteries of the past. It also made history come alive especially since it related to ordinary people such as themselves, not those from some unknown community but those from their own village.

SORTING GAME is an example of a particularly useful type of information handling program for the historian. Essentially, the user 'teaches' the micro to distinguish between different objects by typing in questions whose answers reveal which of the objects is being considered. A completed file is very much like a simple 'expert system'. But all the real work of classification, of deciding how you distinguish between one object and another, has had to be thought through by the children. Programs of this type encourage children into thinking analytically, of considering concepts such as similarity and difference – all things which are necessary adjuncts of the historian.

The usefulness of information retrieval packages to primary historians is apparent. Yet word processor and text handling packages have much more to offer. Bennett (1988) has pointed out that besides helping children write with greater clarity, the redrafting facility of a word processor allows groups of children to restructure and shape a piece of historical writing. She also points to the benefits of newsroom simulations and newspaper-formatting programs. Programs such as these may, at first, seem to lie outside the interests of the primary historians. But they can be remarkably useful to teachers who can discern their qualities as a tool for communication.

In one Londonderry primary school children were intrigued by their elders tales of the last War. They went and interviewed some of the witnesses. From their evidence the children pinpointed areas where the bombs fell. Visits to people living in houses nearby added fresh evidence. The children decided to see what the local press reports had had to say. To their dismay, there were huge discrepancies. Nothing daunted, they tracked down the retired editor. And he explained the constraints that censorship had placed on him. To put it plainly, the newspaper report was not authoritative. The children decided to remedy this state of affairs. Using FRONT PAGE EXTRA they produced versions of what the paper should have said, basing the contents on the fruits of all their research. Some educationists may argue that a computer was not a necessary ingredient in this exercise – maybe not, but it was vital to the children's perceptions. They were reporter/investigators for their newspapers, and it was important that the end product looked like a newspaper.

In a somewhat similar vein teachers have used EXTRA to inject a sense of immediacy into the classroom situation. EXTRA relays messages (previously typed in by the teacher) as a series of news flashes on the computer screen. The teacher has control over the timing and number of these messages. The program makes provision for the printing of multiple copies of each flash. Groups of children attempt to turn these messages into a coherent story, working to a publishing deadline. Thus children are faced with a mass of information, sometimes conflicting, always partial. Experiences such as these encourage children to see that interpretations of events are subject to change and are always tentative.

Some text handling programs have recently appeared which address very real needs of the historian in the primary classroom. Two which spring to mind are TIMELINES and TOUCH EXPLORER.

TIMELINES allows children to create, amend and print out information in the style of the traditional format. The computer offers two especial advantages. First, the micro handles all scaling problems

– and as anyone who has struggled with squared paper and rulers knows, this is a godsend. Secondly, you can choose how the timeline will be displayed. For example, if you decide to display in centuries, only events which have had century significance ascribed to them will appear. The effect of this is that one can scan timelines at different levels of magnification, zooming in to areas which attract attention and observing a greater and greater amount of detail. Conventional timelines pose such problems that few are constructed by children or classroom teachers. And even if one could justify the time, storage difficulties would prevent their creation on any large scale. The micro offers the potential for each child to maintain their own timeline, adding in personal events amongst items of local and national news. Sensitive teachers will be quick to put this type of software to good use.

TOUCH EXPLORER makes use of a Concept keyboard. Until recently the preserve of children with special needs, the Concept keyboard is a flat, touch sensitive rectangle on which paper overlays can be clipped. The overlays can consist of diagrams, pictures, maps or what you will. Pressing on any portion of the rectangle causes a message pertaining to that area to appear on the screen of the micro. The whole is under the control of the teacher who can create and modify both paper overlay and underlying computer messages. This type of program will do little on its own. But in the hands of the enthusiastic teacher, its potential is vast. Teachers have used the same overlay to promote group discussions about choices for settlements, to provoke debate about archaeological sites, and to consider change of land usage over time.

One final class of software which exists for primary use is that of those utilities which form a bridge for the extension of a computer's powers. Communications software such as that offered by COMMUNITEL or CAMPUS 2000 falls into this category; so do some utility programs. These are only of any real value if teachers and children are already comfortable with the use of word processors and information retrieval packages. Communications software offers considerable potential to the historian. It enables schools to communicate with other schools. And not just schools within this country, but also schools across the world. Schools in Devon, twinned with schools in Tasmania, were amazed at the different weight given to the same historical events. The sailing of the First Fleet is something the Devon children were barely aware of. At the same time there were events which schoolchildren in both communities shared a common intepretation. Next year will see the linking of schools in England with a matching number in the Netherlands. Some of the exchanges of information will relate to studies of some common historical theme.

Ten years ago, such exchanges would have been unthinkable, five years ago, they would have been dismissed as theoretical moonshine. Today, they are eminently practicable. All that is required is an appreciation of their educational benefits.

Looking to the future there can be little doubt that we are going to see the micro offering even more support for the primary child who is studying history. Galloping towards us come the convergent technologies of such items as Interactive Video, Compact Disc, Compact Disc Interactive and doubtless others – the key fact is that they all involve large, really large, volumes of information (in words, figures, sounds and pictures) which we can explore, often in conjunction with a suitable microcomputer.

Consider the implications of CD-ROM. Here we have a medium which can store huge quantities of information. Technical people will say it is somewhere around 550 megabytes – but most of us will feel more comfortable with the notion that it could store the text of 500 novels. Better, yet, a CD-ROM can contain a mixture of text, computer graphics, digitized sounds, and a program which allows you to navigate your way around.

Thus the '49 Goldrush might be portrayed in text, sound and graphics. The way in which you explored this treasure-house of information might vary according to the persona you had decided to adopt, maybe a prospector, a newspaper reporter, or perhaps a member of an Indian tribe. Furthermore, the text would be interactive to a degree. Children could request more detail, place chunks of text in an electronic satchel, for later analysis, or make quick notes on a scratchpad. The possibilities are limited only by our imaginations, and the length of the educational purse.

The processing power of the microcomputer and its ability to handle sophisticated graphics and sound is advancing at a dizzy pace. Software, particularly educational software, which makes use of these advances, is still in its infancy. But there are portents of things to come. For example there is at least one spreadsheet which is able to display data in three-dimensional map form. We can look forward to viewing historical sites from any perspective we care to choose.

Of such stuff are dreams or nightmares made of. But what will be the likely impact of IT on primary history over, say, the next five years? One thing is certain. The National Curriculum will cause some very fundamental changes in the way history is taught.

Whilst we can hope that:

The content of history courses has to be continually re-assessed and recast. (DES, 1988) there will equally be a need:

> for teachers in primary, middle and secondary schools to come together and plan for continuity in history courses. (DES, 1988)

Providing that the National Curriculum working party on history shows approval, it is to be hoped that many more primary schools will move away from the Cavemen to Vikings approach and will begin to look more closely at the benefits of local historical studies. History at a local level offers a great opportunity for children to achieve a growing mastery of historical skills. First hand experience of data acquisition, analysis of differing sources of evidence, use of primary and secondary sources to support interpretations of events and the making of imaginative reconstructions of the past are all eminently workable at a local level.

And Information Technology? Well, the National Curriculum is certainly not going to involve primary children studying IT for its own sake. Instead they will be using it as an educational tool. In using it they will both acquire information skills and will begin to see not only benefits but, more importantly, the limitations of this particular dimension of technology. Naturally, if this is to happen, then there are implications for resourcing on a far larger scale than any we have yet seen. You can't really expect children to see IT as just another resource unless they have regular liberal access to it. A micro shared between several classes does not even begin to address the real need.

Will children be using IT within the context of primary history? The crystal ball of prophecy darkens, time alone will tell. The last five years have enabled us to identify fruitful areas where IT can genuinely benefit the delivery of the primary historians availing themselves of this powerful aid to understanding. If they fail to do so, our children will be denied a great opportunity.

References

BANKS, D. (1988) 'Information Interface, *Information Handling Pack*, MESU.

BENNETT, S. (1988) 'Synthesizers', *Times Educational Supplement* 9, 12, 88.

BOARD OF EDUCATION (1931) *Primary Education: The Hadow Report on Primary Education*, London, HMSO.

CENTRAL ADVISORY COUNCIL FOR EDUCATION (1967) *Children and their Primary Schools: The Plowden Report*, London, HMSO.

HOLMES, B., WHITTINGTON, I, FLETCHER, S. (1985) *The Child, the Teacher and the Micro*, Cambridge, Scholastic Services.

DES (1988) *Curriculum Matters: History from 5 to 16*, London, HMSO.

TURKLE, S. (1984) *The Second Self: Computers and the Human Spirit*, London, Granada.

Computer Programs

CARTOON (MESU)
EXTRA (Shropshire Educational Computing Centre)
FLETCHERS CASTLE (Fernleaf)
FRONT PAGE SPECIAL EDITION (Newman College)
MARY ROSE (Cambridgeshire Software House)
SHIELDS (Fernleaf)
SORTING GAME (MESU)
THE GREAT PLAGUE (Tressell)
TIMELINES (unpublished)
TITANIC (esm)
TOUCH EXPLORER PLUS (MESU)
WAGGONS WEST (Tressell)

Addresses

Cambridgeshire Software House
Town Hall
St Ives
Cambs PE17 4AL

esm
32 Bridge Street
Cambridge CB2 1UJ

Fernleaf Education Software
Fernleaf House
31 Old Road West
Gravesend
Kent DA11 0LH

MESU
Sir William Lyons Road
University of Warwick
Coventry CV4 7EZ

Newman College Computer Centre
Newman College
Bartley Green
Birmingham B32 3NT

Shropshire Educational Computing Centre
Shrewsbury
Salops

Tressell Publications
Lower Ground Floor
70 Grand Parade
Brighton BN2 2JA

Chapter 5

Primary History and the National Curriculum

Sallie Purkiss

Introduction

The news that history was to be a foundation subject in the National Curriculum came as a relief to teachers of history in secondary schools and higher education institutions, who had become accustomed to periodic exhortations that their subject was in danger and to seeing their timetable slots slipping away under pressure from integrated humanities, student options and the need for more business, science and technology courses. Their reaction, as Sylvester implies, was not widely shared among primary teachers. To many even the actual listing of subjects appeared threatening, and, coupled with the proposals to introduce testing at the ages of 7 and 11, it looked like the end of an era. The very mention of history was regarded by some as an anachronism. Integrated topic work, environmental or social studies, even humanities seemed far more acceptable. Many feared the return of a uniform diet of dates and facts to be learned by rote in place of process approaches given impetus by the new history.

Certainly much good, genuinely historical work has been seen at primary level over the past few years. Sylvester, Wagstaff and Little, in earlier chapters, indicate some of the forms it should and does take. Higher education selectors know that interest generated by a primary school topic – a study of a local Roman fort for example or the creation of a classroom museum of Second World War memorabilia – is often cited by candidates as an experience which 'turned them on' to history. Nevertheless, expertise in history has not been a good career bet at primary level. In-service funding has been sparse and opportunities for promotion have often led those trained in history to divert their attention to curriculum areas given a higher priority profile.

Several surveys have confirmed a picture of confusion as far as primary history is concerned. Sudworth, from Copperfield County

Middle School, in Milton Keynes, analyzed the changes since 1960 (Sudworth, 1982). Until then the traditional pattern reflected in the ubiquitous Unstead textbooks, *Cavemen to Vikings* in year 1, *The Middle Ages* in year 2, *The Tudors and Stuarts* in year 3 and *The Georgians and Victorians* in year 4 had been universal practice. In the intervening twenty years some teachers had moved from this position to the project method. Some liked the line of development approach, transport being a favourite topic; others had ventured into the local environment to look at tangible remains of the past in their own neighbourhoods. The most popular way of accommodating history however was through children's independent 'research' among library books, a method roundly condemned by HMI, in their survey *Primary Education in England*, (1978). On visits to school they had observed mindless copying and concluded that few children were being stretched or challenged in this area of the curriculum. The most recent survey, from Chester College in 1975, revealed a lack of uniformity in aims, teaching strategies or topics taught. Few schemes were informed by theory, guidelines for the selection of content were non-existent and a vast range of local resources was scarcely exploited, at all.[1] It is unlikely that the new survey, currently awaited from HMI, will show much development in the direction to which their 1978 survey pointed.

The coming of the National Curriculum represents an opportunity for the false dichotomy between content and skills, which has bedevilled curriculum planning in history over the past few years, to be resolved and for time-wasting discontinuities between the primary and secondary sectors to be overcome. Although efforts to make arguments for including history in the primary curriculum are now unnecessary, with history securely nominated as a foundation subject, careful study of the principles on which it should be based is nevertheless essential. In particular, we must continue to be watchful that the content of history, however organized, is not misused.

One aspect of their brief, which will no doubt be exercising the minds of the recently-appointed History working group will be the handling of the national history which the Secretary of State has advised should be 'the core' of the 'programmes of study' they recommend. Socially-aware adults, and we assume the members of the Working Party must be counted among them, know that history can be used to promote a particular set of messages. Media experts call it 'image-making'. In the case of advertizing it is achieved by carefully selecting what is put before the public; in totalitarian states by promoting a particular view of their pasts. How we all laugh when we read in the newspapers of new regimes in other parts of the world, who pull down statues erected by their predecessors, who rename streets and even states, replacing the honoured hero of one generation by another. Such a thing could never happen here, we say. Yet all they are doing is substituting one version of history for another and the history that is taught in schools is usually re-orientated at the same time. When Gorbachev was manouvering his perestroika through the Supreme Soviet, history examinations were suspended. A state system of education can easily be used to uphold the values of one regime rather than another and prescribing a view of history is one way in which this can be done. As George Orwell wrote in *1984*: 'he who controls the past, controls the present'.

Identifying Good Practice

The chief justification for a National Curriculum is that it will extend the good practice evident in some schools to all for the benefit of the children and the Nation. Some recent publications designed to remedy shortcomings in history teaching with the younger age range, cite appropriate examples of good practice, refer to research undertaken in the field of children's capacity for understanding history and offer guidance for the important decisions about organization and content which must now be taken.

HMI themselves have given some examples both in their document published in 1985, *History in the Primary and Secondary Years: an HMI view* and in *Primary Schools: Some aspects of good practice*, (DES, 1987). They point to projects where primary children handled documents, statistics and other evidence to plot change in their own communities. Using evidence to distinguish between what was real and what was story also led, in some schools, to the internalization of a respectful attitude towards versions of the past. The textbook or the TV programme may not provide all the answers; some of these need to be investigated for their authenticity or published versions compared with the experiences of the people who lived in the children's own locality. Even infants are capable of finding out through investigation. *Aspects of Good Practice* gives the example of a class in search of D–Day, forty years after it happened and shows how the TV story could be verified by interviewing some of the local people who had lived through the period.

Some LEAs have also produced publications which lay down standards for good practice. The best of these provide theoretical frameworks, suggest approaches and back up their recommendations by citing examples from their own schools. In some cases LEA advisers drew up the documents, with a supporting team of advisory teachers in response to goverment requests to LEAs to draw up guideline policy documents. In several areas a team of teachers worked together to collect the best examples from among their colleagues. One of the first was from ILEA in 1980. *History in the Primary School* took teachers through the options open to them when planning schemes of work. After a number of statements which emphasized the nature of historical enquiry and the reasons why it is important in the education of all children, suggestions were made for tackling both a period approach, such as the Tudors, (but unlike the Unstead version, this one placed great emphasis on the children experiencing Tudor life) and schemes which emphasized skills, such as sequencing or putting things in a time order, hypothesizing or making guesses about the evidence as well as the cross-curricular skills relating to observation, recording and researching in the library. Shortly afterwards, Avon's two pamphlets *In Search of the Past* and *In Touch with the Locality* (Avon, RLDU, 1983) appeared. These gave more examples of approaching history as a problem-solving activity and showed the challenges which could be put to children through the use of artefacts and documents.

Wiltshire's publication *History-based Topic Work* (1987), reports on work done in the county and shows how history topics can all draw on authentic evidence from each period with the addition of secondary sources, including historical novels as back up material. It is full of practical examples of active history from the pre-historic period up to the twentieth century and shows how historical starting points develop and inspire cross-curricular work of a demanding standard.

Teaching History, too, has published articles describing successful classroom projects. Hall, (1980), bought some old postcards from a flea market and set the children the task of making some assumptions about Rose, the recipient of the postcards. Young children are naturally curious and become motivated when set a problem. Wright, (1984), in his article 'A small local investigation' described the outcomes of a project which began when the class found some old pieces of china in a ditch at the bottom of the school field. What they learned about the past from their finds, thanks to the skill of a teacher who knew how to capitalize on their enthusiasm, they could not have learnt as effectively from any book.

— In the past there were no plastics or dustbins.
— The school field had once been the garden of a big old house.
— Old bricks were made with pebbles as well as clay.
— More rubbish rotted in the past than it does today.

The project led them to invite a museum education officer to view their finds. She showed them other ways to catalogue them and invited them to see 'her' collection in the museum. Such infant experiences can lead not only to an understanding of evidence but to an appreciation of the value of those who work in history as archaeologists, as curators and as conservators. Their understanding of heritage and the need to value it will have been considerably enhanced by practical experience.

Another project which makes *Cavement to Vikings* look like a comic strip has been undertaken in the Southampton area by Woodhouse and Wilson (1988). With students from La Sainte Union College of Higher Education and teachers and children from local schools they organize history through drama days which represent the culmination of a term's work in school reading, talking and investigating. Finally children experience imaginatively what, for example it may have been like living in their area 2,000 years earlier.

There also exists a small body of research in the field of primary history. West, (1981), asked questions about young children's awareness of the past and found they were much more knowledgeable than teachers often realized. Blyth (1987), Cooper (1986) and Knight (1988), are concerned with finding out how far children can understand concepts such as cause, conflict and power. More definite data on this are needed, but such information is crucial for the identification of how children may make progress within the structure of a National Curriculum.

A Plea to the Working Party

At the time of writing the Working Group for history has not published its interim report. This, like those already published for other subjects, will, we assume, be a document for consultation. What considerations should guide the group's thinking? A first concern, and one which they are charged to deliver by the Secretary of State, is the preservation of that enthusiasm for history which early study of the subject can undoubtedly generate in the young. Ross (1986) illustrates this well when he examines his own feelings, as an adult historian, and what he learned from this about planning work with children: 'I remember the pounding of my heart, the blood singing in my ears, the drying of my mouth. It is perfectly possible for primary children to achieve the same sense of excitement in original research in the classroom'.

The use of locally-generated resources is also extremely popular with children and adults, including parents and governors. Although these may start with the near and familiar they can lead to the realization that people and places are not islands. Almost everyone and everywhere has links to other parts of the world. How were the handloom weavers of Lancashire connected to the producers of cotton in Lancashire (Searle-Chatterjee, 1985). Where did the battalion featured on the war memorial actually fight and why? What is the story behind that curious inscription in the cemetery? Why did twenty-six couples get married on Saturday afternoon. What was it really like in the Second World War? Was it like the TV version of Eastenders in 1940, recently produced as a TV film, or does Mrs Smith at the pensioner's club have a more accurate account of the experience? She didn't live in Albert Square. Is this important?

Local sources give children and teachers 'hands on' experience. Many museum officers can help provide resources through lessons at the museum or as loan boxes for the classroom. Activity methods do not exclude the use of books, as gullible media reporters sometimes insinuate. We all use books to find further information if we have been working in the field of history for six weeks or sixty years. But books are only of use if you have some idea of the questions you seek to answer and young children need to be schooled to articulate the questions as well as to use indexes, libraries and catalogues to find some of the answers. Sylvester has suggested how this can be done (*see* Chapter 2).

Ways of recording and reflecting on knowledge and experience in history topics fit easily into the pattern of good primary practice. Language activities of all kinds – factual reporting, talk, story writing, simulated diaries, writing books – are all part of history. Historians are forced back on language all the time. Creative activities, music-making, cooking, artwork and model-making all help children interpret what they have learned. Insufficient connections have perhaps been made at the time of writing between history and the more publicized curriculum subjects – science, mathematics, craft, design and technology. Closer consideration will reveal that all share similar aims. A pamphlet from the Engineering Council, *Problem Solving: Science and Technology in Primary Schools* (1985), makes explicit some of these links. The case study included shows a project work based on the Abbeydale Industrial Hamlet in Sheffield. In *Design and Primary Education* (Design Council, 1987) the relevance of the historical example again prevails. One class is shown deliberating on the best materials to use for castle building. Well, what would you use if you wanted to get a castle up in a hurry and how permanent would your structure be?

Many of the objectives listed in the two publications in the *Curriculum Matters* series *History from 5 to 16* and *Classics from 5 to 16*, (DES, 1988) emphasize the variety of approaches open to teachers when teaching about the past. They can be grouped so that children, both by the age of 7 and by the age of 11 can learn something of the nature of history and acquire some knowledge which will help them understand the world in which they are growing up. For example:

By the age of 7:

> use basic vocabulary related to time such as 'now', 'long ago', 'before', 'after'.
> understand that evidence of the past comes in many forms.
> begin to distinguish between myths and legends about the past and real events and real people.
> develop an understanding of their own and their family's past.

By the age of 11:

> use chronological conventions such as BC, AD, century.
> make use of primary and secondary sources to support interpretations of historical events.
> develop an understanding of the history of their immediate neighbourhood and relate this to wider themes.
> demonstrate that they have some understanding of the development of British society and other societies over long periods; illuminated by shorter periods in greater depth.

These objectives are some help when considering the most controversial issue for debate surrounding history in the National Curriculum, the selection of content.

Identifying Content

The debate about history in schools which has raged in the popular press over the past two years has been remarkable for its inability to pose the significant questions. Some of the most uninformed comment has come from those who have not been inside a primary classroom since they left it as a pupil,[2] yet they feel sufficiently confident to offer a formula which prevailed in the 1940s and 1950s for the young people of the 1990s and beyond. Two other factors are confusing the issue. While many can see the relevance of introducing 16-year-olds to the historical background to current modern world issues of which they will need knowledge in order to act as literate adults in a participant democracy, they seek to find a slot for 'the rest' of history and simplistically decide that all you have to do is move down the age range. Primary school pupils can learn all about the Greeks, Romans, early civilizations and so on, so that the 11–14 syllabus can fit nicely into four years of chronological sequence.[3]

Some of those who advocate this, justify the choice in terms of the presentation of history as story, just as no doubt they would consider the transmission of Old Testament stories a viable method of teaching religious education. Narrative has its place in education at all levels, but as a method of communication, not as a substitute for investigation and analysis. Would these same people suggest that science teaching should be limited to teachers telling children stories about scientific discoveries and facts? There may well be a place for young children to learn some very ancient history, but let them do it by contact with the archaeological evidence and by understating the fragmentary nature of the conclusions that can be drawn. If they are denied access to periods of history for which there is more evidence, many will leave the primary school believing that history is a story, most of which has been invented, and uninitiated into the processes and skills which will help them to make progress in the further phases of their education.

The second consideration is the requirement, included in the brief to the History Working Group, that British history should influence content choice at every stage from age 5 to 16.

This second is perhaps the most important to open out for debate. British history clearly means different things to different people. The leader writer of the *Times* (23 January 1989) thinks it is:

> The opportunity, from primary school onwards, to gain a smattering of the shape of their country's history ... Britons, Anglo-Saxons and Danes ... and something of fundamental importance that happened in 1066.

Samuel, on the other hand, writing in the *Guardian* (21 January 1989) argues:

> One possible object of national history would be to identify the minority communities of which, at any time, the majority community of the British was composed

and goes on to question whether we really want every child in the country to: 'parrot the same set of answers to the same set of questions'.

The necessity to define 'British' history is obvious. Local history cannot be anything else but British. Excursions to historic sites are British – an activity the Working Group could do much to preserve if they had the guts to recommend access to these and to museum education services as a free entitlement for every child. British involvement in every part of the world must be seen as British, just as the stories of every individual who has travelled from anywhere to set up home in Britain must be British.

The good practice identified above may help in this dilemma. Wherever it is taught the content of the British history must stand up to analysis and be capable of verification. Anecdotes about 'Our Island Story' can only be a substitute for good history teaching and will seriously undermine the potential that history teaching has for stretching the young child intellectually. Some useful suggestions for determining the content of the history curriculum from 5 to 16 have been produced by Brown (1988) in a pertinent pamphlet from the Historical Association. These were extensively discussed at the series of regional conferences prior to the Association drawing up its own submission to the Working Party. He argues that any content selected should allow all pupils to understand how historians examine the past, that the content of history should allow pupils to understand people in the past and that every pupil should have access to local, national and global history. The pamphlet identifies criteria for selecting content across the compulsory years of study, and argues that it is those which emphasize people, their communities, social organization and contributions to society which are most suited to younger children. Its author notes that the national dimension should be truly British, not just English, and include the role of women and ethnic minorities as well as white men.

However British history is eventually defined, it is essential that opportunities for the small in-depth study be retained, even at the cost of the national 'overview'. This can provide a framework for further study since it offers opportunities for children to do some history, know some history and gain some understanding about a small microcosmic aspect of the past. Small studies in depth allow pupils and their teachers to take part in the process of historical enquiry, just as good science teaching involves everyone in investigation and verification. The children themselves can write up 'the story', learn skills and concepts specific to history – about evidence, about time, about change and cause – which will provide them with a jumping-off point to consolidate their progress in the next phase of their learning. During the years from 5 to 11 pupils can build up their knowledge of where evidence from the past can be found. The flexibility of the timetable, the cross–curricular nature of much of the work, invites teachers to take advantage of opportunities for learning outside the classroom. All pupils can get to know something of historic buildings in their neighbourhood. If they are living in a new town or new estate then they should learn how to look for clues about the way the land was used before the advent of urban development. The history of the locality is a perfect vehicle for learning about chronology and sequence and for extending vocabulary used to describe the past, time and age. Children will become knowledgeable on the function performed by libraries and Record offices and the work of the people employed there. Such experiences provide children with a historical 'language' and 'framework' as well as opportunities for really knowing something about the past.

It would not preclude the possibility of good local history project work in the secondary school, indeed it would help prepare for it, if pupils were familiar with the people and places in their own area where evidence is to be found. Some areas are richer in resources than others, but once a properly-financed national support system were established as an adjunct to the National Curriculum, and its British history core, there would be nothing to prevent schools from visiting other areas as part of their excursion programme. Television too could take into the classroom places of exceptional interest, which would enrich the historical 'language' of all children, who would have the experience derived from their own locality as a reference point. We have said that local resources are rich for British history in many areas, but they also provide international dimensions. Many of the souvenirs brought back by eighteenth- and nineteenth-century travellers and collectors have found their way into museum collections. Until recently, many of these have been put into reserve, so we should welcome the efforts of those museums which are now seeking to display such treasures to advantage, in particular the Victoria and Albert Museum Indian Collection which is to go to Bradford. It is surely desirable that at least one study in the junior school should promote children's global awareness and encourage respect for other cultural traditions. It is here that the stereotyped story version can be as damaging as that of the 'Island Story' presentation of British history. While active history methods are less possible, even if the children are near a museum with ancient Chinese bronzes or Egyptian mummies, they cannot handle them and documentary work is not possible – television and books are crucial and each study can be fitted into the chronological framework established by constant use of the local resources.

Sylvester (Chapter 2) has reminded us again of the historical questions which can be posed. There are numerous variations to suit all age groups:

> What was it like?
> How did it work?
> Which is the oldest?
> What happened first?
> Why did it change?
> How did it happen?

The same key historical questions first listed in *History in the Primary and Secondary Years* (DES, 1985) and repeated in *History from 5 to 16* (1988) apply to any historical study and the core of knowledge of British history and of the kinds of evidence from which conclusions are drawn should enable children to approach more distant environments, whether in time or space, with confidence.

There is a strong case to be made for the selection of content to be left to local communities – teachers from all sectors of education, museum education officers and others funded to supply support services under a nationally-agreed quality control standard. Broad guidelines could be prescribed which, ideally, would ensure that all children were introduced to authentic historical evidence and initiated into the activity of history through a local study. Such study should begin to build a conceptual and chronological framework and provide children with the necessary language, questioning techniques, and skills to move outwards from the locality to widen their horizons in time and space.

Making Progress

The government is pledged to raise standards and believes that the National Curriculum will be one way to achieve this.

Regular testing at the ages of 7, 11, 14 and 16 will allow teachers, parents and governors to monitor achievement.

Standard assessment tasks (SATs) may incorporate a variety of assessment methods and are intended to 'complement teachers' own assessments' (DES, 1989). There will be ten different levels of achievement defined within each attainment target, reflecting differences in ability and in progress according to age and it is expected that in the primary school pupils may advance from level 1 to level 5.

Teachers will be familiar with proposals for attainment targets and levels of achievement already published as statutory orders in maths, science and English. The history Working Group is expected to make proposals along similar lines.

There is room for a degree of cautious optimism. Those who originally feared that classroom assessment would be of the factual, 'Mastermind' type, will by now have realized that attainment targets published so far are formulated so as to encourage teachers to allow children to demonstrate what they can do and understand as well as what they know. TGAT (1988) recommends that discussion and practical activities such as sorting and sequencing be permitted as well as the more formal writing and drawing. We conclude from this that it should be possible to create classroom assessment activities in the form of historical problems which will allow children to show their understanding of historical language, skills and concepts as well as knowledge of the topic which has been selected.

At the time of writing, I can only speculate on the Working Group's thoughts, but offer the following as possible models.

Attainment Target 1

Children should be able to talk and write about the past using appropriate historical language.

Level 1
- Be able to recognize old things and old buildings.
- Be able to match pictures or objects using the words 'now' and 'then'.

Level 2
- Know a range of words to describe old things and old buildings using terms like 'before', 'after', 'earlier than', 'later than'.
- Put objects or pictures of old things or old buildings into a rudimentary time order.

Level 3
- Demonstrate that they understand the terms 'past' and 'present'. Point to some of the evidence which exists in the present, but which tells us about the past.

Level 4
- Be able to use the term 'century' by reference to the current date and the term 'twentieth century'.
- Recognize the relationship between dates and centuries other than the twentieth, according to the period of history studied.
- Be able to recognize some of the conventional labels given to specific periods of time, such as Viking, Tudor, according to the period of history studied.

Level 5
- Be able to discuss historical periods, centuries or terms such as medieval, Tudor, according to the period studied by reference to evidence about the period which differentiates it from another period in the past or the present.

Attainment Target 2

Children should know that history is a subject which depends on evidence. They should be aware of the fragmentary nature of evidence and the variety of interpretations which can be drawn about the past from evidence.

Level 1   – They should be able to talk about evidence of the past collected from family sources – their own or someone else's.

         – They should be able to point out which buildings in the neighbourhood are 'old'.

Level 2   – They should be able to pair modern objects or picture objects with similar things from the past e.g. a candle with an electric light.

         – They should be able to discuss, by handling or observing, why some things last longer than others.

Level 3   – They should be able to answer the question 'How do we know?' about any period studied. They should be able to speculate on what we do not know.

Level 4   – They should be able to point to places in the neighbourhood where historical evidence can be found e.g. the church, museum or library.

         – They should be able to make a guess about the period from which certain pieces of evidence come, according to the period studied.

Level 5   – They should be able to distinguish history which is a story from history which is based on evidence.

         – They should be able to suggest ways of finding out about people, places or historical periods, which they have not studied.

Tasks along these lines could be set around whatever topic the teacher had chosen for study. Over the primary years children would become familiar with the key historical questions and learn what the study of history involved. They would be introduced to the structure, rules and 'language' of the subject, just as they are in maths and science. Secondary teachers would have something to build on.

Few teachers would regret the passing of the kind of assessment which allows only for pupils' cognitive performance to be recorded, but many would wish to see an opportunity for recording and reporting children's attitudes to learning in general and subjects in particular. TGAT is against this. Pupils' experience of history in the primary school should lay the foundation for their secondary years, not only in terms of knowledge gained but in raising enthusiasm for the subject. Kenneth Baker, the Secretary of State for Education, asked the Working Group to produce a formula which will allow this to develop. They have an awesome responsibility and can make or break the subject, switch children 'on' to the subject or switch them 'off' at an early age. Failing to give proper attention to the primary school could be their most fatal mistake.

Notes

1 The full survey is available from the Department of History, Chester College of Higher Education, Cheney Road, Chester. Part of it is reprinted in *Teaching History, No. 49*, Historical Association.
2 This seems to be a view shared by both the Centre for Policy Studies, and the Campaign for Real Education, reported repeatedly in the press during 1987 and 1988.

References

Avon Resources for Learning Development Unit (1983) *In Search of the Past, In Touch with the Locality* Bishop Rd, Bristol BS7 8LD.

Blyth, J. (1987) *Place and Time with Children 5–9*, London, Croom Helm.

Brown, R. (1988) *The Future of the Past: Occasional Paper 1*, Historical Association.

Cooper, H. (1986) 'Historical concepts 5–11' in Fairbrother, R. (ed) *History in the Primary School*, School of Education, Manchester Polytechnic.

DES (1978) Primary Education in England, London, HMSO.

DES (1985) *History in the Primary and Secondary Years: an HMI View*, London, DES.

DES (1987) *Primary Schools: some aspects of Good Practice*, London, DES.

DES (1988) *History from 5 to 16: Curriculum Matters Series*, HMSO.

DES (1989) *National Curriculum: from Policy to Practice*, London, DES.

Design Council (1987) *Design and Primary Education*, London SW1Y 4SU.

Engineering Council (1985) *Problem-solving: Science & Technology in the Primary School*, London, Engineering Council.

Hall, A. (1980) 'Rose's Life' in *Teaching History, No. 26*, Historical Association.

ILEA (1980) *History in the Primary School*, London, ILEA.

Knight, P. (1988) Unpublished thesis, Liverpool, University of Liverpool.

Rose, A. (1986) 'The Place of History in the Primary School' in Fairbrother, R. (ed) *History in the Primary School*, School of Education, Manchester Polytechnic.

Samuel, R. (1989) 'History's battle for "a new past"', *The Guardian*, 21 January 1989.

Searle-Chatterjee, M. (1985) 'Lancashire textiles and the Indian Connection' in *Teaching History, No. 43*, Historical Association.

Sudworth, P. (1982) 'An analysis of history teaching in the primary school since 1960', in *Teaching History, No. 33*, Historical Association.

Task Group on Assessment and Testing (TGAT) 1988. *First Report*, London, DES.

West, J. (1981) *History 7–13*, Dudley, Dudley Metropolitan Borough.

Wright, D. (1984) 'A small local investigation', in *Teaching History, No. 51*, Historical Association.

Woodhouse, J. and Wilson, V. (1988) 'Celebrating the Solstice: a history through drama project,' in *Teaching History, No. 51*, Historical Association.

Wiltshire County Council Education Department (1987) *History Based Topic Work*, Education Offices, The Sea Road, Trowbridge.

Part Three
Investigating The Environment

Chapter 6

Primary School Geography: The Question of Balance

Bill Marsden

Introduction

The position of geography in the primary school is delicately poised. At face value, its case has been officially approved by its acceptance as a foundation subject in the National Curriculum. This enshrinement would appear to subvert the classic Hadow maxim: 'Work in the primary school in geography, as in other subjects, must "be thought of in terms of activity and experience rather than of knowledge to be acquired and facts to be stored . . ."' (Board of Education, 1931). But the National Curriculum documentation, at a point in time prior to the establishment of a Geography Working Group has, no more than Hadow, made explicit any commitment to the subject being offered a separate slot in the primary school timetable.

This chapter is built on the premise that the separate subject timetabling issue is not the key question. It does, however, support the view that geography justifies a place in the primary curriculum as a foundation 'element', but more in the sense of a resource than a body of content (Blyth, *et al.*, 1976). It does not support the view that there is a necessary clash between so-called subject–centred and child–centred approaches, arguing that geography, like other subjects, can be taught in a child–centred way, as it can didactically. By the same token, integrated studies can be taught formally and prescriptively, though it is tacitly assumed that in practice this will not be the case. More important questions relate to the quality of input, broadly defined. The quality of input not least reflects the expertise of the people providing it. As HMI surveys in the last decade have shown, in this respect geography in the primary and middle years of schooling has not been well served (DES, 1978, 1983, 1985).

A framework for good education, I suggest, needs to be derived from a balance of three components, relating the child, the discipline and society. Three crudely defined questions may be asked of curriculum material:

1 Is it good pedagogy, in terms of such variables as match, progression, coherence, appropriate language, and appeal to the interests and the emotions of the children?
2 Is it good (in this case) geography, accurate, idiomatic, and up-to-date in terms of content and conceptual frameworks?
3 It is good social education, bearing in mind a range of aims from the narrowly utilitarian (like achieving attainment targets or passing examinations) to promoting a more just global society?

Therefore, I shall not explore the basic issues in terms of dichotomies: of progressivism and reaction, of the child and society. Rather I shall attempt to survey the internal complexities, and in particular to identify the historical changes in the balance of the components that can provide an illuminative context for current debates.

In the development of geography in mass elementary or primary education four stages can be distinguished.

Stage 1: Most of the Nineteenth Century

In this stage, a strong imbalance was created by the primacy of the social education component, evident in the underlying utilitarianism and political control ideology, as much the responsibility of the church as of the state. For much of the period, the discipline of geography was split into physical and political components, the former of the greater intellectual standing, the latter deployed primarily, especially in elementary education, as a medium for communicating the richness of God's world, the excitement of new geographical discoveries and, increasingly, pride in colonial expansion. The pedagogy was largely derived from religious instruction, catechitical modes being readily applied to geographical content, as exemplified in the so-called 'interrogatory' technique developed under the monitorial system:

EMIGRATE
Q. What is to emigrate?
A. Remove from one country to another.
Q. What are people called who emigrate?
A. Emigrants.
Q. Where do they go to?
A. A colony.

Q. What is a colony?
A. A place peopled by people from another country.
Q. Name some colonies.
A. West Indies, Van Diemen's Land, Pennsylvania.
Q. Who founded that colony?
A. William Penn.
Q. How did he get the land?
A. Bought it off the Indians.
Q. Did all do so who founded colonies?
A. No.
Q. Who did not?
A. The 'Spaniards.
Q. How did they obtain them?
A. By force of arms.
Q. Was this right?
A. No.
Q. How do we know it was not right?
A. Because Christ would not even let Peter defend him, but made him'put up his sword. (Ward, 1911)

Thus religious certainties made it legitimate to present unfavourable value judgments of other peoples as being as factual as the names of the founders of colonies. There was much more to geography and history than lists of countries and capitals, or dates of battles. Whether the above extract is history or geography is not important. In effect it integrates the two. More significantly, it reflects an early politicization of the curriculum, the prime objective being to inculcate prescribed values. The twin thrusts are religious fundamentalism and nationalism. The closed pedagogy is potent reinforcement.

This extract is symptomatic of a dominating pedagogic framework which endured into the second half of the century, though there was a shift of emphasis from using geography as a handmaiden of religious instruction to an important component in disseminating imperial knowledge and attitudes. A contradictory element was, however, the coexistence of a more progressive tradition based on visual realism, local study and the involvement of the child. For Joshua Fitch, the concentric approach was the key: 'we should begin with what is known and what is near, and let our knowledge radiate from that centre until it comprehends what is larger and more remote' (Fitch, 1854). But while Fitch was relatively progressive in terms of content and pedagogy, the political underpinning was also explicit:

Of Geography and History I need say very little. The reasons for teaching them are so obvious and so universally acknowledged, that there is probably no great danger of our neglecting or undervaluing them. They are both becoming of more and more importance as our civilization advances. Both have especial claims on a community of Englishmen: the former, because our relations with distant parts of the globe are so numerous and important; and the latter, because in a country which affords political privileges to all classes, it behoves every man to know at least so much of the past history of the State as shall guide him in the formation of his opinions.

Stage 2: From about 1890 to 1960

In the last two decades of the nineteenth century the discipline of geography was transformed by a major change of paradigm. Prior to this date there had, as we have seen, been a gulf between the political and physical dimensions of the subject. Academically, political geography was seen almost as a necessary evil, suited to the elementary curriculum in its stress on memory, but of low academic status. By contrast, physical geography was linked with geology, at the cutting edge of scientific development, associated on the one hand with the Darwinian revolution and on the other with overturning fundamentalist views on the origins of the universe.

One of the great earth scientists of the time was Sir Archibald Geikie, one of the few who saw the connection between scientific research methods and good pedagogy. He wrote of his first fossil collecting excursion to a local quarry as leaving a sense 'of the enormous advantage which a boy or girl may derive from any pursuit that stimulates the imagination' (Geikie, 1882). Here good geology (for which read geography) and good pedagogy were combined, for Geikie's skills ranged from the writing of advanced geological texts, to school primers on *Geology* and *Physical Geography* and a progressive methodological text, *The Teaching of Geography*. But the stress on local field work, integrated study and environmental education it contained had little impact on the development of the subject in school.

Instead a more academic approach followed Halford Mackinder's celebrated paper 'On the Scope and Methods of Geography' (1887), which sought both a unifying structure within the discipline, and the use of the discipline as a bridging subject between humanities and sciences. On the basis of its ideas, Herbertson (1905) constructed a new paradigm: the 'major natural regions of the world'. Involved in the university extension movement, both Mackinder and Herbertson were effective disseminators. Herbertson and his followers wrote highly successful text-books based on the regional framework. While particularly designed for older children, regional geography also established a hold in junior texts. It was argued that the framework simplified geography in that instead of covering hundreds of different countries, the student could concentrate on fourteen major natural regions.

But Herbertson himself recognized that 'the best logical order is not necessarily the best pedagogical order' (1906). Good geography was not of necessity good pedagogy. Indeed it could be argued that for younger children in particular the regional system had the lethal disadvantages of emphasizing abstract generalization, promoting inert, de-humanized language, and indirectly encouraging environmental determinism and social stereotyping.

That is not to say that Herbertson and his followers did not recognize the need to provide differentiated material for older and younger pupils. Thus for the study of distant lands Herbertson initiated the idea of the case study, an in-depth treatment of particular groups of 'primitive' peoples, in simple relationship with their environment. But the negative shift from a tenable pedagogical position to bad social education could be devastatingly direct, as demonstrated by an early twentieth-century geographical educationist, whose argument can be paraphrased as follows:

1 Education is the record of teachers erecting barriers between real things and the pupil.
2 The answer is to go to first-hand sources such as travel books, full of human interest and motivating to children.
3 Thus the child will have no difficulty in remembering that Hong Kong has a 'China Type' of climate, producing dampness, on reading that mushrooms are inclined to grow on the boots of the residents. (Page, 1909)

Page was in fact in advance of many of his peers in condemning negative stereotyping of peoples. Even the more benign stereotypes were serious distortions, repressing similarities and promoting theoretically sound pedagogy but socially suspect 'contrasts'. This led to concentration, in junior texts in particular, on strange dress, strange food, strange homes and strange customs. An omnipresent stereotype was that children the world over were happy (Wright, 1981). Thus in one series Spain was described as 'a land of sunshine and happiness'; for Ireland 'the wonder is that Irish boys and girls can find it in their hearts to leave their beautiful loving land of the shamrock'. But the most favoured of all were the Japanese:

> Happy children! Who are always laughing and never crying; who are taught filial respect, reverence, and unquestioning obedience, but are surrounded in their homes with an atmosphere of kindness, cheerfulness, and loving care. (McDonald and Dalrymple, 1910)

For older children in the primary school, and for boys in particular, a more warlike approach was needed to incite interest. The stress was on the heroic exploits of explorers, missionaries and military men meeting with, trading with, converting, or suppressing hostile tribes in hostile environments (Bramwell, 1961). As Jones put it in her survey of the differences in interests in geography of boys and girls: 'Boys seem to find in geography some outlet for their greater adventurousness, their stronger fighting, hunting and migratory instincts . . .' (Jones, 1933). In order to make the subject more vivid and human, bibliographies of travellers' tales and fictional works were provided in methodological texts. Yet even in so progressive a work as Welpton's, the stress was on male prowess in one form or another, with writers such as Winston Churchill (*The Malakand Campaign*), Rudyard Kipling (*Captains Courageous*), and Jack London *(White Fang)* in the forefront (Welpton, 1923).

It was generally agreed that the study of the geography of the British Empire had a triple advantage. It was good geography in that British colonies were so widespread that all the major natural regions of the world were covered, without the need to deal with the plethora of unimportant countries outside the realm. It was good also in motivational terms, because it was seen as natural that Empire countries were of special significance and therefore interest for English children. And of course such study was a vital aspect of social education. Teachers were advised to seek out pictorial and other aids from Dominion governments, Empire commercial associations, different emigration bureaux, and the Imperial Institute (Board of Education, 1930). In such an atmosphere, it is no great surprise that even so forward-looking an educationist as Garnett was ready to justify geography in this way.

> There is no need, in these days, to stress the reasons for including geography in the school curriculum, especially for future citizens of Britain – a democracy with colonial and mandatory responsibilities. (Garnett, 1940)

Thus the regional approach was seen as beneficial in achieving academic respectability and a place for geography in secondary schools and universities, in providing a framework for the study of imperial geography, and in cutting down the amount of rote learning required under the old 'political geography'. A kind of balance, though not what we would today define as a desirable one, was achieved between content, pedagogy and social education. But the pull was inexorably away from an earlier progressive tradition, based on direct observation in local study, as advocated by Geikie (*op. cit.*).

Yet the progressive flame was by no means extinguished. One problem was that by the end of the nineteenth century most school children lived in towns and towns were not seen as good places in which to conduct field work. Field work was regarded by some writers not as geography as such, but as an amalgam of geography, physiography and nature study (Cowham, 1900). The logistics of transporting large numbers of children into the countryside were considerable (Reynolds, 1901). But Geikie had long before argued that while the countryside was obviously advantageous for field work, 'the skilful teacher' would none the less find topics of interest 'even in a wilderness of streets and houses' and 'the most crowded thoroughfares' (1887). The Board of Education (1905) urged the study of home surroundings whether in town or country. But the only substantial text on urban field work was Penstone's *Town Study*, sub-titled *an Introduction to the Study of Civics* (1910).

The notion of urban field work continued to be resisted post-World War I. Even Hadow strangely saw the country child having an advantage in being able to observe objects before recognizing their representation on maps, as though only the countryside provided features worth observing (Hadow, 1931). Integrated work on the local urban community continued to be neglected until the 1930s, when Cons and Fletcher's influential text, *Actuality in School*, (1938) appeared, offering ideas on how to study a working-class London community and its services. At the same time, the work of Coulthard in Bishop Auckland was designed not only to promote geographical skills but also to develop a community involvement (Geographical Association, 1935; and Ministry of Education, 1948).

These ventures were clearly curricular breakthroughs but, so far as both the subject element and social education were concerned, provoked tensions. In the first place, in their extreme form local studies could be said to be too bound up with parochial matters, and could unduly dominate the integrated timetable, leaving little scope for decentration. As Garnett put it:

Geography should develop from the biological and community studies of the locality into a subject studied for its own sake . . . Children must learn about maps, places, peoples and things beyond their immediate experience. (Geographical Association, 1945)

Another writer quoted directly a ten-year old's view that beginning with your own neighbourhood kept you 'waiting to find out all about the world', and asked why this broader coverage could not 'be allowed to develop side by side with placing the nearest post office in its proper relationship to the nearest public house' (MacMunn, 1926).

The second tension was created by the increasing inter-war stress on the 'human' or 'social' aspects of geography, exemplified in Fairgrieve's famous dictum on training future citizens to think sanely about the political and social problems of the world around (1926), and Forsaith's plea for extending geography into the moral domain (1932). Such developments, and the transmission of American integrated approaches through the Dalton Plan (Selleck, 1972) were seen as capable of destroying the perceived unity of geography and indeed its status as a distinctive subject in the curriculum. As Honeybone later summarized:

> . . . by 1939 geography had become grievously out of balance, the geographical synthesis had been abandoned, and the unique educational value of the subject lost in a flurry of social and economic generalizations . . . (Honeybone, 1954).

The post-World War II period predictably led to new demands for education for international understanding and, in part to cope with less able children in the secondary modern school, labelled as uninterested in 'subjects', a renewed proselytization of social studies. The geographical establishment launched into a counter-offensive and successfully repulsed the intruder, so far as the secondary system was concerned (Royal Geographical Society, 1950; Scarfe, 1950; Stamps, 1951; Brooks, 1952).

The dispute was symptomatic of a division that had opened up between academic geography, thought of as a critical component for the secondary grammar sector, and a watered-down version, seen as acceptable for less able and younger children. It is significant that very little attention was paid to the potential contribution of educational research to the geography for the more able. This group did not need pedagogy. Grammar school teachers hardly required 'training', though those of the young and less able did. Academic geographers were prone on occasions to refer to pedagogical aspects of teaching in derogatory terms: 'mere class management' (Lyde, 1928), or 'cranky ideas and devices' (Wooldridge, 1955).

These divisions generated different sorts of textbooks. It is interesting that the famous geographer Dudley Stamp (1930), prepared a junior school series, with his wife Elsa Stamp, which was far more progressive in style than the many secondary texts he wrote by himself. Thus advertisement for books for the secondary modern sector advised that the material was kept as simple as possible (Fairgrieve and Young, 1952). Brooks stressed that in such texts academic methods should be avoided: the life and work of the people should take priority over cause and effect relationships (Brooks, 1929). At the primary level, stock-in-trade geography was epitomized by the Archer and Thomas series, explicitly justified in the following terms:

1 Small children are more interested in people and places wholly foreign to them than in those more familiar.
2 So-called backward people have simple relationships between their environment and life activities than more advanced and thus are easier for beginners to grasp. (Thomas, 1937)

Our second stage was therefore characterized by sharp divisions in the thinking of geographers and geographical educationists. There was a greater consensus of ideas, though a negative one, so far as social education was concerned. Most writers of texts were people of their time and, however progressive in pedagogical terms on the one hand, or hard–line in keeping the discipline pure on the other, were thoroughly ingrained with imperialist values. And while the lobby for using geography in the cause of advancing international understanding gained ground, there were obvious gaps between the confident rhetoric of such writers as Archer and his colleagues (1910), Forsaith (1951) who seemed to think, for example, that commodities geography, very popular in the primary school, *per se* generated international understanding, and successful delivery, an even less likely possibility in the case of the grander vision of Walker:

> Geography has thus a well–established and important place in the training of our future citizens. The extensive nature of the field which this subject covers, and the facts and relationships with which it deals undoubtedly afford many opportunities for the development of such an intelligent and sympathetic interest in lands and their peoples throughout the world that one more link may be forged in that golden chain that will bind the world in brotherhood. (Walker, 1953)

Stage 3: From about 1960 to 1980

Stage 3 can be regarded as a spell of rapid and generally positive change, though the context was confusing. At one level a rapport was established between the conceptual revolutions in the discipline and in curriculum thinking, a synthesis being achieved in Schools Council Projects, methodological texts, and later examination syllabuses, which from the 1970s required a much broader educational justification than the previous content-dominated statements. For the primary level, there appeared on the face of it a divergence between the new science and mathematics-driven frameworks of the so-called quantitative revolution in geography, and the reaffirmation of progressive values in the Plowden Report, where history and geography were consigned to 'topic work', with reference to geography confined to its role in developing mapping skills (Plowden, 1967).

In fact there was a quite speedy revulsion in the geographical world against the threatening dehumanization of the subject which the quantitative revolution had injected. There was a shift in priority towards concepts of social welfare and territorial justice. But clearly both changes tended to pull geography away from the Mackinder position of prioritizing the unity of the subject as a study of regions and places. Competing pulls were in the direction of mathematics and the pure sciences on the one hand, and on the other of the social sciences. There was in fact a third strong pull, towards earth science or, more particularly, environmental science.

Digging deeper, it can be argued that both in principle and practice most of these changes represented moves away from geography as a body of content to be acquired, towards a 'process' subject compatible with a progressive pedagogy and intent on bridging gaps. This conclusion can be justified on the following grounds:

1 The stress on pre-structured conceptual frameworks, which tended to cross over boundaries of knowledge and bring to notice integrative possibilities.

2 Emphasis on the development of skills, especially the notion of graphicacy, as the geographer's major contribution to education (Balchin and Coleman, 1965).

3 A re-emphasis on direct observation as a process, based on ideas of scientific induction and personal research. There was an escalation of local field work in the 1960s, for example, and children having had this experience are now the norm, rather than an experimental vanguard.

The 1960s and 1970s also witnessed convergence in the social education dimension. In geography text-books, while stereotyping remained (Marsden, 1976) and evidence of Eurocentric, racist and sexist attitudes was all too easy to find (Fisher and Hicks, 1985; Wright, 1983), there was still an enormous advance on earlier jingoism and xenophobia, which declined as the generation of teachers nurtured on ideas of imperial greatness died out. Discussions of social welfare, territorial justice, and environmental concerns at the frontiers of the discipline were quickly placed on school geography agendas. But how far could geographers legitimately lay claim to these as discrete areas of study? At the same time, for example, environmental studies was receiving a new impetus (Watts, 1969; Masterton, 1969; Schools Council, 1972), and was being translated into integrated primary school projects (Hammersley *et al.*, 1968; Lines, 1971).

Similarly, a 'new' social studies movement emerged, anxious to side-step the problems the earlier academically soft-centred civics movement had faced and failed to overcome. This embodied a tougher-minded approach, social science discipline-based, and concerned about the gaps left in cultural transmission if geography and history held a monopoly over this field (Lawton, 1971; Lawton and Dufour, 1974). Broadly, one target was the emerging curriculum of the comprehensive school, with new head teachers not necessarily as committed to traditional subject divisions as their predecessors. Another was the curriculum of the middle school, towards which a significant number of local authorities were moving (Blyth and Derricott, 1977).

On this occasion, geographers were in no position either politically, academically or, it might be added, by internal preference, to be as disdainful of moves towards integration as they had been in the immediate post-war period. There was predictable scepticism, but the discussion was certainly couched in more considered and less confrontational terms (Williams, 1976). At the same time, geographers continue to be seen from the outside as thwarting integrative curricular initiatives (Goodson, 1983).

Curiously, the integrative mode in which some geographers see the subject fitting least easily is the one in which in practice they most frequently find themselves, and that mode the least precisely defined (Blyth, 1987). This may be because the developments in their subject since the 1960s have given geographers a greater commonality of interest with environmental and social scientists, than with arts areas that pull geography towards a more literary tradition, one redolent of a period which geographers now view as of low academic repute for their discipline and outside the scientific mainstream. On the other hand geographers, like historians and religious educationists, have become strongly committed to playing a part in values education, with the development of more empathetic attitudes to foreign peoples and less favoured groups being brought to the forefront of aims.

Notwithstanding the greater success of this generation of integrated study approaches, which have tended to associate history and geography with often not well-structured topic work (Alexander, 1984), the 'new geography' of the 1960s and 1970s has found a toe-hold in the primary curriculum. Thus the quantitative dimension was very quickly transmitted in an innovative skill-building series, *New Ways in Geography*, by Cole and Beynon (1968–1972), though the major breakthrough has had to wait until the 1980s.

But as we shall see, primary geography by the end of the 1970s was in crisis. In terms of the balance between subject, pedagogical and social education dimensions, it can be argued that child-centred progressivism held sway, certainly in the opinion of geographers (Catling, 1987) and of the new force for change from the late 1970s, the inspectorate.

Stage 4: the 1980s

A major problem posed by the radical changes of approach at the frontiers of the discipline and in curriculum theory in the 1960s and 1970s was that evident over half a century previously with the onset of the first 'new geography': the need for a sophisticated teaching force. Clearly primary teachers could readily cope with the simplified but outmoded and distorting stereotypes embodied in studies of primitive peoples. The capacity to use texts like Cole and Beynon effectively was less apparent. HMI surveys of primary and middle school practice (DES, 1978a, 1983a and 1985) found geography was one of the worst-served subjects. The need was argued for specialist teaching input at the primary level:

> The national primary and secondary surveys demonstrated the overwhelming importance of teachers' knowledge base and confidence in the subjects which they teach . . . Primary schools expect, and primary teachers need to have, a particular strength in one aspect of the curriculum . . . Many such teachers will come to be used as subject leaders or consultants in the primary school. It follows therefore that all BEd students preparing for the primary phase should follow one main curriculum area in some depth . . . . (DES, 1983b)

Concurrently, geographers, represented by their subject association, the *Geographical Association*, became alarmed when official statements following Callaghan's 'Great Debate' speech of 1976 implied that the DES was not supportive of the claims of geography for a distinct place in the school curriculum (DES, 1978b and 1981). A period of intense and successful lobbying on the part of the Geographical Association followed, culminating in the acceptance of geography as a foundation subject in the National Curriculum at all levels (DES, 1987). Meanwhile, the Geographical Association (1981) pulled together its case, which basically is that geography has four special contributions to make to the school curriculum at all phases, in promoting:

Graphicacy – the communication and understanding of spatial information through maps and other forms of illustration as of crucial importance.
World knowledge.
International understanding.
Environmental awareness.

It may be added that a recent authoritative HMI statement in its 'Curriculum Matters' series, *Geography from 5 to 16* (DES, 1986) is very much in harmony with the Geographical Association's views, which have been strongly presented in its *The Case for Geography*, (Bailey and Binns, 1987).

Away from the political debate, earlier changes in subject paradigms and the increasing commitment to social and environmental education have been translated in the 1980s into stimulating new primary texts. Thus a frontal attack on social stereotyping can be found in the *Into Geography* series (Harrison, Harrison and Pearson, 1986–7). There is a powerful environmental education input here and in, for example, the *Going Places* series (Renwik and Pick, 1982). Equally impressive is the trend towards texts which have skilfully linked local study with the progressive development of graphicacy skills, particularly by Catling and colleagues in the *Outset Geography* series (1981–4), and alternatively in moving out in classic concentric style from large scale local to smaller scale maps and atlas maps in the *Mapstart* series, also by Catling (1985). Despite recent work by Elliott and Martin in the *Discovering our World* texts (1986) and Jennings, adopting a more traditional but certainly coherent 'natural regions' line in *The Young Geographer Investigates* series (1986), the study of distant lands is less well served and a problem still to be resolved with the demise of old models of treatment.

So the National Curriculum has established geography as a foundation subject at the primary phase. But does this necessarily demand that it be taught as a separate subject on the timetable? It is part of the remit of the National Curriculum subject working groups to explore cross-curricular initiatives, and indeed some of the new 'profile components' are required to be of this nature. Thus the terms of reference of the Science Working Group make clear that the Secretary of State accepts it would not be sensible to teach science and technology as separate subjects in the primary school (DES, 1987). How thus can geography make such a claim, albeit a geography component of the National Curriculum having been approved?

The plot thickens when it is found that in mapping its territory the Science Working Group has identified as one of the major science themes a significant part of the earth science area of geography: 'Earth, Atmosphere and Space', including sub-topics such as the atmosphere, soils, and volcanoes and earthquakes (DES, 1987). This is in fact a salutary lesson for geographers, who have long been prone to incorporating a vast range of topics. It can be predicted that if they stray too indiscriminately away from their heartland into environmental science, or social science, they can anticipate that environmental scientists and social scientists will argue that *they* can do the job better. While geographers can indeed make a distinctive contribution to, among other things, the promotion of international understanding and to the development of environmental awareness, these are critical examples of areas which demand an integrated, even interdisciplinary attack, of a sort demonstrated in, for example, the Schools Council 8–13 History, Geography and Social Science Project (Blyth *et al.*, 1976), and in Fisher and Hicks' *World Studies 8–13* (1985).

Geography should therefore seek to clarify the nature of its place in the new primary curriculum. First, what it has to offer which is not only demonstrably worthwhile but which it can legitimately claim to do more effectively than any other subject; and, secondly, what expertise it can contribute, in conjunction with other subjects, to important cross-curricular issues, particularly in the areas of social, environmental, political and values education.

Taking these issues further it can be argued that the four areas identified by the Geographical Association as those in which a special contribution to the curriculum can be made by the subject might well be divided into two:

1 Even the strongest proponents of child–centredness and curriculum integration accept that geography has a distinctive role to play in the development of skills of map interpretation: 'Of making maps there should be no end', as an early protagonist put it (Burrows, 1900). But while there were honourable exceptions, such as Dudley and Elsa Stamp's *A First Atlas* (1935), in general younger children have in the past been introduced too early to complex small-scale atlas maps, and small, before large-scale, Ordnance Survey maps. The myth developed that mapping and map interpretation was a mode of cognition beyond the powers of most primary children. The 1970s saw the publication of research suggesting that, through the use for example of surrogate

toys such as Lego, children could be effective map makers even in the pre-school stage (Blaut and Stea, 1971 and 1974; Blades and Spencer, 1986). The potential use of children's maps as diagnostic both of cognitive progression and in creatively developing images of their local environment is more fully appreciated (Catling, 1978; Gerber, 1981; Piche, 1981; Matthews, 1983). The literature on spatial cognition is now rich and of obvious application and indeed as typology of the nature and level of skills of graphicacy that might be expected of children at different ages has been offered by Boardman (1983). Further, as we have seen, the findings have been translated into text-books which in terms of match and progression are a major advance on what has gone before.

2 If geography is about maps it is also about the world: about places and peoples. World geography is, however, a problematic area: 'How can the geographer "cover the world" yet not over-simplify to the point of dull triviality or even untruth?' (Marchant, 1964). We have seen how in the first stage of development of geography as a school subject its world coverage was either associated with the pedagogically unacceptable gazetteer approach often termed 'capes and bays', or what we would see today as equally unacceptable inculcation of doctrinaire religious and colonial values. In the second stage the regional paradigm produced an equally suspect pedagogy. On the one hand, particularly for younger and less able children, its language and generalizations were too abstract. On the other, attempts at simplification led to untenable social stereotyping. In the third stage geographers have become more aware of these problems, but in their place have tended to replace regional with thematic courses, particularly on great world issues. These are socially more relevant, but depart from the distinctiveness of the subject, and have shifted the content balance in a direction which has aroused the suspicions of parent and government. Well may parents ask what geography is now all about, on finding their children in their homework asked to resolve the population problems of the Indian sub-continent, tease out the machinations of multi-national companies, analyze the environmental impact of acid rain and oil slicks, and empathize with the inhabitants of Soweto (*see* Storm, in Bale, 1983), and especially when they find these issues repeated, though not in any planned way, in other subjects as well.

An alternative view is that geography's discrete contribution is not to prioritize or colonize themes such as energy, or industry, or community, nor key concepts such as conflict and consensus, or empathy. These are indeed cross-curricular. No one subject can claim them as its domain. On the other hand, no subject other than geography has a more logical claim to developing mapping skills and studying distance places.

The idea of shifting geography away from relevant themes may sound reactionary. Obviously a return to 'capes and bays' is not being suggested. That does not mean that building up place knowledge is a 'trivial pursuit', without cultural significance. Conscious of this, the Geographical Association has launched a national world-wide quiz competition to stimulate the acquisition of world knowledge. Knowledge of continents and oceans, countries and capitals can, it is argued, at a limited level, as a means to an end, be justified (Bale, 1987). It is surely not hard to draw up thresholds and say that beyond these the knowledge accumulation is becoming too much an end in itself.

It is evident that in the study of distant places an important objective must be to stress indirect observation: bringing the wider world into the classroom. This requires the collection of rich and first-hand materials, and particularly visual, materials. These should above all emphasize a sense of place, rather than thematic constructs such as 'energy', which have, in themselves, no obvious 'location'. Thus in pre-specification of content the curriculum matrix must have an axis which deals not just with (a) concepts, skills, attitudes to be developed, and (b) general themes, but also demonstrates (c) over the syllabus as a whole a balanced coverage of world places. It should show a balance, both quantitatively and qualitatively, between the North–South economic divide, and the East–West political divide. Key questions for each local topic might be as laid out in the HMI *Geography from 5 to 16* document: 'Where is this place? What does the place look like? What is it like to live there? What important links does it have with other places? What do we find attractive or unattractive about the place?' (DES, 1986). These are not questions that would be regarded as central in other areas of the curriculum. They are, nevertheless, still important broad cultural as well as specifically geographical questions.

The complaint that a return to the study of places would detract from recent progress in achieving a more socially and environmentally oriented georaphy can be countered by the argument that these indeed are of overarching importance, but too wide-ranging for geography to cope with alone.

If, then, the third stage of development we have identified was that in which the progressive educational dimension came into the forefront, it was also one in which there developed a convergence of interest between academic geography, pedagogy and social education. In moving so enthusiastically into covering major world issues, there has been a shift from distinctiveness. Indeed in some geography programmes, cartoons, loom as large as cartography, the skills of chairing environmental planning teams supplant efforts to develop a feeling for landscape, or a sense of place. These are entirely proper endeavours but are not discrete to the subject.

The balance here being sought between geography and education in the primary school presupposes in the first place that there is a relatively limited but absolutely critical need for a distinctive, idiomatic geographical contribution, based on the development of graphicacy and a knowledge and understanding of places. Geographers, however, need to refocus their contribution. If they wish to affirm their commitment to social and environmental issues, to political education, that is in order. Such a commitment, however, by definition demands a cross-curricular endeavour. Whether geography is labelled as a separate subject in the primary curriculum is a low order question. That the geographical resource input should be more precisely framed and more expertly fashioned than it has been in the past is, on the other hand, a high order one.

A more fundamental issue of balance relates to the political context. In the nineteenth century there existed an imbalance in the direction of geography as narrowly defined social education. It is clearly vital today to retain a commitment to a social education that is not merely evaluated on utilitarian criteria or criteria of social control.

References

ALEXANDER, R.J. (1984) *Primary Teaching*, London, Holt, Rinehart and Winston.

ARCHER, R.L., LEWIS, W.J. and CHAPMAN A.E. (1910) *The Teaching of Geography in Elementary Schools*, London, A. and C. Black.

BAILEY, P. and BINNS, T. (eds.) (1987) *A Case for Geography*, Sheffield, Geographical Association.

BALCHIN, W.G. and COLEMAN, A.M. (1965) 'Graphicacy should be the fourth ace in the pack', *Times Educational Supplement*, 5 November 1965, reprinted in BALE, J., GRAVES, N. and WALFORD, R. (eds.) (1973) *Perspectives in Geographical Education*, Edinburgh, Oliver and Boyd.

BALE, J. (1987) *Geography in the Primary School*, London, Routledge and Kegan Paul.

BLADES, M. and SPENCER, C. (1986) 'Map use by young children', *Geography*, 71, pp. 47–52.

BLAUT, J.M. and STEA, D. (1971) 'Studies of geographic learning', *Annals of the Association of American Geographers*, 61, 387–393.

BLAUT, J.M. and STEA, D. (1974) 'Mapping at the age of three', *Journal of Geography*, 73, 5–9.

BLYTH, W.A.L. (1987) 'Towards assessment in primary humanities', *Journal of Educational Policy*, 2, 353–360.

BLYTH, W.A.L. DERRICOTT, R., ELLIOTT, G., SUMNER, H. and WAPLINGTON, A. (1976) *Curriculum Planning in History, Geography and Social Science*, London, Collins – ESL Bristol.

BLYTH, W.A.L. and DERRICOTT, R. (1977) *The Social Significance of Middle Schools*, London, B.T. Batsford.

BOARDMAN, D. (1983) *Graphicacy and Geography Teaching*, London, Croom Helm.

BOARD OF EDUCATION (1930) *Report of an Inquiry into the Teaching of the Geography of the British Empire in Certain Types of Schools*, London, HMSO.

BOARD OF EDUCATION (1931) *Report of the Consultative Committee on the Primary School, (Hadow Report)*, London, HMSO.

BRAMWELL, R.D. (1961) *Elementary School Work 1900–1925*, University of Durham Institute of Education.

BROOKS, L. (1929) 'Geography in reorganized schools: the senior school', *Geography*, 15, 305–307. ·

BROOKS, L. (1952) 'Some thoughts on present-day teaching of geography in schools', *Geography*, 37, 63–71.

BURROWS, F.R. (1900) 'The teaching of geography in preparatory schools', in Board of Education, *Preparatory Schools for Boys: Their Place in English Education: Special Reports on Educational Subjects*, Vol. 6, London, HMSO.

CATLING, S.J. (1978) 'Cognitive mapping exercises as a primary geographical experience', *Teaching Geography*, 3, 120–123.

CATLING, S. (1985) *Mapstart Series*, Glasgow and London, Collins-Longman.

CATLING, S. (1987) 'Some challenges for primary geography', *Teaching Geography*, 12, 148.

CATLING, S. FIRTH, T. and ROWBOTHAM, D. (1981–4), *Outset Geography Series*, Edinburgh, Oliver and Boyd.

CENTRAL ADVISORY COUNCIL FOR EDUCATION (1967) *Children and their Primary Schools (Plowden Report)*, London, HMSO.

COLE, J.P. and BEYNON, N.J. (1968–72) *New Ways in Geography*, Oxford, Basil Blackwell.

CONS, G.J. and FLETCHER, C. (1938) *Actuality in School: an Experiment in Social Education*, London, Methuen.

COWHAM, J.H. (1900) *The School Journey: A Means of Teaching Geography, Physiography and Elementary Science*, London, Westminster School Book Depot.

DEPARTMENT OF EDUCATION AND SCIENCE (1978) *Primary Education in England: a Survey by HM Inspectors of Schools*, London, HMSO.

DEPARTMENT OF EDUCATION AND SCIENCE (1981) *Primary Education in England: a Survey by HM Inspecctors of Schools*, London, HMSO.

DEPARTMENT OF EDUCATION AND SCIENCE (1983a) *9–13 Middle Schools: an Illustrative Survey*, London, HMSO.

DEPARTMENT OF EDUCATION AND SCIENCE (1983b) *Teaching in Schools: the Content of Initial Training: an HMI Discussion Paper*, London, DES.

DEPARTMENT OF EDUCATION AND SCIENCE (1985) *Education 8 to 12 in Combined and Middle Schools*, London, HMSO.

DEPARTMENT OF EDUCATION AND SCIENCE (1986) *Geography from 5 to 16: HMI. Curriculum Matters 7*, London, HMSO.

DEPARTMENT OF EDUCATION AND SCIENCE (1987a) *The National Curriculum 5–16: a Consultative Document*, London, DES.

DEPARTMENT OF EDUCATION AND SCIENCE (1987b) *National Curriculum Science Working Group: Interim Report*, London, DES.

ELLIOTT, G. and MARTIN, K. (1986) *Discovering our World Series*, Oxford, Oxford University Press.

FAIRGRIEVE, J. (1926) *Geography in Schools*, London, University of London Press.

FAIRGRIEVE, J. and YOUNG, E. (1939) *Real Geography. Book I*, London, G. Philip and Son.

FISHER, S. and HICKS, D. (1985) *World Studies 8–13: a Teacher's Handbook*, Edinburgh, Oliver and Boyd.

FITCH, J.G. (1854) *The Relative Importance of Subjects Taught in Elementary Schools*, London, Partridge and Oakey.

FORSAITH, D.M. (ed.) (1932) *A Handbook for Geography Teachers*, London, Methuen.

GARNETT, O. (1940) 'Reality in Geography', *The Journal of Education*, 72, 171–3.

GEIKIE, A. (1882) 'My first geological excursion', in GEIKIE, A. *Geological Sketches at Home and Abroad*, London, MacMillan & Co.

GEOGRAPHICAL ASSOCIATION (1935) 'Memorandum to the Board of Education on the place and value of geography in post-elementary education to 16 years', *Geography*, 20, 47–51.

GEOGRAPHICAL ASSOCIATION (1945) 'The future for geography in primary schools', *Geography*, 30, 50–52.

GEOGRAPHICAL ASSOCIATION (1981) *Geography in the School Curriculum*, Sheffield, Geographical Association.

GOODSON, I.F. (1983) *School Subjects and Curriculum Change: Case Studies in Curriculum History*, London, Croom Helm.

HAMMERSLEY, A.D., JONES, E. and PERRY, G.A. (1968) *Approaches to Environmental Studies*, London, Blandford Press.

HARRISON, P., HARRISON, S. and PEARSON, M. (1986–7) *Into Geography: The Geography of the Environment Series*, Leeds, Arnold-Wheaton.

HERBERTSON, A.J. (1905) 'The major natural regions of the world', *Geographical Journal*, 25, 300–310.

HONEYBONE, R.C. (1954) 'Balance in geography and education', *Geography*, 39, 91–101.

JENNINGS, T. (1986) *The Young Geographer Investigates Series*, Oxford, Oxford University Press.

JONES, E.W. (1933) 'Differences in the geographical work of boys and girls', *Geography*, 18, 37–54.

LAWTON, D., CAMPBELL, J. and BURKITT, V. (1971) *Social Studies 8–13: Schools Council Working Paper No. 39*, London, Evans: Methuen Educational.

LAWTON, D. and DUFOUR, B. (1974) *The New Social Studies: a Handbook for Teachers in Primary, Secondary, and Further Education*, London, Heinemann.

LINES, C. (1971) *Teaching Environmental Studies in Primary and Middle Schools*, London, Ginn and Co.

LYDE, L.W. (1928) 'BA Honours students and training colleges', *Geography*, 14, 329–332.

McDONALD, E.H.B. and DALRYMPLE, J. (1910) *Little People Everywhere Series: Ume San in Japan*, London, Wells, Gardner, Darton and Co.

MACKINDER, H.J. (1887) 'On the scope and methods of geography', *Proceedings of the Royal Geographical Society*, New Series, 9, 141–173.

MacMunn, N. (1926) *The Child's Path to Freedom*, London, J. Curwen and Sons.

Marchant, E.C. (1964) 'Geography in education in England and Wales', *Geography*, vol. 49, 173–191.

Marsden, W.E. (1976) 'Stereotyping and third world geography', *Teaching Geography*, 1, 228–230.

Masterton, T.H. (1969) *Environmental Studies: a Concentric Approach*, Edinburgh, Oliver and Boyd.

Matthews, H. (1986) 'Children on map makers', *Geographical Magazine*, 58, 124–16.

Ministry of Education (1948) *Local Studies: Pamphlet No. 10*, London, HMSO.

Page, J.W. (1909) 'Geography', in Hayward, F.H. (ed.) *The Primary Curriculum*, London, Ralph, Holland and Co.

Penstone, M.M. (1910) *Town Study: Suggestions for a Course of Lessons Preliminary to the Study of Civics*, London, National Society.

Piche, D. (1981) 'The spontaneous geography of the urban child', in Herbert, D.T. and Johston, J. (eds.) *Geography and the Urban Environment: Progress in Research and Applications, Vol. IV*, London, John Wiley and Sons.

Renwick, M. and Pick, B. (1982) *Going Places Series*, London, Nelson.

Reynolds, J.B. (1901) 'Class excursions in England and Wales', *The Geographical Teacher*, 1, 32–36.

Royal Geographical Society (1950) 'Memorandum on Geography and "Social Studies" in Schools', *Geography*, 35, 181–185.

Scarfe, N.V. (1950) 'Geography and social studies in the USA', *Geography*, 35, 86–93.

Schools Council (1972) *Environmental Studies 5–13: Teacher's Guide*, London, Rupert Hart-Davis.

Stamp, L.D. (1951) 'Some neglected aspects of geography', *Geography*, 36, 1–14.

Stamp, L.D. and E.C. (1930) *The New Age Geographies Junior Series: Book I. At Home: Book II. Far Away: Book IIIa. Round the World: Book IIIb. More Travels round the World*, London, Longmans, Green & Co.

Stamp. L.D. and E.C. (1935) *A First Atlas*, London, G. Gill and Sons.

Storm, M. (1983) 'Geographical development education: a metropolitan view', in Bale, J. (ed.) *The Third World: Issues and Approaches*, Sheffield, Geographical Association.

Thomas, H.G. (1937) *Teaching Geography*, London, Ginn and Co.

Walker, J. (1953) *Aspects of Geography Teaching in School*, Edinburgh, Oliver and Boyd.

Welpton, W.P. (1923) *The Teaching of Geography*, London, University Tutorial Press.

Ward, H. (1911) 'Monitorial Schools and their Successors', quoting from Dunn, H. (1837) 'Principles of Teaching', *Education Record*, 18, 253–259.

Watts, D.G. (1976) *Environmental Studies*, London, Routledge and Kegan Paul.

William, M. (ed.) (1976) *Geography and the Integrated Curriculum*, London, Heinemann.

Wooldridge, S.W. (1955) 'The status of geography and the role of field work', *Geography*, 40, 73–83.

Wright, D. (1983) '"Colourful South Africa"?: an analysis of textbook images', *Multi-racial Education*, 10, 27–36.

Chapter 7

Industry and Humanities

Alistair Ross

Introduction

The past decade has seen an increasing political emphasis on bringing industry into the education system. From James Callaghan's Ruskin Speech in October 1976 to the launch of the Enterprise and Education Initiative by Lord Young, Kenneth Baker and Norman Fowler in September 1988, educationists, including those working in the primary sector, have been urged to get in touch with the 'real world'. The objective of these advocates seems to be wholly instrumental in nature. So what, then, is a chapter on industry in the curriculum doing in a volume on the humanities in the primary school?

In this chapter I will explore this question and suggest that there are three quite different arguments for involving a 'world of work' dimension in the primary curriculum. These three alternative views provide perspective on the wider debate of the role of the humanities in the curriculum, offering clearly different values about the nature of education that curiously converge at the point of industry education. However, these viewpoints are sufficiently disparate that, however much there may be apparent unity on including an industry-related element within the curriculum, there will be quite different expectations and evaluations of the results of these initiatives.

Teachers' Objectives

Primary schools' work with industry has grown dramatically in the past decade. In his survey of primary school activities in 1982, made for the Schools Curriculum Industry Project (SCIP), Jamieson (1984) concluded that there were 'hardly a dozen examples of primary schools engaged in clear-cut work on industry'. By 1984, SCIP was actively beginning to broaden its attentions to include the primary sector; in 1986 Industry

Year placed a special emphasis on primary education. A DES survey (DES, 1987) found that about half of the primary schools surveyed had organized links with industries. Links tended to have been organized for junior children rather than infant classes, although about a third of five year olds were involved. Both manufacturing and service industries were equally involved. A parallel report noted that primary schools had a significantly lower level of involvement than secondary schools, and had fewer formal or regular links (Industry Matters, Arney, 1987). Since that year, Industry Matters, now the Enterprise and Education Initiative, has focused attention on developing primary as well as secondary school links.

What exactly is primary schools–industry work? Smith (1988) suggests that there are two approaches, drawing on an earlier formulation by Blyth (1984). Smith distinguishes *education about industry* as focusing on 'what it is that children of the primary age range need to know about "the world of work"', whereas *education through industry* sees industry education 'as a process which helps young children develop some of the intellectual and social skills appropriate to their age and ability'. Blyth's distinction was that *education about industry* is 'part of social or environmental studies in a fairly conventional mode', while *education through industry* is 'a particularly vivid way of coming into contact with the realities of competition, conflict, enterprise and achievement'. Blyth's original categorization also identified *education for industry* as the instrumental view of education intended to encourage favourable attitudes to particular enterprises.

An examination of the practice of primary schools–industry work seems to confirm this categorization. While most teachers seem to admit a variety of aims into their planning of this kind of work, an analysis of the expressed aims of primary teachers engaged in schools–industry work (Ross, 1985) showed a distinct polarization. Some teachers stress knowledge-based objectives, such as 'understanding the structure of industry', 'knowing that industry creates wealth', or that it 'pays for services', while rather more teachers focus on the human and social dimensions possible through industry work, such as 'experience in meeting new people', 'understanding how people work together' and 'experiencing problem-solving at first hand'. However, both approaches might be seen as reproducing in children an uncritical acceptance of the values of the free market economy (Campbell, 1986).

Primary Schools–Industry Work: Practice

Some examples of the kind of work taking place in schools may illustrate some of these divergent ambitions:

1 Exploring Class and Gender Divisions at Work

In a south London primary school, 10 year-olds made a case study of a local factory. They interviewed many of the workers, trying to find out how the various departments worked together, and the hierarchical relationships that held the enterprise together. Some of them were particularly concerned at the role of the managers, whom they saw as parasitic on the labours of the production line workers. 'I don't think they need directors,' said one child. 'The workers could organize the factory themselves.' 'Could you work without the directors?' they asked a charge hand. 'Have you ever tried?' As for differential rewards at the workplace, one child summarized the views of his group as follows: 'All the directors might work in the office and so on . . . but they don't work on a bench, on machines and that, so I don't think that none of the directors should get no more money than the workers.'

Other children were more interested in gender roles in the workplace. 'Why can't a women do that job?', 'Why are you called a fore*man*?' were some of the questions asked (Ross, 1984).

The focus of the work was the development of a critical awareness of social inequalities. One of the class discussions with a worker was videotaped (ILEA, 1983), and this shows the children using the worker as an incidental resource in their own debate on their own social and economic experiences and observations. At times the perceptions and awareness of these predominantly working-class children were clearly beyond those of the worker.

2 Investigating Hierarchical Relationships

Another London primary school made a whole school approach to industry. Ten classes made case studies of local workplaces. The staff's objectives in this were four-fold:

1 To develop in staff and children an awareness of the interdependence of industrial society.
2 To develop particular economic and social concepts associated with work and industry, which the staff believe would be of value to children's understanding of industry: co-operation, the division of labour, interdependence, hierarchies of power and authority, tradition, social change and exchange.
3 To develop children's skills in observing, investigating and evaluating social and economic activities in their everyday lives.

4 To report on how a whole school can work together to develop such concepts, skills and understandings, using an industrial focus, within the primary curriculum. (Fox Primary School, 1984)

The emphasis here was on using industry as a convenient vehicle for more general social cognitive and skill development, rather than specific knowledge about local workplaces. Classes examined the hierarchical organization of the workplaces they had chosen. Thus one first-year junior class made several visits to a magazine's offices, and, among other aspects, looked at the relationship of the editor to designers, writers, sub-editors and illustrators. A second-year class looked at the organization of a hotel, and a third-year class made a detailed study of the hierarchy of a medium sized light engineering works. They made a diagram of the relationships, and interviewed different people about their perceptions of who was in control. A fourth-year class studied a local National Health Service hospital, and constructed a mobile showing the rigid hierarchical patterns of the medical, nursing and administrative staff.

After these projects, children were asked to construct organizational patterns of an imaginary factory. It was found that younger children tended to develop linear hierarchies, while older children were able to formulate more complex branching patterns (Ross, 1989). It also appeared that younger girls developed their linear patterns along status-determined lines (forming one group of shopfloor workers, another of supervisors, another of managers, etc.), while younger boys emphasized functional relationships (forming one group of all the sales staff and managers, another of all the design workers and managers, etc.). Older girls were better able to transfer their linear status pattern to branching hierarchical structures than were older boys.

This group of projects had placed a premium on the understanding of social relationships in relatively complex organizations. The emphasis was more on analysis than on developing a sharp critical focus, but the children emerged aware that social patterns of inequality could be explored and sometimes challenged.

3 The Firm as a Provider of Goods or Services

Mini-enterprises are now a fairly common primary school activity. A class of seven and eight year olds in Bedfordshire made a study of a small row of shops opposite the school. They interviewed the shopkeepers, surveyed the customers, and generally explored how a retailer organized the enterprise to meet consumer needs. They then organized their own store, baking and selling a variety of biscuits. To do this, they formed a company, 'The Crunchiest Cookie Company', each child contributing the same amount of capital, and were given shares in the company. They collectively shared the organization and labour tasks, making market surveys, taking orders, and organizing the selling and book-keeping. The shares were not transferable, and at the end of the company's life, each share was redeemed at its face value. The children had decided in advance to give the profits to the school to buy a disc-drive for their microcomputer (Grant, 1987).

In this instance, the children in effect formed a co-operative. The capital necessary for the enterprise was held equally and mutually. The nature of the enterprise was not to generate surpluses for individuals: its prime purpose was to produce goods that customers needed at a price that they could afford.

There is a frequent assumption amongst some critics of industry that the purpose of any enterprise is to produce a profit on capital. This is not so: the purpose of the firm is to produce goods and services, to satisfy a need. In a capitalist economy, the owners of capital may well see it as a way of accumulating further capital; and the workers may well see it as providing them with wages but the function of the firm is neither to produce a profit or to provide jobs, but to meet the public's needs.

4 Capital as a Marketable Commodity

Another example of a mini-enterprise, reported by Waite (1988), shows a different emphasis. In a Newcastle primary school the children organized a company growing and selling house plants. Capital was raised through the issue of 100 ten-penny shares bought by the children. There was a market in trading shares, with the price fluctuating according to the anticipated profit levels. In two months the price of a share rose to 65p, and five months later shares were redeemed at 71p each.

In this example, the concept of a market economy is extended beyond the simple notion of production, supply and demand. A market has been established for capital itself. Shares fluctuate in value, respond to demand, and are traded. These seemingly small changes in emphasis from the previous example have shifted the whole focus of the project, from one in which the business was concerned with meeting a need to one in which the return on capital is stressed.

5 The Company as a Wealth Creator

A number of primary schools in Staffordshire worked with a Shell onshore oil exploration rig. The principal aim was defined as:

> To develop an approach to the study of onshore oil exploration as a vehicle for introducing children to:
>
> (i) the role of major companies like Shell UK in creating wealth;
> (ii) the concern of such companies to protect the environment;
> (iii) the technology of the onshore oil industry.

The work arising out of visits to the rig emphasized the scientific and technological aspects of the industry, perhaps at the expense of personal values. There was science work on the properties of oils, work on the transmission of sound waves and the designing and testing of rigs, as well as map making and role play planning enquiries (Carter, 1988).

The aims clearly stress the development of a positive view of the industry, and of this company in particular. The industrialist's view of the project was instrumental, rather than any wider concern, and the teachers involved apparently accepted this. The achievement of these aims is furthered by stressing the technological aspects of the work at the expense of more humanistic elements. Such a project, for example, could have examined the working conditions of the drillers, or their concern with health and safety, and the potential conflict with managers on this. This would not, however, have helped the aim of viewing the industry as a wealth generator.

6 Reproducing Capitalist Values

Examining a schools–industry project in a Staffordshire primary school, Campbell (1986) suggested that children might have picked up alternative value systems from industry: leadership, equated with decision making and the exercise of authority, and loyalty, associated with passivity and obedience. The project had at least the potential of 'reproducing in children the polarized values characteristic of relations between workers and management.' Children in the project were seen to be subscribing to the view of industry as competitive and profit making.

This project exemplifies a recurrent problem that is inherent in school studies of the social environment. If one works from the immediate and specific experiences of the child towards a more generalized and abstract representation, then the teacher must inevitably start by encouraging the close observation of the local community. However, in contemporary society such observations are bound to reflect the unequal nature of society: sexist, racist, and in this instance, capitalist. It can be argued that making such studies naturally reinforces children's stereotypical views of society. If they always see women and blacks in low grade jobs, and they will believe that this is 'natural' or perhaps accept some pseudo-rational argument for these phenomena. On the other hand, to represent some ideal type to children will be difficult, it will not match their own observations and may well be discounted. The duty of the teacher in this situation is to foster skills of critical awareness of the issues so that children reflect upon their findings rather than just mirror them.

7 Establishing a Monopoly Position

In a Hampshire primary school, children engaged in a simulation of running rival airline companies, with the help of a computer. The children bought planes, chose routes and fixed prices. The lessons of free market competition were not missed. One boy observed, 'All we had to do was undercut the other airlines for a while till they were out of business, and then we could charge what we liked.'

This final example takes the model of capitalist organization to its ultimate conclusion. In this simulation the objective has moved beyond the provision of a service, and beyond the establishment of trading in capital, to the elimination of competition and the establishment of a monopoly in order to maximize profits at the expense of the consumer.

Three Arguments For Schools – Industry Work

In Chapter 1, Campbell argues that there are various rationales for including the humanities within the curriculum, one of which concerns the children's relationship to society. Translated into the schools–industry field, this becomes the argument that learning about industry is to the general good of society (in that the population will appreciate the advantages of industrial goods and services) and to the specific advantage of the individual (in that they will be better placed to make career choices and will better understand their role and status in the workplace). This instrumental view of the role of schools–industry work would appear to be held by many industrial managers (CBI, 1988). There may also be a sizeable minority of teachers who subscribe to these arguments. In terms of Blyth's (*op. cit.*) analysis, these arguments are essentially for *education for industry*.

The second group of arguments for the humanities is that there is something intrinsic to the study of these subjects that makes them of value. In the schools–industry area, this provides some dilemmas, in that there is a variety of value systems at work. Many teachers would see the process of studying a local industry as valuable; one in which children develop skills and conceptual understanding of their social environment. Because the social environment of our society is so dominated by the work process, the study of work becomes an essential element of the education process. Many teachers would share this view.

This argument that the study of industry is intrinsically valuable is also used by some politicians in a rather different way. They hold that industry is essentially an enterprise, and that children studying industry will become more 'enterprise minded'. This is the philosophy behind the Enterprise in Education Initiative, which stems in part from Wiener's (1981) thesis that education lost touch with the 'real' worlds of manufacturing and commerce, promoting value systems that ran counter to wealth production. Enterprise is thus narrowly defined, and is implicitly always 'private' enterprise. This has led to some extraordinary debates within the Department of Trade as to what exactly constitutes an industry: is it purely manufacturing (a view subscribed to originally by both the DTI and Industry Year) or does it also include services provided by the private sector? Does it include hospitals? (at the time of writing, probably), or local authorities? (no).

Behind this semantic juggling lie two notions. Firstly, that wealth consists of material objects, as opposed to services. It is argued, by many industrialists and some politicians, that it is the manufacturing base of the country which supports the services, which could not exist without these 'wealth creators'. This curious scale of values would, taken to its logical conclusion, mean that the printer of pornography was of more value to society than, say, a nurse. The second notion is the politically polemical view that the distinction lies not between services and production, but between privately owned and publicly owned workplaces. The former are seen as true enterprises, in that they are motivated by the search for profits (and all the competitive values that this implies), while public utilities are defined as non–enterprising. Fiddy (1986) provides a background to the beginnings of this debate.

Both these groups – the teachers, and the industrialists and politicians, – however, agree that there is something intrinsic to industry that is of value. Their debate is over which elements are intrinsic, what industry actually is, and, ultimately, what value system should prevail. They are at one, though, advocating *education about industry*.

The third set of arguments for the humanities generally is that they help children to organize and reconstruct their experience of the world. By providing models and conceptual frameworks to analyze experience, children come to the ability to share and to extend their understanding. Using these justifications for schools-industry work, teachers and liberal educators argue that the needs of both the individual in terms of self-fulfilment, and society in terms of critical and reflective membership, are best met through developing skills of analyzing personal relationships. One of the most vivid fields for such analysis lies in the relationships of the workplace, where individuals come together to co-operate and are interdependent, yet also in conflict over their different needs; where individuals develop (or have developed for them) different roles, and where the division of labour is linked with hierarchies of power and authority, which are in turn linked to gender, class and racial differences. Industry, in its broadest sense, offers a rich and unique ground for such learning, as can be seen in some of the examples above. Going back again to the Blyth-Smith analysis, this group falls into the *education through industry* category.

There is a variety of people promoting primary schools-industry work. Each offers a quite different rationale and set of aims for this. There are those politically to the right, who believe it is possible (and necessary) to inculcate positive views of free market capitalism. There is a variety of industrialists, ranging from those in large firms who welcome a liberal and broad humanistic education, provided that it develops a more positive view of wealth creation, to the small scale entrepreneur and trader, who generally favours a more narrowly and traditionally defined curriculum (*pace* the subject based nature of the National Curriculum defined in the Educational Reform Act). There is a number of trade unionists anxious to counter negative media images by involving children in the day to day work of negotiating health, safety and other conditions of employment. There are teachers who view the curriculum as knowledge based, and see the industrial world as part of the core of information that must be transmitted. And there are teachers who are concerned with the process of enhancing critical cognitive skills, and who use industry as a powerful vehicle for such development. There is a noticeable tendency to semantic drift, as new emphases are brought in. 'Industry' as a concept has been challenged by 'economic awareness' and recent government initiatives have variously stressed 'business', 'employers' and, in particular, 'enterprise'.

Much of the development of the schools-industry movement in secondary education can be seen in terms of the alliances formed between these competing individuals. The plethora of formal groups promoting this work is partly the result of such alliances and partly the result of the realization that their objectives, although employing rather similar broad strategies for encouraging schools and industries to liaise, are ultimately incompatible. The debate over the place of the humanities in the curriculum, and the reasons for it being there, is seen in sharp focus in issues raised by the education and industry debate.

Industry, the Social Sciences and Humanities

Whilst one can, to an extent, understand the motivations of primary teachers who argue for industry education on intrinsic grounds, to concede this ground would make it difficult to resist the pressures of others with different but equally valid reasons. In my view, the study of industry is a useful vehicle, if but one of several, to the broader understanding of social relationships. If one of the aims of education is to make sense of one's environment, and the human environment is essentially social, then teachers must be concerned to help children make sense of society. Almost without exceptions, societies are organized around the need to work together to provide the level of goods and services which society aspires.

Understanding society, and in particular the economic and political dynamics in the organization of work, depends on the development of a series of related social concepts. Lists of such concepts for primary aged children have been suggested, for example, by Blyth *et al.* (1976), Wagstaff (1979), Ross and Smith (1985), Waite (1988) and King (1989). The Appendix gives these. They include power and authority, the division of labour, conflict, money, price and value.

These concepts are useful tools for organizing our perceptions and thoughts about the way in which our lives are organized and they are found in and extend beyond the workplace. It is, however, in the study of work that we can see them all clearly operating together. A broad definition of industry might well be situations in which individuals and groups work. As Pahl has described (1984, 1988), work itself is a complex and often ambiguous concept.

The social sciences and the humanities are mutually supportive in this, and can be used together particularly fruitfully in the primary school curriculum. The older disciplines of history and social geography can be seen as particular dimensions in which the social sciences of sociology, economics, political science and anthropology can be explored (Burke, 1983). And, as Campbell has argued (Chapter 1), a justification for the humanities in the primary curriculum is that they can encourage children to reconstruct their experiences in a social framework. The same reasoning holds good for schools-industry education.

A Pattern for Development

This chapter, as well as exploring the competing forms of primary schools-industry work, has suggested that one set of arguments is more satisfying than the others. The notion of education *through* industry has a firm grounding in theories of children's conceptual development, has the ability to rebuff ideological challenges, and probably represents the most attractive argument to primary teachers. How can these humanistic justifications best be translated into practice?

There seem to be three types of industry work that fit into the humanities tradition. Firstly, there is the case study. Children make a study of a local workplace, visiting it several times (with intervals, to develop reflections on their observations), and inviting workers into the school. In a good example of a case study, the children will meet a variety of people at work, not just managers but also shop floor workers, trade unionists, owners and office staff. The children will analyze what is happening both in terms of a process (making goods, providing a service) and in terms of personal relationships and how they are developed. The children will, for example, ask questions about who controls whom, about what the rewards are and pose questions about inequalities and fairness. Their work will extend over a wide area of the curriculum.

The potential utilitarian and intrinsic arguments that may run counter to this work would be the presentation of a wholly company view ('This firm and its product is best'), or a management view ('We need to control the workers and we don't need trade unions here'), or a false consensus view ('This firm is rather like a football team, all working together'). There is also the possibility of children having ideological views such as, 'The nature of the enterprise is to put competitors out of business, and to keep the workers in place' or 'Of course workers like us need bosses; it's their company, isn't it?'. The role of the teacher is not to avoid such viewpoints, but to encourage children to question them, and to pose alternatives. In my experience, this depends on creating an inquisitive and challenging ethos to the work, not on prompting the children.

The second kind of activity is the mini-enterprise. Here a group of children plan to provide a service or produce some goods, make decisions about how the enterprise will operate, and then actually see it through. The examples given earlier indicate some of the potential. The organization of these mini-enterprises should largely be left to the children. In the right atmosphere, they will to an extent naturally model themselves on what they have seen adults do but will also be prepared to challenge this at times, particularly on the grounds of fairness.

The potential difficulties here are that the product may run away with the process, and in so doing competitive and profit-making values dominate everything else. The ideological view of enterprise would, of course, welcome such a development. One way around this, which calls for some careful management by the teacher, is to arrange for a variety of organizational forms: co-operatives (all children equally owning the enterprise), school-funded projects (perhaps equivalent to state capitalism) and enterprises funded by borrowing (as from a high street bank, for example).

Thirdly, children can simulate various forms of work, for example, in role play or in some other enactive process. Simulations are usually more short-lived than case studies and mini-enterprises, but can often focus on a particular concept or issue, such as the advantages and disadvantages of production lines or the equity of world trading patterns. The value of simulations emerges through the discussions that follow, when children explain not just what they did but their reasoning and feelings. It is in this debriefing that the teacher ensures that concepts and issues are debated.

The variety in approaches outlined above embodies implicit disagreement about aims, which if made explicit, might lead to open conflict. Because the area is relatively new, most assessments have been concerned with the nature and type of contacts being made, rather than its purpose. There have been only limited attempts to evaluate the results of this work. Between some of the parties concerned there may even be a tacit conspiracy not to enquire too deeply into objectives, lest they expose too clearly conflict over fundamental purposes. But this is to side-step the main issue. Until the participants of industry-education initiatives clarify to themselves what purposes such initiatives serve, their contribution to the humanities in primary schools will also remain unclear.

Appendix

Checklists of social, economic and industrial concepts

Blyth (1976)	Wagstaff (1979)	Ross & Smith (1985)	Waite (1988)	King (1989)
values/beliefs				fairness income & its distribution
power	power & authority social control	authority		government
conflict/ consensus	conflict			conflict
causality			choices	scarcity
similarity/ difference				
continuity/ change	(social change) (tradition) co-operation inter- dependence division of labour	co-operation inter- dependence division of labour structure		inter- dependence specialization
communi- cation		location		local economy
			money	money
	value		value	
			cost	opportunity cost
	price			price
			exchange	transactions enterprise supply/demand
	capital			
				tools and technology

References

BLYTH, A. *et al.* (1976) *Curriculum Planning in History, Geography and Social Science*, London, ESL/Collins.

BLYTH, A. (1984) 'Industry education: case studies from the North West' in JAMIESON, I. (ed.) *We Make Kettles: Studying Industry in the Primary School*, London, Longmans.

BURKE, P. (1983) *Sociology and History*, London, Allen and Unwin.

CAMPBELL, J. (1986), quoted at a National Association for Pastoral Care in Education conference, *Times Educational Supplement*, 12 December.

CARTER, R. (1988) 'The Staffordshire/Shell UK Project: an alternative model for school-industry co-operation' in SMITH, D. (ed.) *Industry in the Primary School Curriculum: Principles and Practice*, Lewes, Falmer Press.

CONFEDERATION OF BRITISH INDUSTRY (1988) *Survey of Schools-industry links*, September.

DEPARTMENT OF EDUCATION AND SCIENCE (1987) *Statistical Bulletin, 12/87: Survey of school-industry links in Industry Year 1986*, London, DES.

FIDDY, R. (1986) 'Education for employment and unemployment: is this the age of the trained?' in WELLINGTON, J. (ed.) *Controversial issues in the curriculum*, Oxford, Blackwell.

FOX PRIMARY SCHOOL (1984) *The Fox School Industry Report: a brief report*, mimeo, ILEA.

GRANT, S. (1987) 'From "Some kind of business" to "a life system"', *Primary Teaching Studies* 2, 2.

INDUSTRY MATTERS/ARNEY, N. (1987) *A survey of schools-industry links in England, Wales and Northern Ireland*, London, Industry Matters/RSA.

KING, B. (1989) 'Charting the territory of economic awareness' in ROSS, A. (ed.) *Economic and Industrial Awareness in Primary Education*, London, National Curriculum Council, forthcoming.

PAHL, R. (1984) *Divisions of Labour*, Oxford, Blackwell.

PAHL, R. (ed.) (1988) *On Work*, Oxford, Blackwell.

ROSS, A. (1984) in 'A case-study of a junior class investigating a local factory during social studies work' in JAMIESON, I. (ed.) *We Make Kettles: Studying Industry in the Primary School*, London, Longmans.

ROSS, A. (1985) 'Primary school teachers' aims in introducing industry into the classroom', *Curriculum* 6, 3.

ROSS, A. and SMITH D. (1985) *Schools and Industry 5–13: Looking at the world of work: Questions teachers ask*, London, Schools Curriculum Industry Project/SCDC.

SMITH, D. (1988) 'Industry and the Primary School Curriculum' in SMITH, D. (ed.) *Industry in the Primary School Curriculum: Principles and Practice*, Lewes, Falmer Press.

WAGSTAFF, S. (1979) *People Around Us: Families – Teacher's Guide*, ILEA.

WAITE, P. (1988) 'Economic Awareness: context, issues and concepts' in SMITH, D. (ed.) *Industry in the Primary School Curriculum: Principles and Practice*, Lewes, Falmer Press.

WEINER, M. (1981) *English culture and the decline of the industrial spirit 1850–1980*, Cambridge, Cambridge University Press.

Chapter 8

World Studies: The Global Dimension

David Hicks

Definitions and Concerns

We live in a world of increasingly rapid social and technological change.
Such change is immediately evident in our own lives and those of our
pupils and is, in turn, the result of both political and economic decision
making. However, these processes can now only be fully understood
in a planetary context. One essential ingredient in the humanities
curriculum therefore has to be the global dimension. Some idea of what
this may actually look like in practice is given by the following glimpses
of five clasrooms in which a world studies approach to teaching and
learning is being used (Hicks and Steiner, 1989).

A Bird's Eye View

The first classroom is actually empty because the children are outside
on a woodland walk. To be precise they are in the local park making
a study of different trees. Each child has chosen one tree for observation
that she or he particularly likes. The teacher asks them to record what
they can see, what they can smell and what sounds they can hear. From
this appreciation of trees in their own environment they will go on to
look at the current destruction of the world's rainforests. They will explore
why this is happening, what the long-term consequences are and what
people are doing to reverse this trend.

In the second classroom children have been doing project work on
Australia. In particular they are looking at different accounts and
photographs of the Australian Bicentenary celebrations in 1988. On the
one hand they find that many white Australians are very proud of their
country's 200 year history and greatly enjoyed the festivities. On the other
hand they find that the Aboriginal community felt insulted by the way

in which their 50,000 year presence on the continent was largely ignored. Such different views of Australian history lead on to questioning how other minority groups have faced up to racial discrimination in multicultural societies such as our own.

In the next classroom pupils are working in small groups studying a close-up photograph of a woman working. Collectively they write a description of everything that they can see and then try to establish what the woman is actually doing. What assumptions do they make about her and what sort of work she is doing? Next they are given a second photograph and find that the first one gave them a less than complete picture. Are they surprised by what they now see? Did they make stereotyped assumptions when faced with the limited evidence in the first photograph? What issues does this raise about sexual discrimination in our own society?

In the fourth classroom children are involved in drama. They are thinking about how to create an imaginary machine which recycles waste into something useful. What waste material do they choose and what will it be turned into? How well are they able to co-operate over this task, since each group will eventually have to show its machine working to the rest of the class for two or three minutes? This activity is part of a project on the world's waste. Pupils began by looking at the nature of rubbish in the home and what then happens to it. They are going on to look at the environmental hazards created by waste, such as the holes in the ozone layer and what is being done to prevent such damage.

In the last classroom pupils are exploring some of the popular misconceptions about world food today. They have completed a short questionnaire which asks them to identify some of the main reasons for recent famines in Africa. After this they compare their answers with a checklist on popular myths about world food in order to re-evaluate their earlier answers. In particular they make a study of Ethiopia which helps them to see that hunger is really a question of poverty and that poverty has many causes. These include the country's history, its geography, the current war and what other countries may do or not do to help.

All of these classroom glimpses have three things in common. Firstly, they all pay careful attention to the process involved in children's learning. They are developing children's skills of observation, hypothesis testing, co-operation, enquiry, empathy and research via a wide range of active learning methods and techniques. Secondly, they all relate to issues which are of immediate interest to the children, either in their daily lives or in their local environment. Thirdly, however, they also set these concerns in a wider context. They show that the local and the global are essentially interlinked, that we are all part of a complex planetary web of interaction.

Global Education

There has long been a tradition of education for international understanding in British schools, a tradition which goes back to international initiatives from progressive educators in the 1920s. Their concerns were two-fold: on the one hand 'world understanding' and on the other 'child-centredness'. The Council for Education in World Citizenship was established in the late 1930s to promote these ideals, followed by the One World Trust in the 1950s. The latter set up the first World Studies Project which ran from 1973 to 1980 under the influential leadership of Robin Richardson. Its publications and workshops had a catalytic effect on a small but influential number of educators.

At the same time the voluntary agencies were arguing the need for development education, that both adults and pupils in school needed to learn about the gross global inequalities of wealth between the rich North and the poor South. Organizations such as Oxfam and Christian Aid took on trained educational staff to help provide well-researched and appropriate materials for schools. One important offshoot of this was the setting up of several Development Education Centres in the 1980s, such as those in Manchester, Birmingham and Leeds. They have a high reputation for their production of excellent teaching materials.

During the 1980s common strands of concern were increasingly noted between world studies, development education, multicultural education and education for peace (Hicks, 1982). The practitioners of each highlighted different aspects of the global condition. The continuous demand from teachers, both primary and secondary, for classroom materials and in-service training gave considerable impetus to the work of bodies such as the Centre for Global Education at York University and national curriculum projects such as *World Studies 8–13* initially at St Martin's College in Lancaster.

The latter has been one of the most innovative curriculum projects of the 1980s. It has a network of contacts in half of the LEAs in England and Wales and at the time of writing is in its ninth year of operation. Its first publication *World Studies 8–13: A Teacher's Handbook* (Fisher and Hicks, 1985) has been well-received by both teachers and advisory staff because of its practical focus on classroom activities. The project defines the aim of world studies as 'helping children develop the knowledge, attitudes and skills which are relevant to living responsibly in a multicultural society and an interdependent world'. Such a concern is clearly cross-curricular, whilst at the same time each subject area will have specific contributions to make to the overall global thread in the curriculum. Certainly the humanities have a major part to play here.

David Hicks

Education Rationale

The educational justification for world studies derives from at least four critical areas:

1 Aims of Education

World studies is in direct harmony with several of the broad aims of education set out in *The Curriculum from 5 to 16* (HMSO, 1985), e.g.

> to help pupils develop lively, enquiring minds, the ability to question and argue rationally;
> to instil respect for religious and moral values, and tolerance of other races, religions and ways of life;
> to help pupils to understand the world in which they live, and the interdependence of individuals, groups and nations.

Whilst there was some concern that these widely agreed aims were not set out in the Education Reform Bill, subsequent debate in the House of Lords clarified the omission. The Earl of Arran, speaking for the Government, pointed out that 'an awareness of global concerns . . . is thus implied automatically in our reference to "society"' and went on to say that the existing wording of the Bill did cover 'the concomitant need to understand the world and the complex interrelationships on which our existence depends' (Hansard, 1988).

2 Children's Interests

One prime reason why pupils enjoy world studies is that active learning is so much more engaging, and fun, than passive learning. World studies also constantly relates their own immediate world and interests to events in the news and in the wider world. One early evaluation of the *World Studies 8–13* project talked of teachers teaching unteachable ideas. This referred to the fact that many teachers were initially surprised at (a) how interested their pupils could be in global issues, and (b) how knowledgeable they were, at their own level. There was thus an initial tendency for teachers to underestimate both their pupils' potential interest and their learning abilities in this context.

There is also often a tension in primary education between the belief that we must always start with the pupil's immediate experiences and the fact that they also have an interest in the wider world. Whilst they may find it *easier* to grasp the immediate, it does not follow that they are uninterested in the wider world. Both teachers and researchers report varying degrees of interest in a wide range of issues, ranging from animal rights and pollution to world famine and the threat of nuclear war. Children can hardly *not* notice these issues given their exposure in the media. They may well be confused about them, but this is precisely one of the problems that world studies directly addresses.

3 Needs of Democracy

It is also important to recall the long 'reconstructionist' tradition in education traceable to Dewey. This, in contrast to the narrow dictates of utilitarianism, looks at the wider needs of society and sees education as having a role to play in bringing about appropriate change. In a democratic society education at all levels should encourage wide-ranging debate about contemporary social, political and economic issues. It should encourage the development of critical thinking in all pupils so that they can recognize propaganda and indoctrination as much from governments as from pressure groups. Kozol (1980) makes the point abruptly clear:

> There is no such thing as a 'neutral' skill, nor is there 'neutral education'. Children can learn to read and write in order to understand instructions, dictates and commands. Or they can read in order to grasp the subtle devices of their own manipulation – the methods and means by which a people may be subjugated and controlled.
> . . . Oppenheimer, working on the final stages of development of the atom bomb, and his co-worker Fermi (said) that they were 'without special competence on the moral question' . . . It is this, not basic skills but basic competence for basic ethical enquiry and indignation, which is most dangerously absent in our schools and our society today.

If we do not help young people to understand the major debates occurring in the world around them we do them and ourselves a grave disservice. Our young adult citizens will be signally uninformed about trends and events that are directly and indirectly affecting their lives. Nor can this process be left until the secondary school, for children's attitudes to other groups and countries, to issues of race and gender, war and peace, are often well established by the junior school stage.

4 State of the Planet

World studies also draws attention to the global condition. Whilst for some this may seem unnecessary or a curriculum luxury that we can ill afford, there is a growing consensus that the state of our planet in the late twentieth century is an issue of urgent concern. Over the last two decades it has become increasingly clear that we are facing a multifaceted global crisis (Spretnak and Capra, 1984) which is now affecting our, and our children's, futures. In broad terms this crisis embraces five main areas.

Firstly, there is the problem of *inequality*. In global terms this is marked by the ever-increasing gap between, and within, the countries of the rich North and the poor South. It is about issues of underdevelopment and overdevelopment. It is about the fact that the minority takes by far the largest slice of the global cake.

Secondly, there is the problem of *violence* and conflict. In global terms this manifests itself as the nuclear arms race with all its absurdities and gross misuse of resources. But it is also about superpower intervention in the countries of the South, about the black struggle in South Africa, about terrorism and increasing violence in our society.

Thirdly, there is the problem of *injustice*. These times are marked by numerous struggles for human rights, in many countries of different political persuasions, where torture and abuse of official power are commonplace. It is important too to recall that issues of injustice, and the erosion of civil liberties, can occur just as easily in our own society as elsewhere.

Fourthly, there is the problem of *environmental damage*. For too long we have treated the natural environment as if it can withstand any assault. Yet the destruction of the rainforests, acid rain, the holes in the ozone layer, the greenhouse effect, are all indicators that we have reached the ecological limits. All economic activity has an environmental and human cost which needs to be made explicit.

Lastly, there is the problem of *alienation*. Particularly in the industrialized societies of the North we find increasing vandalism, drug abuse and teenage suicide. Society is suffering from a general loss of meaning and an often acrimonious debate about the values which we should adhere to. In societies which institutionalize self-interest the marginalized are increasingly disempowered.

The justification for a global perspective in the curriculum is thus a rich and varied, if controversial, one. What this looks like and what this may involve in the primary school can be better appreciated if we set our earlier classroom activities in their broader context.

Teaching and Learning

Many teachers may, of course, be using activities of the kind mentioned above, without calling them World Studies. However, it is important to be clear about the principles and practices of World Studies. The *World Studies 8–13* Project (Fisher and Hicks, 1985) offers a framework for curriculum planning based on the use of key concepts and of knowledge, attitudes and skill objectives. These objectives and concepts also provide the framework underpinning *Making Global Connections* (Hicks and Steiner, 1989), a framework which can be related to many of the attainment targets of the National Curriculum.

The Content of Learning

The content of World Studies is varied. It includes i) studying countries and cultures other than one's own, and the ways in which they differ from, and are similar to, one's own; ii) studying major issues which face different countries and cultures, such as those to do with development, the environment and human rights; iii) studying the ways in which our everyday life and experience affect, and are affected by, the wider world. How teachers tackle themes such as these will vary enormously depending on the age and ability of pupils. Whilst there is no sample 'syllabus' for the 8–13 age range, there is a GCSE World Studies syllabus from the Southern Examining Group.

An idea of appropriate content can be gained by noting the chapter headings in the two 8–13 handbooks mentioned above. These include: Here is the World, Getting on With Others, Other Worlds, and The World Tomorrow; Forest Environments, Aboriginal Perspectives, Gender Issues, Wasted Wealth, and Food Comes First. In each case the emphasis is on drawing out local and global links via a range of active learning techniques. In particular it is about studying not only the problems, but also the suggested solutions. It is about looking at what individuals, groups and governments are doing to create a better world and in so doing helping pupils to clarify their own value preferences. These issues can be addressed in both project work and through subject areas. Some good examples of subject-based approaches are given in Pike and Selby (1988).

The Process of Learning

World Studies is committed to experiential and participatory learning because it achieves both the best results for children and the most appropriate mode for the subject matter in question. Didactic and passive methods do not encourage discussion and debate, reflection and critical thinking. Since active learning gives some measure of ownership to the pupil, it is more likely to result in a high level of interest and commitment, and to be challenging and fun (Rogers, 1983).

Much of this is, as we know, at the heart of good primary practice. It is undoubtedly one reason why World Studies approaches have been taken up so enthusiastically in junior schools. It has sometimes, perhaps, been more difficult for teachers in the 11–13 age range to adapt to, although such methods are equally appropriate here. Detailed examples of the theory and practice of student-centred learning have been admirably illustrated by Brandes and Ginnis (1986).

A World of Change

One of the major themes of this chapter has been that of change. It is important to recall that change is created by humans beings, that different changes relate to differing value assumptions and that we can make choices about the sorts of change we want, or at least those of us who are amongst the well-off minority on this planet, can.

Global Change

The twentieth century has seen an explosion in the *rate* of change: social, scientific, technological, economic, political and cultural. Whilst on the one hand this can be confusing, it is also possible to discern several major underlying trends. In essence, writers such as Capra (1983) and others, have suggested that we are witnessing in the Western World a major paradigm shift. Thus it is argued that the essential worldview through which we interpret and analyze reality is beginning to shift.

The old worldview or paradigm stems primarily from the scientific revolution of the seventeenth and eighteenth centuries. It interprets life and the universe in a very mechanistic and reductionist way. Whilst major social and technological progress has been made by the scientific method, it also tried to treat reality as a set of discrete and separate parts. It causes fragmentation. The new worldview or paradigm draws on the insights both of ecology and, for example, the 'new' physics. It stresses the holistic and systemic nature of reality, in which the parts are seen to be inextricably related. It focuses on the nature of wholeness. Many of the struggles and debates in society today make more sense when set in this context of changing paradigms.

National Change

The last decade has also seen many changes in Britain. For example, the percentage of the population below the poverty line has grown from 10.8 per cent to 16.6 per cent. The percentage of the workforce unemployed has grown from 5.2 per cent to 9.2 per cent. Spending on overseas aid as a percentage of Gross National Product has dropped from 0.48 per cent to 0.28 per cent (*New Internationalist*, 1988).

Trends such as these do not bode well, but as Hall (1988) writes:

> The critical thing to understand is that this restructuring of society has been, at every turn, coupled with an ideological offensive designed to win hearts and minds and gradually to reshape culture itself. Every move has been ideologically packaged so as to appeal to the narrow self-interest of particular groups . . . It aims to win popular consent and authority by a strategic struggle – by fighting on many different fronts at once (the economy, the family, education, sexuality, the realm of ideas . . .) and by promulgating a whole new social philosophy. Its aim, in short, is not simply to remodel society but to undermine the philosophy of social co-operation, mutual aid and care for the underprivileged . . .

To stress self-interest and individualism above all other values is to encourage a fragmented view of the world. Whilst this may appear to make sense in the short-term, the long-term consequences are bound to be damaging to the overall system.

Educational Change

Education too has been in a state of flux over the last decade. It is, therefore, increasingly important that we are clear about the values and principles with which we want to underpin our work. This chapter, and indeed this book, has argued that reductionist and instrumentalist views of education are not in the best interests of children or of the country's future. One reason for the popularity of global education is that it embodies all that is the antithesis of such narrow utilitarianism.

Yet the National Curriculum may not be as constricting as some have thought. Several of the attainment targets that are proposed in *Science for Ages 5 to 16* (DES, 1988), for example, are entirely consonant with the concerns of world studies.

> Target 4 – Pupils should develop knowledge and understanding of the ways in which human activities affect the Earth.
> Target 18 – Pupils should develop the ability to work effectively as part of a group in the planning, carrying out, reporting and evaluation of an investigation or task.
> Target 21 – Pupils should develop a critical awareness of the ways that science is applied in their own lives and in industry and society, of its personal, social and economic implications, benefits and drawbacks.

There is great scope for bringing in a global dimension here, for example by studying the benefits and drawbacks of nuclear power or alternative energy sources.

Above all, we need to be asking ourselves, and helping our pupils to ask, 'What sort of world do we want?' We need to focus on the future as much as on the present and the past, to be clear about our visions and ideals.

> A map without Utopia on it, it has been said, is not worth consulting. Admittedly there are disadvantages in dreams and ideals, the disadvantages of unreality and abstractions. But frequently it also clears and strengthens your mind if you venture to dream for a while, as concretely and as practically as possible, about the ideal situation to which all your current efforts are, you hope, directed. (Richardson, 1985)

It is essential that we reclaim in ourselves, and our pupils, the ability to so dream and envision. It is a key ingredient in global education. Without it we may well not survive in the third millennium.

Resources for Teachers

It is only possible here to describe a selection of the numerous resources that are available for the teacher to use in her work. What follows is my own choice of key texts: details of nine books (and one pamphlet), all of which are addressed directly to teachers and which blend theory and practice in illuminating and challenging ways.

Books for Teachers

World Studies 8–13: A Teachers' Handbook, (Fisher and Hicks, 1985). This is one of the most popular and widely used teachers' handbooks. It is divided into three parts. The first looks at curriculum planning and includes a series of detailed learning objectives. The second contains a wide range of classroom activities and the chapter headings are listed above under 'The Content of Education'. The third part focuses on activities for in-service and professional development.

Themework: Approaches for Teaching with a Global Perspective, (McFarlane, 1986a). This, and the following two books, arose out of the Primary Education Project run by Birmingham Development Education Centre. The book contains ideas and guidelines and groupwork, discussion skills and other activities. It focuses on working with images, attitudes and perceptions, particularly in relation to the themes of change, transport and the notion of a country.

Hidden Messages: Activities for Exploring Bias, (McFarlane, 1986b). This book helpfully and practically explores issues of bias, whether in the media, in teaching materials or in language. Ideas are set out for planning groupwork, for using checklists and analyzing both words and pictures. Starting points are suggested for exploring different points of view and for dealing with stereotypes.

A Sense of School: An Active Approach to In-service, (McFarlane, 1986c). What does global education look like when we work with colleagues in, or outside, school? This, the third book in the series, focuses on inset facilitation, groupwork with adults, and ways of establishing priorities and clarifying policies in school. It clearly shows the way in which world studies in-service matches the classroom processes it advocates.

Earthrights: Education as if the Planet Really Mattered, (Grieg, Pike and Selby, 1987). An exciting mix of photographs, facts, figures, poems and quotations in support of global education. It contains thumbnail sketches by teachers of their work in school, a strong rationale for global education and a very succinct resource section entitled 'Ten Starting Points for Teachers'.

Coping With Conflict: A Resource Book for the Middle School Years, (Nicholas, 1987). This book is divided into four parts all of which contain classroom activities. The first deals with children's immediate experience of conflict and co-operation; the second with conflict and violence seen in the media; the third looks at prejudice and different attitudes to aggression; the last looks at change and scenarios for the future.

Education for Peace: Issues, Principles and Practice in the Classroom, (Hicks, 1988). A detailed study of the field of peace education with case studies on conflict, peace, war, nuclear issues, development, power, gender, race, environment and futures. Contains some twenty classroom activities and useful contributions on both curriculum change and global change.

Teaching Resources for Education in International Understanding, Justice and Peace, (Brewer, 1988). A comprehensive, cross-referenced and age-related, resource catalogue. The main sections cover problem-solving and conflict resolution; war, peace and violence; human rights, race and gender; development and environmental issues; games and drama; audiovisual aids; references and organizations.

Global Teacher, Global Learner, (Pike and Selby, 1988). An excellent handbook for teachers with numerous classroom activities. It sets out in a wealth of detail what being a global learner entails, what the global classroom looks like, what the global curriculum involves and a profile of the global teacher. It contains a very useful select bibliography.

Making Global Connections: A World Studies Workbook, (Hicks and Steiner, 1989). The chapter headings on classroom activities have been listed above under 'The Content of Education'. For each case study there are three sections: Understanding the Issue, Planning the Work and Classroom Activities. Other chapters are on making sense of the world, political education, whole-school approaches and issues of evaluation.

There are also many other books which, whilst not directly written for teachers, provide a wealth of back-up ideas and support. For a major overview of the current human condition Capra's *The Turning Point: Science, Society and the Rising Culture* (1983) is excellent. *The Gaia Atlas of Planet Management* (Myers, 1987) provides a detailed and beautiful reference book for any staffroom. The 'green' scene is also well worth watching and two really useful books to help plan practical project work are *Blueprint for a Green Planet: How You Can Take Practical Steps to Fight Pollution* (Seymour and Girardet, 1987) and *The Green Consumer Guide: High-street Shopping for a Better Environment* (Elkington and Hailes, 1988). The first of these is beautifully illustrated with cut-away drawings; both set out the full environmental and social costs of different products and activities, as well as indicating appropriate alternatives. Finally, three journals which many teachers find valuable are the *World Studies Journal*, *Green Teacher*, and *The New Internationalist*.

References

BRANDES, D. and GINNIS, P. (1986) *A Guide to Student-Centred Learning*, Oxford, Blackwell.

BREWER, A. (1988) *Teaching Resources for Education in International Understanding, Justice and Peace*, University of London Institute of Education, Marc Goldstein Trust.

CAPRA, F. (1983) *The Turning Point: Science, Society and the Rising Culture*, London, Flamingo/Fontana.

DES (1988) *Science for Ages 5 to 16*, London, HMSO.

DES (1985) *The Curriculum from 5 to 16*, London, HMSO.

ELKINGTON, J. and HAILES, J. (1988) *The Green Consumer Guide*, London, Gollancz.'

FISHER, S. and HICKS, D. (1985) *World Studies 8–13: A Teacher's Handbook*, Edinburgh, Oliver & Boyd.

GREIG, S., PIKE, G., SELBY, D. (1987) *Earthrights: Education as if the Planet Really Mattered*, London, Worldwide Fund for Nature/Kogan Page.

HALL, S. (1988) 'The bitter death of the welfare state', *The New Internationalist*, No. 188, October.

HANSARD (1988) Debate on the Education Reform Bill, 21 June.

HICKS, D. (1982) *Teaching World Studies: An Introduction to Global Perspectives in the Curriculum*, Harlow, Longman.

HICKS, D. (ed.) (1988) *Education for Peace: Issues, Principles and Practice in the Classroom*, London Routledge.

HICKS, D. and STEINER, M. (eds.) (1989) *Making Global Connections: A World Studies Workbook*, Edinburgh, Oliver & Boyd.

KOZOL, J. (1980) *The Night is Dark and I am Far From Home*, New York, Continuum.

McFARLANE, C. (1986a) *Themework: Approaches for Teaching With a Global Perspective*, Birmingham, The Development Education Centre.

McFARLANE, C. (1986b) *Hidden Messages: Activities for Exploring Bias*, Birmingham, The Development Education Centre.

McFARLANE, C. (1986c) *A Sense of School: An Active Approach to In-service*, Birmingham, The Development Education Centre.

MYERS, N. (ed.) (1987) *The Gaia Atlas of Planet Management*, London, Pan. *The New Internationalist* (1980) No. 188, October.

NICHOLAS, F. (1987) *Coping With Conflict: A Resource Book for the Middle School Years*, Cambridge, Learning Development Aids.

PIKE, G. and SELBY, D. (1988) *Global Teacher, Global Learner*, London, Hodder and Stoughton.

RICHARDSON, R. (1985) 'Each and every school: responding, reviewing, planning and doing', *Multicultural Teaching*, 3 (2).

ROGER, C. (1983) *Freedom to Learn for the Eighties*, Columbus, Ohio, Merril.

SEYMOUR, J. and GIRARDET, H. (1987) *Blueprint for a Green Planet*, London, Dorling Kindersley.

SPRETNAK, C. and CAPRA, F. (1985) *Green Politics: The Global Promise*, London, Paladin/Grafton.

Journals

World Studies Journal, Centre for Global Education, York University, York YO1 5DD.
Green Teacher, Llys Awel, 22 Pentrerhedyn, Machynlleth, Powys SY20 8DN.
The New Internationalist 120–6 Lavender Ave., Mitcham, Surrey CR4 3HP.

Part Four
Investigating Culture And Language

Chapter 9

Writing, Social Learning and Gender Roles

Carolyn Steedman

Prologue

Teacher: When you come to write, you all do different things. In a minute, you're all going to write, aren't you? How do you make up your minds what you're going to . . .?

Prakash: When we . . . in the night a . . . in the night we thinks about stories, and when we finished about our stories I – we like to say

Once upon a time there was a dragon . . .

Once upon a time there was a . . . man . . .

Once upon a time there was two three.

So on on like that. So when we come to school we reminds our minds to make a story, and when we make a story, it's all there then . . . In the next morning we . . . we reminds our names – our minds – then we do our story . . . You must think . . . you must think very hard . . . Then you must know . . . Then if you make a mistake we – I rub out the mistake and I write it again so it'll be alright; it'll be done . . . so it'll be finished.

Teacher: Sometimes when you're writing though, do you change your mind about the story?

Prakash: If . . . if we done a mistake we must . . . if we . . . if we thought again in the night we . . . have not done a mistake in our books . . . and in the next morning we come to school in class so we rubs . . . we rubs the words out and we put another word in the book.

> *Teacher:* Luxme, how do you do yours? – because sometimes you haven't made up your mind?
> *Luxme:* Sometimes I go to sleep and I think about it.
> *Anita:* Miss, in the night I think everytime ... I was looking in the night and finishing by breakfast ... in the morning I think ... I wakes up and I sleep and I think ...[1]

Introduction

Here a group of Cardiff seven-year-olds talk to their teacher about writing, about the effort they put into it, and its importance in their life. Writing for them, it seems, crosses the boundary between school and home: the children think about their stories in bed at night; the stories enter into their dreams. The children know that writing is to do with power and change: they are in charge of the story they invent, and if they go wrong, they can rub the words out and do it again. Does writing introduce children to the idea of change in a more general sense? If you can change the words on the page, do you understand that what those words represent is also subject to change?

This chapter is about writing, and what it can do for children as well as what they do with it. It concerns a story – not, in fact, a story written by Prakash, Luxme and Anita – but one composed by another three children, in a different classroom, another city, another time. The story that is the subject of this chapter, 'The Tidy House', was written by three eight-year-old girls, and on the face of it, it looks like a semi-fictional account of life as they know it. It catalogues the life of two young mothers bringing up noisy and demanding children in the dreary wastes of a council estate. It looks like a story that rehearses the items of a life that the girls would inherit one day; it looks at the learning, in writing, of adult roles, particularly the roles of working-class women and mothers. This then, is a chapter about writing, and gender – and about the idea of role itself.

Writing and the Humanities

Writing has a dual function in this area of the primary school curriculum. First, it is one of the central ways in which everything else children are asked to understand and learn is mediated. Children write imaginative accounts of living in Norman castles , list the types of building they have just seen in a film about Indian cities, close their eyes, listen, and then put down on paper what it felt like to listen to a piece of music. But at exactly the same time as writing functions as a medium of expression, it is a process and a way of thinking. It is much more than speech written down – though in the early stages of writing development children have to believe that speech *can* be written down, or they would never get anywhere at all. But once they have begun to operate with even the most minimal competence, they find that they can do things in writing that simply cannot be done in spoken language. These differences between the two systems are most apparent to children when they invent narratives. They can tell a story in the voice of other people for instance, or tell a story in the present tense.

The developmental importance of writing has been located as the means it gives to children to detach themselves from actual concrete situations, and to replace words with images of words.[2] This is a step on the road to abstract thinking, and what it means for the eight-year-old perhaps, is that she can symbolize in writing the ideas, entities, and events that make up her world – and play around with them, manipulate them and change them – in a way that she cannot do with reality. The argument that follows is to do with three little girls symbolizing, playing about with, and manipulating the idea of their mothers, and the idea of women in general. This is a story then, about another story, which was itself about the active process of becoming a gendered human being, becoming in this particular case, a woman.

Gender Roles?

Is gender a role? – a part to play, a script that children pick up and learn in the classroom, just as they pick up and learn other bits and pieces of the part called being a boy, or being a girl, elsewhere, by watching telly, or mum hoovering the stairs, or dad finally fixing the bathroom tap? Role-theory, which has provided the vocabulary for educationists' discussion of gender over the last ten years or so, finds its roots in the field of social psychology, and implies the whole complex of attitudes, beliefs, practices and attributes that belong to an individual occupying a particular social position. A teacher for instance, or a bank-clerk, have in the course of their work, to perform in line with the expectations of their audience (five-year-olds listening to a story; an impatient queue during Saturday morning opening) in a way that may have nothing to do with how they are feeling at that particular moment. This notion of a role, taken from the sociology of everyday life, was elaborated and refined during the 1960s and 1970s. This was the time it entered the ordinary lexicon of social workers, journalists and television reporters, and became a broader and vaguer term the more it was used.[3] It was also taken up by those whose attention had been drawn by the women's movement to questions about women's position in society; and so the question was asked: what are the attitudes, attributes, beliefs, and practices that belong to the person who occupies the social position labelled 'woman' or 'girl'? It was at this time too, that it became one of the paradigms of educational research into unequal opportunity in classrooms, and into sexism in schools and of curricula.

The idea of a role implies the transmission of patterns of behaviour and structures of belief, and suggests that they are a list of attributes that can be learned – by watching mum hoovering the stairs, or the boys rather than the girls being asked by their teacher to move the tables for a drama session. But the idea of gender roles may be unhelpful in considering the everyday life of classrooms, for it suggests that if only the teacher could behave in a different way, and give the children a different script to follow (by getting the girls to move the tables and the boys to wash the paintbrushes, stop lining them up by sex, and being vigilant about the sex roles shown in the reading scheme) then things would change. Things do not of course, always change and the role theory sometimes allows those who consciously or unconsciously work within its framework sadly to conclude that there is not much to be done about it all, that boys will be boys, and girls will be girls!

The idea of a *genered identity*, and the *acquisition of gendered identities* on the other hand may actually take us closer to the children in the classroom, and help us see more clearly what they *do* in the process of growing up. Acquisition of a gendered identity is a tale of passion, love, despair, desire; of sex as well as sexuality – in the classroom as well as in all other places that children live their lives. Certainly, classrooms are not places where we expect to find such tales, but we must see them being enacted there, if we are to understand the child's engagement with its own socialization and aculturalization. We need to apprehend the passionate involvement of children in the whole process of becoming a human being of a particular kind. Once we have recognized that passion and that involvement on the part of children then those aspects of classroom life that allow children to work on what they know, to actively transform their experience into something else, through a drama, a story or a painting, and in the process think about that experience, become strikingly important. What this chapter will finally be about is the way in which writing allows children that active transformation of reality.

What we all Know about Gender

It is the classroom door that we need to open if we want to understand how children take part in this process; the door of the classroom rather than of the school, for it is in this interactive community that some thirty odd children and one adult spend time together, six hours a day, five days a week, forty weeks a year. The classroom provides both a social and an emotional setting for long stretches of children's lives, and there are things that most teachers know about the questions of gender and sexism that are raised in it.

Unlike our Victorian forebears, we who live in this society do not believe absolutely that sex-differences are innate, are fixed at birth. We are aware, from a wide range of research that filters into public consciousness (through the channels of television, women's magazines and newpaper articles) that children are made into boys and girls through the processes of socialization. More precise understanding indicates the way in which parents and other carers treat male and female children in very different ways from the first minutes of life – handle them differently, use their voices in different ways with them.[4] This behaviour, largely unconscious, feeds into more *conscious* attitudes and beliefs about what boys and girls should wear, what toys they should play with, what kind of behaviour is appropriate from them. To sum up the wide range of research, and recognizing the force of the argument from biological determinism, from the perspective of the classroom the environmentalist argument pretty much wins the day.

We know as well, that schools are part of that whole social array that shows children what boys and girls, men and women are like, or should be like. Mums may go out to work, but they still do most of the housework; most of the active roles in life and in all the fictions children encounter, are reserved for men; when women work, their jobs are usually the menial ones. In schools, they are dinner ladies and most primary schools are staffed by women with many presided over by male heads. Schools confirm what children learn from everywhere else: that this is the way the world is. This now is taken-for-granted gender knowledge among most primary school teachers.

So are the questions raised at the beginning of the 1980s, by Dale Spender in particular, who alerted the teaching profession to the fact that boys in classrooms receive a disproportionate amount of teacher attention, are asked more questions by their teachers and are responded to more positively by them.[5] Researchers have argued about her findings for eight years now, but in a recent issue of *Research in Education*, Alison Kelly surveys everything that has ever been written on the question of gender in teacher pupil interaction, and concludes that:

> It is now beyond dispute that girls receive less of the teacher's attention in class, and that this is true across a wide range of different conditions. It applies in all age groups . . . in several different countries, in various socio-economic and ethnic groupings, across all subjects in the curriculum, and with both male and female teachers (though more with males). Boys get more of all kinds of classroom interaction.[6]

Classrooms are indeed one of the places where little girls learn to be self-effacing, and silent. We all know this.

What we all know as well is that the teaching profession has responded to findings like this in a variety of positive ways. These have taken the form of formal anti-sexist teaching policies (more particularly in secondary schools), and junior school teachers have described the way in which they have tried to raise children's awareness of sex roles and sexist attitudes.[7] Above all else, the content of the school curriculum has been considered, and in the primary school, reading schemes have been scrutinized, and the extraordinary passivity of girls, in text and illustration, has been outlined and condemned.[8] Writers and publishers are aware of this changed climate of opinion, and beyond the reading scheme there are books like Robert Munch's *Paper Bag Princess*, a hilarious reworking and subversion of the fairy-tale, to help teachers help children become aware of the sex-role stereotyping that surrounds them.[9] There is no denying that educational research has had an effect on primary school teachers' practice, and that many of them feel that it is important not to divide their register into a block of boys and a block of girls, and not to say things like 'I want two strong boys to help me lift this desk' and not just let it happen that somehow it's the girls who always wash the paintbrushes!

The theoretical framework of much of the research influencing practice in this way has been that of role theory; actual research in classrooms has been largely ethnographic in design and approach, that is to say, it has watched and observed children as the *subjects* of various social forces and social processes. It has made little effort to see children as interactive with their environments and interactive with sets of ideas, nor has it asked children questions about gender.

Teachers often get depressed, in spite of their best efforts, because they still seem to turn out sexist little monsters in the boys and quiet, well-behaved little women in the girls! Would we be so depressed if we understood the classroom in a different way, not just as a place that passively reflects the wider society, but one that has its own structures of time and relationship and affect; a place where things happen *because it is that place*, and nowhere else; a place called a classroom that has children and a teacher in it?

Women and Children in Classrooms

A different way of seeing might be provided by making the simple observation that the majority of teachers of young children are women. This social and historical fact is almost never questioned, or treated as a matter for comment. The other part of this simple observation is that this teacher, this woman, is doing a job of work called teaching, though from the way we talk about it conventionally, in schools and in other institutions of education, it appears as a role, or a mission, as anything but a system of wage-labour. Recently, in a range of accounts that can only be referenced here, women have started to write about the job of teaching.[10] In this culture, as in all known cultures, woman's identity is bound up with the idea of children. Most women have children, or they are child*less* . . . What happens when this pivotal point of our identity – children – is also the means by which you earn your living?

There is a history to show how very *particular* and *historically specific* is the female teacher, and how through her development over two centuries, the idea of work has got lost in assumptions about the nature of womanhood, and mothering. I have written about this history in detail elsewhere, but, in summary, we may think of teaching as women's work now, but it is a fairly recent development. In the early years of the nineteenth century, the majority of teachers of infants were male. In the educational text-books of the 1820s and 1830s, the advantages of the male teacher were made quite clear: he was able to exercise what was called a kind of judicious tenderness, a quality he would have learned as head of a family, and through *governing* that family.

Whilst it is clear that women assisted these male pedagogues, it was not until about 1870 that there were equal numbers of men and women teaching in the elementary schools of England. By the beginning of the First World war, in a striking reversal of earlier figures, women numbered 70 per cent of staff in maintained schools. According to recent figures from DES, the proportion is now closer to 90 per cent. This history reveals the feminization of a trade.[11] I have described how the way in which this society came to define what a good woman and a good mother is, has been bound up with ideas about the suitability of women as teachers of young children. I have argued that our general, late twentieth century understanding of good mothering (empathy with children, an attention to their needs, the desirability of consistent presence in their lives, the efficacy of love in bringing them up) was forged in the way teachers were trained. So if we walk – historically speaking – into the primary classroom, we can see at work a process by which, over the last century and a half, the relationship between women and children has been established as natural, and understood to exist between all women and all children, irrespective of biological ties. Some historians of the family argue that all the ideas we hold about women's 'natural' relationship with children, are, historically specific; it seems likely that the primary school classroom is one of the places where this historical perception has been established (and is still being established).[12]

A teacher as a kind of mother is a historical legacy; for the women teachers who carry it as baggage into the classroom and for the children, in that a certain construction of feminity, embodied in their teacher, is signficant of their own acquisition of a gendered identity. Conclusions like this have been reached by very different research routes. In her work on girls and mathematical learning, Walkerdine has attempted to account for girls' early superior performance compared with boys', by showing how familiar and secure the classroom is as a learning environment for little girls compared with little boys, how familiar is the relationship they have with their teacher, how very much like home that place appears to be.[13]

The Tidy House Revisited

Some time ago, I published a book called *The Tidy House*,[14] a title which I took from a story written by three eight-year-old girls I had taught. 'The Tidy House' – the original Tidy House, the children's story – was written collaboratively in a classroom, during one hot July week of 1976. It was a story that allowed the children concerned (Carla, Lindie and Melissa) both to represent the social world they knew – neglected housing estate on the outskirts of a town, high unemployment even in the mid-70s, very young partnerships and marriages producing many children – and, at the same time, to explore the *meaning* of that world. The story was structured around the uneventful fictional life of two young married couples, Jamie and Jason, and Jo and Mark, their children, and the opposing views of childcare that the two female characters held. Jamie and Jason have a small son called Carl when the children's story opens. Jo (who is childless) indulges her best friend's little boy with 10p pieces and ice-creams, is criticized by his mother Jamie for spoiling him, and contrives to conceive a child to prove that she does indeed, know how to bring up children.

There is a riveting and pivotal scene in the children's story that we see as the place where a baby gets conceived in words, and in which the sense of antagonism between the two women is palpable. The three girls had an extraordinarily good ear for the nuances of adult dialogue with the social tension it often embodies, and they were able to reproduce their observations in written language.

Here, Jamie takes her little boy to visit her friend at the end of his first day at school:

> When they came to Jo's house he ran in the gate and in the house and hugged her.
> 'Hello Jo', he said.
> 'Hello Jo', said Jamie. 'How are you.'
> 'Oh fine', said Jo. 'How are you?'
> 'All right', said Jamie, 'but Carl is getting on my nerves. I am really fed up with him'.
> And Jo said, 'Don't be mean'.
> 'I'm not. It's because he's so spoilt. I don't like children being spoilt.'

'She's up in competition', said Carla, the author of this piece by way of explanation. With grim satisfaction, the three writers have Jo produce twin boys, Simon and Scott. They called the last part of their story 'The Tidy House That is No More a Tidy House', and went on to dourly catalogue the strain and tension involved in bringing up noisy, demanding little boys.

All the fictional children produced in the story are little boys. In my account of 1982, I argued (and would still argue) that here the children found a highly effective way of dealing with one of the pressing psychological and social facts of their life. They knew from experience that children were both loved *and* resented; were desirable objects and difficult items of expenditure; they knew that children cost their parents (particularly their mothers) a great deal, both in financial terms, and in terms of labour and effort; they knew that children were those who untidied the tidy house. They were told this often at home, and told something very like it at school, about untidying the tidy classroom. Making their fictional children boys, was both a way of acknowledging the force of the complaint, and, at the same time, distancing it, deflecting the *personal* accusation. It is not possible to do this sort of thing when telling a story verbally, it was the freedom that *writing* gave them to manipulate the ideas they encounterd that is one of the most important aspects of this account.

'The Tidy House' was an unusual narrative for eight- and nine-year-olds to produce – unusual from the perspective of written narrative. For the most part, the children abandoned the use of the simple past tense, which is the habitual tense of young children when writing – it is characteristic of diary-writing, other reporting, and of most narratives that begin 'Once upon a time'. Most of 'The Tidy House' by way of contrast, was written in a timeless, present dialogue. The dark nights of whispering, the hesitations and reluctances involved in the conception of children (overheard by an eight-year-old through the thin wall of her 1930s council house bedroom) was represented like this:

> 'What time is it?
> Eleven o'clock at night.
> Oh no! Let's go to bed.
> OK.
> Night sweetheart. See you in the morning.
> Turn the light off, Mark.
> I'm going to.
> Sorry.
> All right.
> I want to get asleep.
> Don't worry, you'll get to sleep in time.
> Don't let us, really, this time of the night.
> Shall I wait till the morning?
> Oh stop it.'

Carla wrote this scene and Melissa tried to make it visible. She drew a picture for the cover of their second volume,[15] which depicted the most secret recess of the tidy house, the bedroom of the childless couple, Jo and Mark. There are hearts everywhere: they make the shape of the lamps, the outline of the flowers in a vase. On the floor is what appears to be a circular rug, covered with a random pattern of hearts. Carla commented about the hearts:

> *Carla:* Miss, never seen heart flowers . . .
> *Teacher:* [pointing to Melissa's picture] That's the rug, is it?
> *Melissa:* No, that's a nest of babies.
> *Teacher:* [taken aback] Oh. [recovers herself] A nest of babies! Of course, in every bedroom, a nest of babies.
> *Lindie:* Yes, of course, there is. [Quotes] 'What is the mother without them' . . .

As this was a story written by little girls, the symbolism of the house, the nest and the baby is particularly interesting. For all three children, writing their story was an attempt to understand life's mysteries. They knew indeed how babies were conceived and born, and they knew that I knew that. It is clear that at one level, they were using the hearts, those conventional symbols of romantic love, to think about, and work through this exciting and mystifying knowledge. In the tidy house bedroom, the rug/nest occupies a position opposite the bed. Within a wide brown border is that random scattering of little red hearts, one large red heart and a small ovoid brown blob. The bed in fact, is not shown in full, being cut off by the right-hand side of the page. Yet it was to the bed that the children wanted to draw the observer's attention. The conversation transcribed above continued like this:

Lindie: ... 'What is the mother without them'.
All: Mmm.
Teacher: But your mum hasn't got a nest. She's only got –
Melissa: No, not a nest, but she's got a big bed, and she's got all these cuddly toys around it. She's got a teddy that big.

I had understood 'nest' as 'a houseful of children; a lot of children in fact; but Melissa was not to be deflected by this misinterpretation. There may not have been an actual nest, she agreed with that; but there *was* a bed, and it was her mother's bed; the cuddly toys, the teddies that decorated it, were like the babies in the nest. The large, flamboyant red heart on the rug (in the nest) has, in the context of the child's analogy, to be seen as the mother. The brown blob may be a blocked-out error (but it is a very carefully executed drawing), or it may be the father. The children, through writing and drawing, worked the conventional symbol of the heart into their own metaphor for the central meaning of the house they were writing about – a mother, their mother, and the role of mothers in the production of children.

In the children's life, their mother was an important and powerful figure. In their story, they expressed their apprehension of female power by giving the women the initiative in the conception of the children: it is Jamie and Jo who turn out the light, make the sexual advances, *have* the children. But Carla, Lindie and Melissa also knew that women were not powerful in every way, and that the burden of work, and tiredness, and frustration in the upbringing of children fell on them. Was it out of such contradictory knowledge, and their feelings of betrayal by their actual mothers, that they punished their fictional ones, and had them produce boys instead of girls in the text?[16]

This story then, was not a pretty one, and it certainly wasn't a good piece of 'creative writing'. Three working-class eight-year-old-girls living on a depressed and depressing council estate watched the world around them, saw a pattern of life that they were likely to inherit, and used written language to hold a future up to scrutiny, think about it, feel and express ambivalence about it. They wrote thus, about romantic love, sexual relations, women's desire for children, and their eventual resentment of them. But their writing was no mere rehearsal of what they saw and heard; it was not a way of more thoroughly learning what was transmitted to them concerning the sexual and social world around them. It *was* that of course but it was also a way of resisting what was seen and heard, of feeling angry and resentful, albeit in complicated and convoluted ways. It was writing that set them particularly free to do this, because the writer is not constrained by the presence of an audience, asking questions about who is doing what to whom, where it is happening, suggesting the response 'so what?' by facial gesture and body language.

If the children had attempted to *tell* this story they would constantly have had to stop to explain things. They would also have had to tell the story in the past tense, implying that at some level it *had happened*, and that *they had seen it happen*. The dialogue they used, on the other hand, placed the story in a realm of nowhere and everywhere, now and not-now. What is more, writing allowed them to adopt different persona in rapid succession, to be noisy demanding four-year-olds, tired and irritable mothers and eight-year-old author directing a cast of characters. Even imaginative play does not allow children to move as rapidly as this, between different perspectives.

It would seem then, because writing allowed them to operate in a timeless present, that they achieved an abstract manipulation of ideas and meanings. These points about writing, and its role in the cultural and psychic development of children are general points that apply to both sexes. But my interpretation of 'The Tidy House' offers an insight, I hope, into the ways in which – in different places and at different times – little girls have made themselves into the women they are expected to be. But of course . . . I wasn't sure. I prefaced the book with a line from Henry James: 'Mrs Wix gave a sidelong look. She still had room for wonder at what Maisie knew'.

Entering the Tidy House

You learn things through the process of writing. In particular, you come to see what it is you have suppressed during composition. The moment the finished book was put into my hands, I knew that I was Jo, the childless wife in the children's story, representative particularly, of a principle of child care that was different from that of their mothers. Had I allowed myself to see how *personally* implicated I was in the children's composition, I do not think that I could have written the book. To have known that I was a figure in the children's imaginative universe, that my meaning was to be manipulated, just like the meaning of their mothers – and of houses, and babies – would have exercised the most inhibiting effect. And yet, because of that repression, there is something missing from my own understanding of the Tidy House and the bedroom that lies at its heart; something that I did not think through at my own level of understanding. I was willing at the time to acknowledge the usefulness of psychoanalytic theory in seeing the bedroom, the useful dream-symbolism that makes the connection between houses and bodies, between rooms and wombs. But I turned away (I still do) from the hearts so flamboyantly displayed, and their connection with the bed on the right, cut off by the edge of the page. I understand the hearts, those little pictures of romance, for I grew up, like Carla, Lindie and Melissa, to be a woman in this culture. I did not want to pursue though, the question that their drawing and story raised, about sexual and social truth of that romance: with Mrs Wix, I sent that half-admitted bed only a sideways glance. I recognize now that I was there too, in the picture and in the story – because I was there in the classroom as the children's teacher. I was part of the material out of which the children constructed a gendered identity.

In Conclusion

So is gender a role, a part to play, a script that you can pick up and learn? The script is there, but the children rewrite it. They see the story surrounding them, and they do not like all they see. So they do what they can, with the materials they have to hand, to change the script, though of course, they would not be able to tell you that was what they were doing, and you would not be able to organize for its happening. But the circumstances in which it may happen can be organized; children can be invited to write at length, without the immediate pressure of getting it right, (so that they know this first time is a draft and that details of spelling, punctuation and presentation will be sorted out later). The day, the room and the time available can be organized, so that children can work together if they want and an interested adult can talk to them about their written productions, to let them know that this is something people do: talk about the words they've just put on the page, the world they've tried to alter, discover in this way a little more of what it is they mean.

Notes

1 This transcript was collected as part of the Schools Council 'Language in the Multicultural Primary School' Project, 1981–1982.

2 For the classic theoretical statements of this argument, see Vygotsky, L. *Thought and Language* (1934), MIT Press, Cambridge, Mass., 1986, See also 'The Prehistory of Written Language', in Vygotsky, L.S., *Mind in Society*, Harvard University Press, Cambridge, Mass., 1978.

3 For role-theory, see Jackson, J.A., *Roles*, Cambridge University Press, 1972. See Chetwynd, J. and Oonagh Harnett, *The Sex Role System*, Routledge and Kegan Paul, 1978; see Delamont, S. *The Sociology of Women, An Introduction*, George Allen and Unwin, 1980.

4 For a recent account of this process, see Grabrucker, M. *There's a Good Girl*, Women's Press, 1988.

5 Spender, D. *Invisible Women: the schooling scandal*, Writers and Readers, 1982.

6 Kelly, A. 'Gender Differences in teacher–pupil interactions: a meta-analytic review', *Research in Education*, 39, 1988.

7 Minns, H. 'Girls don't get holes in their clothes', in National Association for the Teaching of English, *Alice in Genderland*, NATE, 1985.

8 Harland, L. 'Why doesn't Johnny skip?', in Minns, H. *ibid.*

9 Munch, R.R. *The Paperbag Princess*, Hippo Books, 1982.

10 Spencer, D.A. 'The Home and School Lives of Women teachers', *Elementary School Journal*, 83:8 (1984), 283–214. Lawn, M. and Grace, G. (eds.), *Teachers: the Culture and Politics of Work*, Falmer Press, Lewes, 1987.

11 For a more detailed account of this argument, see Steedman, C. 'Prisonhouses', *Feminist Review*, 20 (Summer 1985), 7–21. Also reproduced in M. Lawn and G. Grace, *op. cit.* and Steedman, C. ' "The Mother Made Conscious": the history of a primary school pedagogy', *History Workshop Journal*, 20 (Autumn 1985), 149–163.

12 For a discussion of modern construction of motherhood, see Helterline, M. 'The Emergence of Modern Motherhood in England', *International Journal of Women's Studies*, 3:6 (1980), 590–615.

13 Walkerdine, V. 'Sex, Power and Pedagogics', *Screen Education*, 38 (Spring 1981), 14–24.

14 Steedman, C. *The Tidy House: Little Girls Writing*, Virago, 1982.

15 The children called the books that were produced out of their story either 'episodes' or 'volumes'. For the interest of literate children of this age in the forms and structure of written language, see Bissex, G.L. *Gnys at Wrk: a child learns to read and write*, Harvard University Press, Cambridge, Mass., 1980.

16 For one account of the Freudian paradigm, that has little girls feeling angry and betrayed at their mother's making them little girls rather than little boys, see Rose, J. 'Feminity and Its Discontents', *Feminist Review*, 14 (June 1983), 5–21. See also Mitchell, J. *Women: the Longest Revolution*, Virago, 1984.

Chapter 10

Sharing Bilingualism

Sarah Campbell

Introduction

> I speak English at school to my friends and Panjabi at home to
> my family. I can listen and understand Hindi, but I can't speak
> it, and I'm learning French.

The boy who said this to me is one of my pupils. His experience is not
rare; many other examples of children with multilingual backgrounds
and skills can be found in the majority of our urban schools. The Linguistic
Minorities Project, set up in 1979 and funded by the DES to investigate
the use of languages other than English, reported its findings in 1983.
The Project included research into language use among schoolchildren
in five metropolitan areas, and found that the proportion of children in
those areas who had a home language other than English ranged from
7 per cent to 30 per cent (Linguistic Minorities Project, 1985). In the
1987 ILEA Language Census, it was established that in ILEA 64,987
schoolchildren (23 per cent of ILEA's school population) used a language
other than, or in addition to, English at home. Both the number of children
and the percentage of the total were greater than the comparable figures
for 1985, representing an increase which the authors of the Census Report
believe will continue, at least in the immediate future. Within any urban
LEA the proportions of such children in schools will vary enormously.
ILEA no doubt includes monolingual schools as well as schools where
90 per cent of the children have a home language other than English.
In other, perhaps more rural areas of England, but not Wales, monolingual
English-speaking children predominate, and other languages may be few
and far between.

It has become common practice to call pupils with a home language
other than English (or PHLOE, the acronym used in the ILEA census)
'bilingual'. The accuracy of this designation is questionable, as the

individual child's competence in two languages may be unequal, and the balance of competence may shift from one language to the other in the course of her school years, but it is a useful shorthand.

The presence of such bilingual children in the classroom raises challenges and possibilities as yet not fully explored. They have often been regarded as 'problems' for their schools because they have needed specialist help with English on arrival at school and extra support for the development of their English skills as they continue their school careers. Their bilingualism has great potential. It can enable both them and their monolingual classmates to develop and value their language abilities; and thereby to understand and value the culture in which such abilities have been developed.

English as a Second Language: New Methods

Over the last twenty years English as a second language has developed, with Section 11 funding, into a very interesting and innovative branch of language teaching. Successive new developments in language teaching methodology and organization (direct method, functional language teaching, communicative methodology, intensive language teaching) have been common practice for English as a second language specialists long before their modern language colleagues discovered and hailed them as exciting initiatives.

Both the urgency of the task confronting English as a second language teachers and the flexibility with which they have had to respond to each changing situation has meant the constant re-examination of methods and materials.

The report of the Swann Committee (1985) on the education of minority ethnic children, in its recommendations on the teaching of English as a second language, favoured co-operative teaching, where a language support teacher (possibly from a central team of such teachers) works alongside the class teacher in primary schools or the subject teacher in secondary schools. Working together, the two teachers develop both the children's language skills and teach the normal curriculum. This co-operative approach can be used to deliver language support in a community language or in English as a second language. A bilingual teacher can work in both capacities. This practice is now fairly well-established in Section 11 support teaching; it certainly predates the modern linguists' similar 'section bilingue', (Hawkins, 1988) whereby children learn geography, or cooking, through the medium of French.

The Politics of the Bilingual Classroom: Denial, Loss or Support?

The history of educational provision for minority ethnic children is an interesting mirror of social and political attitudes over the last thirty years. The provision of English as a second language has been a constant need since the arrival of the first groups of non-English speaking children in the early 1960s. Multicultural and anti-racist perspectives now highlight the necessity to provide for the support and development of bilingualism or, more specifically, of the bilingual children's home or community languages, but many questions about the nature of language teaching provision for bilinguals remain unanswered.

The importance of a fluent and skilful command of English for every child in British schools is not in dispute, (ILEA, 1985) but the educational implications of the provision of support for other first languages have not yet been fully explored. The provision of bilingual support has implications both for the individual bilingual child and for the entire school population. There has been research into the cognitive advantages of bilingualism for the individual (Miller, 1983), but as Miller points out:

> We should remain wary of tests which seek to isolate cognitive attributes from affective ones and from the social context in which both operate and grow together.

Even with that note of caution in mind, however, it is likely that bilingual children have an advantage over monolingual children in certain areas of the school curriculum, and certainly in the area of language. Clearly, bilingual children are aware of the social context of the languages they speak (high or low status languages), and research suggests that their earlier attempts to avoid the embarrassment of speaking the wrong language – the infant school is probably the setting for this particular struggle – may well make them conscious at an early age of details of language structure (Ben-Zeev, S., 1977). Further, the understanding that two entirely different sets of sounds may refer to the same thing serves to focus the child's attention on the conceptual attributes of the object, and make her aware of the seemingly arbitrary nature of signifiers. The bilingual child can conceptualize the object separately from its name at an earlier age than can the monolingual child (Ianco-Worrall, 1972). It seems likely that awareness of language structure, the early ability to conceptualize, and a consciousness of the relationship of one language to another will have a bearing on the manipulation of speech and the concomitant formulation of thought.

Sarah Campbell

'Me? No, I don't Speak Indian.'

The child who responded thus to my request for a Panjabi word was an 11-year-old-boy who spoke Panjabi frequently and fluently on his way to and from school. His reaction to my question was the typical reaction of many children: the denial of a low-status language of which he was ashamed.

Bilingual childrens' lack of pride in their community language is the product of a set of social, economic and historical circumstances. They perceive their language and culture as less valuable than those of the mainstream majority ethnic group, and less valuable than those of the other European countries whose languages are taught in the school system. In many schools, community languages are completely ignored. In others they are actively discouraged; no one on the staff understands the language and its use is regarded as ill-mannered, or even insulting or threatening. Some children are still forbidden to use their home language at school. An ex-pupil of the primary school I work in was told by a teacher in her secondary school that it was illegal for her to use her home language at school. This was in 1988.

Educationally the denial of language skills is very wasteful. Many teachers engaged in modern language teaching find it ironic to teach a child a new language and simultaneously witness his denial of a language that he is skilled at using:

> I used to speak it, but I can't any more. I can understand mostly what they say but I couldn't, you know talk about anything important. I'm going to learn it again though. (A 23-year-old-teacher, talking about Panjabi.)

It must be a matter of regret to find in adult life that a culture and a literature, which you could have shared with your family and friends, have become closed to you. It is interesting to reflect that the teaching of modern European languages has often been justified, *inter alia*, in terms of access, through the language, to the culture of other societies. It may be that many young people have had expropriated from them, in the course of their school years, their capacity to be bilingual and bicultural; it may even prove to be only in the course of their school years that they are monolingual.

Many young adults who have been born and educated in Britain in the 1960s and 1970s are resolving to re-acquire, to rediscover, their community language skills in adulthood. 'They are losing their first language. We must help them to recover that language.' (An LEA Staff Inspector.) This is the view of those who want to support bilingualism.

But if community language support is to be brought into the mainstream curriculum, it must benefit the whole school community, both multilingual and monolingual. In some primary schools, where the proportion of bilingual children is high and the range of languages is small – the community language is being used as the medium of instruction for quite a large part of the curriculum; up to half the week. The bilingual children in these schools are fortunate. Their community language skills are being developed within the context of the mainstream curriculum.

The question that will inevitably be asked is how this arrangement benefits the monolingual English-speaking child. Grouping children according to their home language is not acceptable in a multiracial school; the needs of our society make it invidious to divide children in this way.

The challenge is to exploit community languages in such a way that all children benefit from studying them. It is in this context that the co-operative team teaching methods developed in English as a second language and bilingual support teaching teams come into play, to ensure that bilingual and monolingual English teachers work together in the normal school setting, with bilingual and monolingual children learning side by side, and having access to two languages. Some schools have found a way of delivering the normal curriculum as well as the community language to both bilingual and monolingual children, as the following example shows.

One School's Response

> The children in the first year Juniors have the opportunity of taking Punjabi to extend their mother-tongue or to be introduced to it as a second language. If you wish your child to take part please fill in the form at the bottom of this letter.

The above quotation is taken from a letter sent to the parents of every child entering the junior stage of a Wolverhampton primary school.[1] For several years, the head teacher and staff of the school have been operating a policy of teaching two lessons a week of topic work (environmental studies) through the medium of Panjabi. About 75 per cent of the school's intake have Panjabi as a home language. The skills and fluency of members of this group, however, will vary considerably. All parents are invited to take up this opportunity for their children to learn Panjabi and generally about two-thirds of the intake opt into the Panjabi-medium lessons. The remaining children are taught the same environmental studies topic in the medium of English. The school is fortunate in that it has at present two Panjabi speakers on the staff, one of whom is the deputy head teacher. It is thus possible to divide the group of children who have opted into the Panjabi-medium lessons into two sets working together in adjacent classrooms. Children who are already fluent Panjabi speakers are taught entirely through the medium of Panjabi; with these children there are few linguistic constraints on the content of the oral work in the lessons, but the children are generally at a very early stage in learning literacy in Panjabi, and the lesson helps them read and write as well as developing their oracy in Panjabi, the content of the lesson – environmental concepts and knowledge – is the same for both groups.

The second set of children who have opted into Panjabi-medium lessons is not homogenous. Some children are monolingual English speakers; there are children of South Asian descent whose Panjabi has fallen into disuse, or whose first language is not Panjabi. The lessons for this set of children are particularly interesting; the course is a simultaneous exploration of language and environmental studies. The children can learn about the life-cycle of insects with vocabulary offered in both English and Panjabi, and with a relaxed, friendly discussion of the similarities and differences between many aspects (including the alphabets) of the two languages. The medium of instruction is generally English but the teacher is bilingual, and can move between languages in mid-sentence. The children are at various stages in second language learning; some are being encouraged to recover a potential bilingualism, or to see the connections between their home language and its close relation, Panjabi; others are only just beginning to perceive that there are other ways of meaning, of expressing oneself, than the traditional one that they have used so far. This perception is an essential first step in second language learning; this is what many 12 or 13-year-old-children appreciate for the first time on their school's introductory visit to France. Bilingual children have grasped this idea at pre-school age, and monolingual children fortunate enough to be in a multilingual school may grasp it much sooner than those in a monolingual environment. In their Panjabi-medium lessons, these junior school children are being trained to think about language and in so doing to understand some quite sophisticated ideas: that language patterns can vary, alphabet systems differ and make transliteration difficult, language changes with mass migration. This grouping together of monolingual and bilingual children to talk about and develop language is in itself guaranteed to produce a heightened awareness of language, both what it is and what it does.

The amount of work involved in preparing and running courses for children of this age in a language other than English should not be underestimated. Even the fluent Panjabi-speaking children are not competent readers, and any written worksheets have to be prepared by the teachers themselves. Dual language books on topic subjects are beginning to make an appearance, fortunately for this school.[2]

Supporting Biliteracy: Dual Language Books

The role of dual language books in community language support teaching, especially in primary schools, is an important and interesting one. As the presence of bilingual children can lead to a reappraisal and adjustment of language teaching methods, so the desire to help such children towards literacy in their community language has produced new approaches to learning to read. The traditional methods of teaching children to read South Asian languages are not appropriate for teaching children in British schools who may be eleven or twelve or older when they begin their task. The mastery of thirty-five letters letters in the Panjabi, Gurmukhi script before attempting to read some simple words, whose meanings may well be obscure even in the British context, is a recipe for boredom and alienation. Access to interesting and colourful modern books, whose meaning can be established from the English text, is a much more promising point of departure.

Learning to read is a quest for the meaningful sound submerged in the shadowy depths of letter and wordshape. In dual language books the English text is a reassuring life-line – an insurance that the book will yield its meaning even if the Panjabi script proves impenetrable. But the desire to decode, to decipher those intriguing shapes and reformulate them into recognizable sounds is fascinating to watch and even more rewarding as a participant. Sometimes several attempts are made at a word; the best reader will dive in to decode the letters and come up with a collection of sounds which may at first be unrecognizable. Attempts may be made to re-arrange the sounds, to shift tone or stress. A sound may be thrown back, and another will reappear – 'That's not "k", it's "kh",' – until they make a phonic combination which matches the meaning they are waiting for, and suspect is there. Occasionally the whole group will resurface, entirely baffled as to the sound combination but with the meaning intact, thanks to the English text:

'It must mean "cart" then. That's the word for "cart".'
'Never heard of it.'

The pleasure in both the book and the script and the fascination of decoding, unlocking the meaning, is almost tangible with these children, and certainly audible, because they are talking about language.

The primary school described above has found a way of offering Panjabi to all its children, and ensuring that all who take up the offer can benefit from it. All the children study the normal school curriculum; of those who 'opt in' to the Panjabi lessons, Panjabi speakers have their home language reinforced and literacy developed and both they and the non-Panjabi speakers learn some Panjabi and quite a lot about the nature of language.

Support from the National Curriculum: Kingman and Cox

Children must learn to use language. Schools should help them to become skilful in speaking, listening, reading and writing, because language is an essential tool in whatever we try to do. The recent Report of the Committee of Inquiry into the Teaching of English Language, (Kingman, 1988) sheds new light on the relationship between teaching children how to use language, and teaching children about language. The Report was not commissioned to investigate community language teaching. However, some of its recommendations are interesting in the light of the multi-lingual nature of many of our schools. An 'explicit knowledge of the structure of the (English) language' is recommended in the letter sent with the Report to the Secretary of State, and Chapter 2 of the Report is entitled 'The Importance of Knowledge about Language'. The Report argues that there is a place for teaching about language, meaning English, in the first instance:

> It is just as important to teach about our language environment as about our physical environment, or about the structure of English as about the structure of the atom. And since we believe that knowledge about language can underpin and promote mastery as well, the argument is even stronger.

> It can only be sensible to make overt comparisons between languages which the pupils know, so that they can be led to see the general principles of language structure and use, through a coherent and consistent approach.

Thus Kingman recommends teaching children about language, and comparing languages the children know, in order to enhance this study of language.

An example of good practice in the primary phase is provided where a multilingual class of 7-year-old-children enjoy a fairy tale and want to label their pictures of the story in both English and in Urdu. This involves discussion of meaning, translation and pronunciation:

> Here was a good example of children being brought to a point of learning where reflection on the nature and use of language was both natural and necessary.

This is the area of the mainstream curriculum where community languages can be located. The example of Panjabi teaching mentioned earlier was possible because members of the school's teaching staff were themselves bilingual. Unless teachers are at least fairly fluent in a language, it is difficult, though not impossible if other bilingual children are present, to teach children to use the language. It is possible, however, to help children to learn about the language, and by comparison and implication, to learn about language in general.

Kingman's view was explicitly drawn upon by the English Working Group, (DES, 1988) appointed by the Secretary of State to make proposals concerning programmes of study and attainment targets in English for the National Curriculum. The Working Group, chaired by Professor Brian Cox of Manchester University, reported first on the 5–11 age range. The Working Group argued:

> Bilingual children should be considered an advantage in the classroom rather than a problem. The evidence shows that such children will make greater progress in English if they know that their knowledge of their mother tongue is valued, if it is recognized that their experience of language is likely to be greater than that of their monoglot peers and, indeed, if their knowledge and experience can be put to good use in the classroom to the benefit of all pupils to provide examples of the structure and syntax of different languages, to provide a focus for discussion about language forms and for contrast and comparison with the structure of the English language. We endorse the view of the Kingman Committee: 'It should be the duty of all teachers to instil in their pupils a civilized respect for other languages and an understanding of the relations between other languages and English. It should be made clear to English-speaking pupils that classmates whose first language is Bengali or Cantonese, or any other of the scores of languages spoken by the school population . . . have languages quite as systematic and rule-governed as their own'.

For this approach to be implemented, primary teachers may need to learn from the 'language awareness' movement currently being developed in some secondary schools. The language awareness courses currently being formulated and taught, often in multilingual schools, have various aims and principles.[3] Most have common features; they aim to set the learning of a modern language in context, and may look at language 'families', with lexical comparisons between members of, for example, the Romance languages, or the Indo-European language family. They may teach about non-verbal and animal communication, and relationship between spoken and written language, and different scripts; they may encourage children to investigate first language acquisition and they often help children to become aware of the demands and skills involved in second language learning. It is an innovative and exciting area of the curriculum, generating much enthusiasm and constant pleas for more timetable space.

The language awareness courses generally slot into a module or proportion of the modern language timetable in the early stages, sometimes the first term of the secondary phase, usually just as the children begin to study a modern language. The approach is ideally suited to middle schools, where a modern language is taught by a specialist language teacher but where, as in other primary schools, the timetable is often flexible enough to allow space for something new, if it can be justified. It could easily be adapted and taught to upper junior children.

The Kingman Report's Recommendation 2, that secondary schools develop a co-ordinated policy for language teaching, is followed by the Committee's Recommendation 3, which urges similar co-ordination in the primary school:

> The Committee recommends that all primary schools should have a member of staff who is designated as a language consultant, and who has the responsibility for advising on and co-ordinating language work, including knowledge about language.

Co-ordination of aims and methods, across the various language teaching activities in a school, whether primary, middle or secondary, should clarify the principles underlying language awareness in any one school, and may also serve to share out the teaching and timetabling of such a course. A co-ordinated policy which results in a sufficient timetable space for a shared, systematic language-awareness course, with a 'coherent and consistent approach', would be the ideal solution. My own work was an attempt to develop a course in language awareness with my bilingual and monolingual pupils.

Language Awareness and Bilingualism: An Example

I am a teacher in an eight to twelve middle school. Two features of the school's intake may be of interest in considering the context of the language work in the school: one is that many of the children appear to be under stress at home and several exhibit symptoms of disturbance in the classroom – their language is often aggressive and used for dominating or controlling others. The other separate, unrelated, feature is that about 45 per cent of the intake is of South Asian descent, with Panjabi as a community language. My job includes responsibility for introducing the 10 to 12-year-old-children to French, but half of my time is designated Section 11-funded, and involves English language support work. My response to the children's denial of skills in Panjabi was to bring Panjabi into the French room and the French lessons. The children start to learn oral French in my school at age 10, and I decided to complement their French with a language awareness course at age 11, and to bring Panjabi in under cover of language awareness. At first my language awareness course was very much overloaded; it included animal communication, non-verbal communication, writing systems, language families, dialects and too much else.

But I remember well the introduction of Panjabi into the classroom. The first steps were very exciting and emotional. I had been trying for several months, but rather sporadically, to teach myself Panjabi, and could manage a few halting phrases. In Panjabi, I asked a Panjabi-speaking girl to tell me her name:

'Tera nam ki he?'

I knew her name, of course, and so did she. Furthermore, we both understood the question, and knew what form the answer should take. But she could not respond. I asked someone else. The Panjabi speakers understood the question. The non-Panjabi speakers did not, and remained baffled onlookers at this incomprehensible drama. After several attempts at putting the question, at last one brave child gave the response I was waiting for:

'Mera nam Parmjit he.'

Now the spell was broken, and we could explain the meaning of the exchange, and teach the question and answer to the non-Panjabi-speakers. The noise level rose immediately, and the excitement and surprise generated was out of all proportion to the actual language used and taught. The teachers who received this class after my lesson were not pleased!

In that lesson a taboo was broken. The use of Panjabi in the classroom had hitherto been unacceptable, and so the children at first dared not respond to my simple question. The appearance of a white teacher speaking a few simple words in Panjabi was a novelty, a signal that something was different, that the rules had changed. What then was appropriate, how should they respond? On a later occasion, when another Panjabi-speaking teacher introduced the use of Panjabi into the classroom to another group of children, I saw a child with her mouth open to respond, incapable of uttering the words she knew, physically inhibited by custom from producing the sounds that signified her own language in the classroom. Neither event was serious – we all laughed at ourselves – but the clash between two linguistic worlds was clear and resounding.

My intention originally had been to introduce Panjabi into the classroom in order to look at some of its features – vocabulary, sounds, some letters from the script. I had in mind the possibility of comparing some aspects of the language with English and with French. I also wanted to encourage the Panjabi speakers to teach some words and phrases to non-Panjabi speakers and so start to raise the status of the language in the school. The impact of the language in the classroom was such, however, that we soon settled on the script as the major area of study. We looked at letter shapes and sounds, did some transliteration and decoded some simple words. The Panjabi speakers did not yet feel secure enough to act as models for the oral work, which would involve monolingual children, who might have proved hostile, in copying new sounds and intonation patterns. The script was interesting to all the children, especially the Panjabi speakers. Most of them hardly knew it at all.

The next year I decided to introduce Russian in the comparative study as well. Russian is a new language for all the children and so its introduction puts the experience of meeting another language into a more normal context. I was fortunate in having learnt Russian myself, and although I had not used it for many years, I could remember enough to run a short 'taster' course for 11-year-olds. Russian also has a different alphabet, one which is new and yet simple enough for the children to be able to deal with. Russian, like Panjabi, is an Indo-European language, which is very useful for lexical comparison.

So the course evolved. With the expert help of a bilingual, Panjabi-language support teacher from the LEA's Intercultural Curriculum Support Service its aims became clearer and leaner. I jettisoned animal communication, non-verbal communication, first-language acquisition and many other fascinating areas in order to ensure sufficient time for the comparative languages study. As the language support teacher and I could work together, we could ensure small groups where children would feel more at ease and able to listen and talk freely about language. An important aspect of the language awareness activity has always been its potential for oral discussion. Rigid rules about listening to others have been applied at the beginning of the course and the children have learnt how to discuss aspects of language and the new languages with each other. They often have much to say. Family experiences, including those of monolingual children, are rich in linguistic anecdote, and although dialect and accent are no longer written into the course, they are inevitably discussed.

The content of the course is continually changing. All the children have been able to learn a little Russian from me, and monolingual children have learnt some Panjabi from the Panjabi-speaking teacher and the bilingual children. The Panjabi-speaking teacher is often able to offer the Panjabi speakers a model of Panjabi which is slightly different from their own. Sometimes the dialect is different, but more often the children's vocabulary has become so anglicized that they do not recognize Panjabi words. A new English-Panjabi creole is developing, as it must in such circumstances. This gives rise to discussion of how languages change as peoples migrate. All the children hear about examples of such change in the course of classroom discussion. The sounds of languages other than English are interesting to explore, and some Panjabi speakers can demonstrate a facility to distinguish between sounds which to the monolingual English ear are identical – the 'k', 'kh', 'g', 'gh', sequence of sounds, presented in that order in the Panjabi alphabet, being one example. The Gurmukhi script in which Panjabi is written is quite different from European scripts, and several children have been introduced to it at home or in a Panjabi evening class, although very few have mastered it. Even so, its intricacies, and its shapes, are interesting to explore. Russian affords similar insights. English is also there as a control or baseline, and of course the lessons often give the opportunity to bring in examples from French – nasal sounds, diacritics and 'silent' letters in written French, the familiar (*tu*) form of the second person pronoun. discussion of similar, simple linguistic concepts ranges far and wide. Apart from the work on scripts, the course has been predominantly oral, with much time in class given over to talk about language.

Development of the Course

In summer 1988, I was given a term's sabbatical leave as a Mary Glasgow Language Teacher Fellow, to enable me to develop materials for the course. Consequently, I was able to think again about the course and reformulate its principles, as well as improve the materials.

The five aims of the course are ambitious. I would not claim that all will be achieved for every child, especially as we only have one period of 45 minutes or an hour – depending on other timetabling factors – per week. The first two aims are equal in importance and I expect them to apply to everyone. The aims are as follows:

(a) to help children understand that all languages have underlying structure; to help them classify components of language and to give them the metalanguage (nouns, syllables) to help clarify their thinking;

(b) to raise the status of Panjabi by using it as an example in the classroom, ranking equally with European languages, and to encourage potentially bilingual children to develop their bilingualism;

(c) to equip the children with strategies for language learning; to give them an opportunity to speak, listen to, read and write a little of a new language, and in doing so reflect on the processes of language learning;

(d) to stimulate children's interest in language by showing them something of the range of human language experience in terms of phonetics, scripts and meanings;

(e) to help the children to understand the social and historical context of the new languages and varieties of language in our community, and to appreciate how language can vary over time, across space and according to the needs and circumstances of the user.

The new revised course has five components one of which is a video tape recording. Of course, I wanted to make materials which children could use in the classroom but I also took the opportunity offered by the fellowship to make a video tape recording of the school's languages in action. I knew that there existed even in a small school many and varied unexplored language skills, and with the help of colleagues who generously gave their time, we made a short video recording of both children and staff at the school either using or learning a variety of different languages. Some could contribute only a few words, while others were revealed as fluent and poetic bilinguals. In the course of making the video, some children were surprised to have their class teacher revealed to them, perhaps for the first time, as an accomplished and fluent Welsh speaker. In the course of an afternoon's recording around the school, we picked up Welsh, French, Czech, Turkish, Italian, Gaelic and Cantonese. It is an amateur recording and technically very flawed. Possibly its greatest value lay in the making of it. It may serve as a challenge to colleagues in neighbouring schools to produce a better version in their own school, or as an initial, undaunting stimulus for the exploration of the languages around us in our schools.

The materials I made during my term's fellowship are based on a comparative study of certain features of the four languages – English, French, Panjabi and Russian – which I have used from the beginning. This work has been divided into four units, roughly corresponding to the four language skills with a study of language structure included. The four units are called:

Speaking.
Listening to Languages.
Reading and Writing.
How Languages Work: Language Structure.

The speaking and listening units are dependent on an audio tape recording. For the speaking unit, the recording has short dialogues in French, Panjabi and Russian, for the children to copy and learn to say. The idea is not simply that they should learn rather random chunks of language, but that they should monitor their own language learning. After spending some time on the dialogue, they should have to think about such questions as:

How long did it take you to learn the dialogue?
How much could you remember before you saw the transcript?
Was the transcript helpful, and why?
Will you still remember this dialogue next week?

The exercise should highlight language-learning strategies which may be helpful to them in the future.

The audio tape recording is also the basis for the exercises in the listening unit. Here the children are to listen for sounds from other languages which may be unfamiliar to them. They will learn and use words such as syllable, consonant, vowel, intonation, stress; they will listen to the phonetic features of each language which go to make up what we think of as its distinctive 'accent'.

The reading and writing unit explores aspects of the written forms of the four languages, including the grapheme-phoneme relationship. The worksheets on English deal with the vagaries of English spelling, with a look at the intitial teaching alphabet (i.t.a.) and some work on the difference between spoken and written language. The French worksheets look at diacritics and making a transcript of a recording. There are five worksheets each for Panjabi and Russian. Both the new alphabets are studied, with some transliterating exercises, using both 'borrowed' words (taxi, cafe) as well as the more authentic spoken Panjabi and Russian which is available in transcript as well as on the audio tape recording.

The unit on language structure, 'How Languages Work', compares and contrasts language structure across the four languages. The unit consists of sets of activities, which the children should be able to work on in groups. Each activity has a set of colour-coded word or sentence cards, and a worksheet with instructions for the children. The children have to manipulate and fit together the coloured cards to find a language pattern – a change in word order, or a morpheme, which signifies a change in meaning. Some of the activities involve writing words or sentences, always using the 'original script' – Roman, Cyrillic or Panjabi. Other activities involve oral work or games. The linguistic concepts exemplified in the eight sets of activities are:

> plurality
> sentence word order
> interrogratives
> negatives
> gender
> tense

Discussion

Firstly, in all of the units, but especially in the speaking and listening units, the role of the Panjabi speakers needs special consideration. They will be at an advantage in much of the work required of the children but it is an interesting comment on the status of their language that one cannot assume that they will want to have their language skills emphasized publicly. Much depends on the make-up of the class and the personalities of the individual children. In some circumstances it may be appropriate to dispense with the tape recording and use the bilingual children's speech as a resource, asking the children to provide the Panjabi model and to take a leading role in teaching non-Panjabi speakers. In other classes, perhaps where fewer speakers are present, it may not be desirable to emphasize Panjabi speakers' skills, and their competence will have to be revealed carefully and sensitively to avoid embarrassment. Many Panjabi speakers who are 10 or 11 years old, do not at first want to use Panjabi in the classroom. They may not wish to bring their private home language into a potentially hostile school environment. It is important that they should not feel threatened.

Second, some children bring into the classroom the racist attitudes of home or street. It is to be hoped that they are few, but the possibility is ever present. One of the major aims of these materials is to confront the learners with linguistic 'realia' in order for them to assess for themselves the relative values of different languages, using criteria that are more objective than emotional: 'what does it sound like? how do you write it? is it easier or harder to say?' These are questions that should be asked about all the languages under study, and the study itself should challenge the simplistic negative attitudes of racism. Every situation is different and any hostility to Panjabi on racist grounds will need to be treated as seems best in the circumstances, although the work would not be viable if racist remarks were allowed to go unchecked in the classroom or indeed in the school. It is a sad truth that we should be constantly aware of the susceptibilities of bilingual children. They themselves may be aware that exposure of the home language can lead to ridicule or rejection.

Third, the materials I use imply a different focus from the normal language awareness course. In order to draw in detail on the four chosen languages, much interesting work, included in other courses, has to be omitted. My course is an exploration of four languages, three of which are very relevant to children growing up in Britain today. English, of course, is the lingua franca, and French is an important language in the EEC as well as the language children are most likely to be offered at secondary school. Panjabi is the language spoken by the largest minority ethnic group in the country. It is spoken by people of both Pakistani and Indian descent, by Sikhs, Moslems and Hindus. Panjabi is closely related to Urdu/Hindi and more distantly to Gujerati. Russian was introduced because it is a new language for all the children and because it has features which make it particularly useful in a comparative language study.

Fourthly, learning about and through language in this way is also learning about culture. Valuing another language is valuing its speakers and its society. Partly, of course, this is because simply by including minority languages in our classrooms, we express our respect for them. It becomes part of the hidden curriculum of the class, the school and society for those children who experience it. But cultural dimensions are also incorporated into the overt curriculum. In learning language, the pupils inevitably learn culture, as the following illustration shows.

A simple conversation in which two children were learning a dialogue in Panjabi offering tea, with or without sugar, turned into a discussion of different ways of making tea. The Panjabi-speaker was at first reluctant to admit that the choice of sugar would be irrelevant as 'his' tea would have sugar added at the start. Gradually he became confident enough to explain that in his family tea, milk, sugar and water are all put in a saucepan together. Other children nodded their heads, and some volunteered information about various spices added. It is unwise to overstate the impact of such relatively mundane classroom linguistic exchanges but as they accumulate they begin routinely to symbolize the school's respect for the cultural experience that children bring with them to school. Interest in languages other than English inevitably generates interest in cultures other than English.

Discussion about the role and practice of community language teaching will continue. The multilingual classroom is a challenge and responses to that challenge are coming in from infant schools, junior and middle schools and secondary modern languages departments. Some infant and junior schools are teaching parts of the curriculum through the medium of a community language, and one or two, including the example outlined earlier, are offering this opportunity to all children. Like most primary school teachers, I am not a fluent Panjabi speaker and so cannot teach in the language. My course aims to use Panjabi to make some general points about language simple enough for the primary school child to grasp and useful to the child in later language study and use. It is one response among many and no doubt more possibilities will emerge. What is certain and urgent is that we must not let the opportunities afforded by the multilingual classroom slip by unnoticed. We can all benefit from sharing the bilingual experience.

Notes

1 I should like to record my gratitude to Mr Brian Milton, Mr Jatar Singh Atwal, and Mrs Pinki Sharma, respectively head, deputy and classteacher at Merridale Primary School, Wolverhampton for their help and advice. I should also like to acknowledge the help of Wolverhampton LEA.
2 Macdonald's list includes several books on environmental subjects. Baker Books, Manfield Park, Cranleigh, Surrey, GU6 8NU, produce an annual catalogue of multi-lingual and dual language books.
3 Some very interesting materials have been published: Hawkins, E. (1984) *Awareness of Language: an Introduction*, Cambridge Educational. This book sets out the principles on which is based the series of pupil's books, edited by Eric Hawkins, entitled *Awareness of Language*, and published by Cambridge Educational, 1983 to 1985; Aplin T.R.W. *et al.* (1981) *Introduction to Language*, Hodder and Stoughton; Mason, M. (1988) *Illuminating English*: Book 1, entitled *Language Awareness*, TRACE; Raleigh. M. and Miller, J. (1981) *The Languages Book*, ILEA English Centre; Strange. D (1982) *Language and Languages*, Oxford University Press. Other courses are being produced by individual schools and teachers.

References

BEN-ZEEV, S. (1977) 'The effects of bilingualism in children from Spanish-English low economic neighbourhoods on cognitive development and cognitive strategy' in *Working Papers on Bilingualism*, No. 14, quoted in Miller, J. (1983).

HAWKINS, E. (1988) *Intensive Language Teaching and Learning: initiatives at school level*, London, Centre for Information on Language Teaching and Research.

IANCO-WORRALL, A. (1972) 'Bilingualism and Cognitive Development' quoted in Miller, J. (1983).

ILEA (1985) *Improving Primary Schools*, London, Inner London Education Authority.

KINGMAN REPORT (1988) *Report of the Committee of Enquiry into the Teaching of English Language*, London, HMSO.

LINGUISTIC MINORITIES PROJECT (1985) *The Other Languages of England*, London, Routledge and Kegan Paul.

MILLER, J. (1983) *Many Voices: Bilingualism, Culture and Education*, London, Routledge and Kegan Paul.

SWANN COMMITTEE (1985) *Education for All*, London, HMSO.

Chapter 11

Religious Education: From Ethnographic Research to Curriculum Development

Robert Jackson

Introduction

This chapter argues that ethnography can be of service to religious education in a number of ways.[1] Firstly, suitably adapted ethnographic methods can be used with and by children as a means to sensitize them to new material being studied and for drawing from children ideas for methods of study. Secondly, ethnographic reports can provide valuable case study material for teachers and pupils in focusing on examples of religion as it is lived and practised by people. Thirdly, ethnographic studies of children in the context of their families and communities can yield material that has particular appeal to child readers who may otherwise have little opportunity for experience of a religious culture or tradition that may be different from their own. This point is illustrated by a research project at the University of Warwick that has linked ethnographic research and the development of curriculum materials for teachers and pupils in the form of books and BBC radio broadcasts.

Religious Education in the Reform Act

The debate about religious education associated with the passage of the Education Reform Bill through Parliament was largely about the content of the subject, with little attention give explicitly to aims and virtually none to method. The clauses on religious education in county schools in the Act reflect the earlier debate, but contrary to some newspaper reports do not limit an open and liberal approach to the subject. The title 'Religious Instruction', used in the 1944 Act and with its implicit suggestion of induction into faith, has been replaced with the name 'Religious Education'. Also, for the first time in law, it is made clear that religions other than Christianity are a legitimate focus for study in religious education and that proper account of their presence in our society should be taken in *all* new Agreed Syllabuses. Any new Agreed Syllabus, regardless of its location in the country, 'must reflect the fact that the religious traditions in Great Britain are in the main Christian, whilst taking account of the teaching and practices of the other principal religions represented in Great Britain'.

The Act also makes it clear that although religious education in county schools should not be distinctive of any particular denomination, different denominations and religions are proper objects of study. It is quite legitimate to study Christianity and the other major religions in their various forms as represented in Britain. This possibility raises interesting methodological questions. How do children from no religious background learn how to understand alternative ways of religious life? How does a young person from a Christian home comprehend the faith of a Hindu or a Muslim? Just as significantly, how does a child with a background in one Christian denomination gain an understanding of others? For a Roman Catholic child to comprehend a Quaker meeting might require as much effort and imagination as understanding the rituals of Muslim public prayer or of a Hindu puja.

Phenomenology and Religious Education

Since the early 1970s many religious educators have answered questions like these by recommending the 'phenomenological approach'. In the words of one influential publication of the time:

> This sees the aim of religious education as the promotion of understanding. It uses the tools of scholarship in order to enter into an empathic relationship with individuals and groups. (Schools Council, 1971)

Phenomenology of religion has its roots in the philosophy of Edmund Husserl and has been especially influential in Europe and in the United States. Although the phenomenology of religion has been conceived in various ways (Waardenburg, 1978), the main writers have aimed to 'bracket out' their own presuppositions when attempting to understand another's faith and to study parallel phenomena in different traditions in order to expose basic forms and structures which give insight into the essence of religion. This second aspect of phenomenology – often referred to, using Husserl's terminology, as 'eidetic vision' – has never been widely used in religious education as a theoretical model for postulating or exposing universal essences of religion. Many RE teachers would in any event wish to leave open the question as to whether there are such essences. Rather this aspect of phenomenology has been adapted by religious educators as a convenient practical tool for selecting and organizing material from a range of religious traditions. Occasionally such thematically arranged material is sensitively put together, as in Olivia Bennett's 'Exploring Religion' series for upper juniors published by Bell and Hyman (1984). All too often, however, thematic books juxtapose material from different traditions taken out of context and cover too much ground in too small a space. In *Family Life* and *Religious Buildings*, two books by John Mayled in Wayland's 'Religious Topics' series (1986), for example, six religions are covered in each book with less than four hundred words per faith. The consequences are superficial treatment, over-simplification and the danger that children will be confused and misled. Books like Mayled's are far distant from the intentions of the phenomenologists but have given ammunition to critics who have caricatured the phenomenological approach as either a 'mish mash' or as mere description.

The other principal element of phenomenology ('epoché' in Husserlian terms) is the capacity to suppress one's own presuppositions and to empathize with those of another tradition or world view, thereby gaining an understanding from the insider's point of view. There are some teachers' and pupils' books available which demonstrate the authors' ability to empathize with members of traditions or denominations different from their own. Patricia Bahree's *The Hindu World* (1982) and Alan Brown's *The Christian World* (1984), both in the Macdonald 'Religions of the World' series, are good examples of pupil texts. What is lacking in the literature on phenomenology and religious education, however, is guidance for teachers and pupils in the methods and skills required for understanding the concepts, beliefs and practices of people whose view of the world is other than their own. My contention is that it is these methods and skills that are of lasting importance to religious education rather than the whole cluster of ideas associated with phenomenology – a term which is hard to separate from its origins in continental philosophy and which is used by some proponents and critics to refer to a total approach to religious education rather than as one of its contributory elements.[2] Further, many of the required methods and skills can be derived from ethnography.

Ethnography as a Source of Methods in Religious Education

Suitably adapted, ethnographic methods can provide tools for children to be sensitized to traditions other than their own and to make sense of religious beliefs, practices and symbols. For most children, attempting to understand an unfamiliar way of life is a difficult challenge and there is an inevitable tendency to reduce it to familiar concepts and categories which usually leads to error. Also the introduction of rituals, customs, beliefs, art and languages which may seem initially strange to children can provoke negative and even hostile responses. Children can be prepared for interpreting a religion or a denomination by the use of imaginative activities designed to allow the children themselves to suggest appropriate methods of study. The following activity for top junior children appears in a recent book (Jackson, 1989):

> Get into a group of between three and five friends and sit facing one another. Have pen and paper ready. You have to imagine that you are aliens from another planet. You are very clever, you have X-ray vision and you are friendly. But you don't know anything about planet Earth, the beings that live on it, or the languages they speak. Your mission is to look for signs of life near your ship and to report back to your base commander with a short message describing what you think is happening. Your craft silently lands near the dwelling place of some earthlings. Using your X-ray vision you look through the walls. The scene you see is the one in the picture (two children placing parcels beneath a decorated Christmas tree). Now, together with your friends, write a short message to your base commander describing what you think is happening. Spend about five minutes preparing the message. Don't read any further until you have written your message.
>
> If other groups in your class have done the same task, take it in turns to read out the messages from the different groups. As you listen to these messages, in your group, do the following tasks:
> - Make a list of the observations that the alien got wrong
> - Make a list of the observations that the alien got right
> - Can you think of some things that the alien would need to do in order to understand what is in the picture? Make a list of them.
>
> You may not have looked at someone else's way of life before. Look again at your lists. What things do you need to do so you don't make the mistakes that the alien made when he observed the earthlings?

The activity works well with adults as well as pupils and the messages tend to be imaginative and humorous. Here is an example from a primary teacher on an in-service course who subsequently used the activity in school with pupils:

> Dominant life-species on the planet is conifera. X-ray examination shows considerably highly developed xylem-phloem interactive memory capacity. The conifera is wearing ritual garments and is receiving tribute from subordinate beings in the form of gifts and adoration. Included in the ritual garb of the conifera is a miniature recognition symbol of the hominid subordinate group, positioned at its apex. It was noted that this procedure is stressful for the dominant species as it loses its green epidermal projections after a period of three wargs.

The discussion following the activity usually includes an awareness among children that intelligence alone is insufficient for understanding another way of life; the alien needed to observe the earthlings over a long period. He should have learned the earthlings' language or had an interpreter in order to ask them what they were doing. He should have contacted his home base to discover whether there were earlier records of explorations of Earth which attempted to explain the practice that had been observed. The point is taken that appropriate attitudes – open mindedness and not jumping to conclusions – and methods – close observation over time, interviewing in order to grasp concepts and the meaning of practices and consultation of written or other source materials – are required in order to avoid serious errors of interpretation when trying to describe an unfamiliar way of life. In other words the pupils often themselves suggest the standard ethnographic methods of participant observation, interviewing and analysis of documentary and other sources. Other related activities in the same book include the interpretation of religious pictures and artefacts and interviewing during the course of a visit to a place of worship.

Ethnography as a Source of Case Studies in Religion

The Canadian Islamicist Cantwell Smith pointed out the inadequacy of the term 'religion' to describe the complex, historically fluid and internally diverse phenomena that are known by names such as Christianity, Islam and Hinduism (Cantwell Smith 1978). Cantwell Smith favoured the use of the terms 'faith' and 'tradition' in preference to 'religion'. Attempting to understand a religion can be a fruitless exercise, involving abstractions and generalizations remote from the power and immediacy of personal devotion. Study of the faith of individuals in the context of their inherited, cumulative tradition, however, might generate a better understanding. This is not to deny that overviews and surveys of traditions have their value but to sound a note of caution about general labels and to assert that it is in the individual Christian, Muslim or Hindu, faced with basic human questions, that each tradition lives.

Cantwell Smith's ideas influenced Killingley and myself when we were faced with the task of writing *Approaches to Hinduism*, (Jackson and Killingley, 1988) a detailed guide to the Hindu tradition for teachers. We eventually decided to include a one chapter overview of Hinduism to introduce readers to issues of terminology, as well as a conceptual, historical and geographical framework together with ten chapters covering general themes in the tradition. There were: family, society, life-cycle rituals, worship, mythology and the gods, festivals and sacred time, pilgrimage and sacred places, sacred literature, theology and philosphy and sects and movements. Each topic is introduced by a case study of one or a small group of Hindus and is followed by a general discussion in which the individual example is related to the wider tradition and concluded by teaching ideas for 'early years', 'middle years' and 'adolescence and post sixteen'.

Since any Hindu inherits the particular traditions of his or her region, caste and lineage, not those of all Hindus, we selected subjects from different ethnic and regional backgrounds in India and included migrants; both settlers in other parts of India and migrants to the United Kingdom. A range of castes, social positions and religious groups is represented, as are women as well as men. Sources are modern, the earliest being Gandhi's autobiography (published 1927) and the latest a piece of unpublished research conducted in 1987.

An analysis of the selection of case studies reveals a number of points. Material which supplies details of personal lives of individual Hindus is principally of two types: biography or autobiography and ethnography. Published autobiographies can be a rich source of material but, inevitably, tend to be of distinguished people. We decided to draw on two, one by Prakash Tandon, a Punjabi writer who wove his own story into an account of a century of his family's memories, and the other by Mahatma Gandhi, to illustrate how his experience was shaped partly by the literature known to him, but also how he helped to form modern attitudes to Hindu sacred literature. We also, incidentally, wanted to show that a distinguished spiritual leader might reasonably have a very limited formal knowledge of the written literature of his own tradition. Of the three biographical sources, one was of unpublished material by a Sanskrit and Religious Studies scholar on T.M.P. Mahadevan, a recent Hindu philosopher and was used to complement philosophical material from Mahadevan himself. The other two were the unpublished work of ethnographers used to writing life histories as part of their research. Sources for all other case studies were ethnographic, derived from the published work of British, American and Indian social or cultural anthropologists, although in one case film was used to complement literary material.

One issue which soon became apparent was the dearth of material on Hindu women. Few Hindu women have written autobiographies, and anthropologists have tended to look mainly at men. Some attempt at balance was achieved by focusing on the character of Satya, the wife and mother in the family studied in Ursula Sharma's book *Rampal and His Family* (1971) and by abandoning a provisionally selected case study on life-cycle rituals in favour of a specially commissioned study done as part of the Hindu Nurture in Coventry Project. In this a Gujarati woman, born in Uganda but now living in England, tells of her marriage, the death of her mother and some of the rituals associated with the development of her children. When appropriate, teaching ideas are related directly to the case studies. Readers wishing to explore the approach in detail are referred to *Approaches to Hinduism* (Jackson and Killingley, *op. cit.*).

At the beginning of the enterprise we had not been at all sure that ethnography would provide our main sources for case studies, so it is worth reflecting on why they were chosen. Good ethnographic material has a ring of truth about it. It is about real people, warts and all, trying to live their lives and practise their devotions in their own way. Whereas publishers generally commission autobiographies or biographies of distinguished people, ethnographers and social anthropologists are interested in a wide range of subjects – often writing about people who in some ways might be very remarkable but who may not have the skills, the inclination, the leisure or the power to record their stories. Further, the authenticity and realism of ethnographic material is often lacking in fictional accounts of Hindu life that have been written for teachers and children. Fictional accounts are tidy, but, however well informed, they tend to reflect the authors' own concerns and presuppositions. Authentic case studies are not so neat – it was impossible to confine each one of ours completely to the theme it was intended to illustrate – but they mirror the preoccupations of their subjects rather than those of the researchers who study them. In selecting and recasting ethnographic material we were inevitably influenced by our own ideas, especially the division of the Hindu tradition into topics, although ideas from the material itself influenced the general discussions and teaching ideas which follow each case study. Finally, Cantwell Smith's dictum that an interplay between personal faith and the cumulative tradition in which it is set provides the basis for grasping a spiritual tradition, required that we use examples from the lives of real people.

Ethnographic Studies of Children for Children

Ethnographic sources have been used in the preparation of curriculum material for children, though outside the field of religious education. A good example is *Man, A Course of Study* (MACOS) which drew on an ethnographic study of Netsilik Eskimo culture to provide textual and film material for schoolchildren.[3]

In the Arts Education Department at Warwick University we set up a series of linked ethnographic studies concerned with the religious nurture of British Hindu children in the 8–13 age range.[4] The term 'religious nurture' was borrowed from American and British Religious Education literature (Bushnell, 1967; Hull, 1984) and is to be distinguished from the term 'religious education' as generally used by educators in the United Kingdom. For our purposes 'religious nurture' denotes the process whereby Hindu children acquire the practices and beliefs characteristic of their ethno–religious community. 'Nurture' became a useful analytic term for our research since it parallels at least one Hindu concept of education grounded in one of the communities we studied.[5]

One of our studies – The Hindu Nurture in Coventry Project – coupled an ethnography of British Hindu children in the 8–13 age range, with the development of curriculum material for use in religious education by pupils in the middle years. The motivation for this project came partly from an ongoing interest in the changing patterns of religious activity in the religious traditions of ethnic minorities in the United Kingdom. (*see* Jackson, 1976, 1981; Kanitkar and Jackson, 1982); and partly through developments in religious education which drew attention to the importance of the life–world of children as a factor to be taken into account by teachers in the process of religious education (*see* Gates, 1977 and Grimmitt, 1982, 1987) and as potential source material for reflection and study by children (Jackson, 1982b, 1984, 1987a).

The limited number of ethnographic studies of South Asian communities in Britain over the last decade suggests changing patterns of religious practice and identity (Brown, 1981, 1987; Jackson, 1981; Ballard and Ballard, 1977; Barton, 1986 and Knott, 1986a). There is a complex interplay of a cluster of factors including 'home' and 'host' traditions, the nature of the migrant group, the nature of the migration process and of the 'host' response to the group (Knott, 1989). Detailed research is necessary to tease out the subtleties of acculturation of each ethno-religious community, for example, Gujarati Hindus or Bengali Muslims. Clearly, the transmission of culture to the young is a crucial aspect of the process, a point brought home by the fact that, according to the 1981 census, over 40 per cent of people of South Asian origin in Britain are under the age of nineteen (CRE, 1985). Our work on the Hindu Nurture in Coventry Project focused on children from two ethnically South Asian Hindu communities.

The Hindu Nurture in Coventry Project began its work in January 1986, with an initial six months of field work devoted to investigating the complexities of Hindu communities in Coventry. The aims were to make contacts, to identify the differentiating factors and to identify boys and girls between the ages of 8 and 13 who might be suitable for detailed follow-up as the subjects of case studies.

Through participant observation in Hindu events such as temple worship, religious functions in homes and public halls and supplementary classes organized by Hindus, an extensive network of contacts was established, spanning the Gujarati and Punjabi Hindu communities. These led to introductions to particular families from a wide range of castes and sectarian groups. It was possible to make a profile of the current patterns of Hindu life in the city. One salient feature of contemporary Hindu life in Coventry is the activity of the following sectarian movements – the Sathya Sai Baba organization, the International Society for Krishna Consciousness (ISKCON popularly known as the Hare Krishna Movement), the Arya Samaj and the Pushti Marga. Contact was made with members of all these groups and religious activities such as festival celebrations, weekly or monthly worship and rites of passage were attended. Of these events some are rarely open to outsiders, in particular those for devotees of Pushti Marga. Records were kept in the form of field notes, colour slides, audio-recording, collections of pictures and printed literature such as educational material, sacred texts and collections of bhajans or devotional songs.

Throughout this field-work period particular attention was paid to the role played by children in religious activities and to the supplementary classes which some of them attended. A list was drawn up of Gujarati and Punjabi Hindu boys and girls between 8 and 13 years of age, from families of as many castes and sectarian orientations as possible. With the intention of coming across hitherto undetected variables and in the hope of finding children from 'less committed' families than those identified through primarily Hindu community events, all (ten) eligible Hindu pupils in one school were interviewed.

In June and July 1986, semi-structured interviews were tape recorded with thirty-four pupils in their schools covering many aspects of the children's religious experience suggested by earlier participant observation in their Hindu environment. The transcripts constitute a rich source of data on children's values, perception of their religious identity, involvement in family worship, and knowledge of hymns and prayers on channels of cultural transmission – notably video – and on the vocabulary and ideas they use to articulate distinctively Hindu experience.

Analysis of the transcripts also facilitated the identification of twelve children, spanning the age range and representing a number of cultural variables, for detailed follow-up. With parents' permission regular visits to these children in their homes began at the Gujarati Hindu New Year, 1 November 1986. The children were given diaries in which to record day-to-day happenings, particularly those which are distinctively Hindu in character. Each child was interviewed informally about the diary entries in order to draw out more detailed comment and explanation. Use was also made of slides, pictures, photographs and artefacts in focused interviews with children relating to Hindu worship and ceremony. Visits to cultural events, religious gatherings and supplementary classes were also maintained and the children's involvement was recorded. Home visits also allowed further photography, informal conversation with older siblings, parents, uncles, aunts and grandparents, and the opportunity to observe the domestic shrine, religious pictures and the Indian videos to which children are exposed.

Field work continued between January and October of 1987 and included regular visits to families; accompanying families on visits outside Coventry, for example, to the ISKCON Rathayatra festival; the visit of Swami Satyamitranand Giri – a sage from India – to Leicester and a pilgrimage to five Hindu temples in the Midlands and South of England – visits with family members to festival celebrations at temples and community centres; attendance at the parents' evening of the Coventry Gujarati school; observation of such domestic rituals as *mundan* – a head shaving ceremony, and community rituals such as *bhumi puja* – the consecration of a site for a new temple.

During November and December 1987 and February–May 1988 the researchers stayed with Indian members of three of the families on the project, in Bombay, Valsad, in Gujarat and Delhi. Interview and photographic material collected during these visits was incorporated into the research data.

Finally, a detailed index of all field notes, an index of all colour transparencies and a calendar of religious occasions affecting Hindus in Coventry between September 1985 and December 1987 were prepared as tools for use in writing research publications, articles for teachers (Nesbitt and Jackson, 1988; Jackson and Nesbitt, 1989a), books for children and for broadcasts and lectures.

Curriculum Material

So far the research material has been used in producing two books for children (Jackson, 1989; Jackson and Nesbitt, 1989a) and five radio broadcasts (*see* Note 6) including one 'radiovision', tape/filmstrip, programme which draws on the project's slide collection as well as on children and parents who contributed to the project.

Publishers and broadcasters showed considerable interest in the research project and its materials, but it soon became clear to us that, in order to get our materials disseminated, we would have to fit in with book and programme series that had already been planned and scheduled. The main disadvantage of this was that we had to conform to the publishers' and producer's choice of themes. In the case of the book *Religions through Festivals: Hinduism* (Jackson, 1989) and four of the radio programmes, the chosen theme was 'festivals'. Although we had plenty of material on festivals (Jackson and Nesbitt, 1989b) we were anxious not to over-emphasize one particular aspect of the tradition at the expense of the many others that had emerged during the research. Fortunately it was possible to negotiate a flexible approach so that, in the case of the book, nine of the twenty-two double page spreads dealt with festivals directly, while the rest provided a context, drawing on topics such as story, domestic worship, visiting a temple, languages and food. Another apparent disadvantage was that publishers wanted both Hinduism in Britain and the Hindu tradition in its Indian setting to be represented. As we experimented with juxtaposing British and Indian subject matter we soon realized that this approach had very positive strengths. We were able to include material about Indian relations to the Coventry families we had studied, showing close family ties that transcend national boundaries and indicating that visits by family members to and from India are common. We were also in a position to select examples of Hindu religious and cultural life from regions of India that most British children would not encounter through meeting the descendants of migrant Hindu families.

In the book *Religions through Festivals: Hinduism* the issue of balance was addressed by featuring one Gujarati Hindu family from the Project to provide characters with whom children could relate and who would reappear at regular intervals. Members of the family are shown praying, eating and taking part in festival celebrations and their words are reproduced explaining practices and beliefs, describing rituals and reminiscing about festivals in the near or more distant past. Readers are also introduced in one spread to relations of the family at their home in Bombay. Transcripts of comments and observations from other British Hindu children and adults, both Gujarati and Punjabi, provide material which complements the contributions from the centrally featured family.

In addition spreads were inserted showing a South Indian celebration, Pongal in Tamil Nadu; a Bengali festival, Durga Puja celebrated by Bengalis living in Delhi; and Ganesha Chaturthi, a festival especially popular in the western state of Maharashtra. One other spread shows a map of India indicating the principal languages and diversity of culture in the subcontinent. Of a total of twenty-one double page spreads, twelve deal directly with Hindus in Britain, eight of these including contributions from the principal Gujarati family. Five spreads use a selection of Indian material, and three show British school children learning about Hinduism through drama, story and visiting a temple. The opening spread includes an activity to help sensitize children to a study of Hinduism and the final spread is a calendar of festivals covered in the book and a glossary. Most spreads are illustrated with photographs, alternately in colour and black and white, over half of them from the project's slide collection.

Direct quotations from children and adults who contributed to the project are featured at regular intervals. The sources are the semi-structured interviews conducted with children during June and July 1986 (e.g. on Raksha Bandhan, p. 31), informal and semi-structured interviews with children, parents and other family members during the main period of fieldwork (e.g. a mother's reminiscences about celebrating Diwali when she was a girl in Uganda) and diary entries by children (e.g. an eleven-year-old-boy's account of his family's celebration of Krishna's birthday – Janmashtami – p. 39).

Two issues concerning language in relation to religion came up as the book was being assembled. The first was the choice of technical terms and names from Indian languages to introduce to junior school readers. On the one hand it would have been a mistake to overload the text with foreign words. On the other hand the research had shown that British Hindu children who are fluent in English habitually use Gujarati, Punjabi or Hindi technical religious terms and names, many of which have no precise English equivalent. We found that sometimes children would resort to gesture to explain a word, or give an English equivalent that was misleading. For example, 'candle' for *diva* – a small oil lamp used particularly in worship. The more common alternative was children's use of terms from the mother tongue or Hindi (Nesbitt and Jackson, 1988).

The decision was made, therefore, to introduce a small, manageable number of key words on each spread, most of them grounded in the experience of the children on the project. These are defined simply at the end of the book.

The second issue was that of correct pronunciation. The research had shown that Hindu children and parents appreciate the coverage of their tradition in religious education. Nevertheless some concern was expressed about the occasional wildly inaccurate mispronunciation of common words in the Indian languages by teachers. Our response to this was to attempt to help readers pronounce a selection of key words by indicating a rhyming word in English such as 'Diwali – it rhymes with barley' or by inserting an explanatory note – 'The book is called the *Ramayana* – pronounced with the stress on the second, not the third 'a'.[7]

There is also an explanatory note at the beginning of the glossary offering further advice on pronunciation:

> Many Indian names come from the ancient language of Sanskrit. Speakers of modern Indian languages such as Hindi do not usually pronounce the last 'a' in names such as Dasratha, Ganesha, Prahlada, Vasudeva. In fact, Rama and Shiva often rhyme with 'calm' and 'give' (not 'calmer' and 'giver'). In some names the final 'a' is essential and must be heard clearly; examples are Sita, Radha, Yashoda.

The '*Listening to . . .*' series, (Jackson and Nesbitt, 1989a) aimed at the 9 to 14 age range, aims to develop 'a spirit of enquiry and an open mind towards all peoples and religions, a knowledge of the fabric of different religions, and an increased level of self-knowledge and understanding', and uses as the basis for its rationale the Swann Report's view that 'the concept of pluralism implies seeing the very diversity of such a society, in terms, for example, of the range of religions experience, . . . as an enrichment of the experience of all those within it' (Swann, 1985). Each book was planned by the general editor and consultant adviser to deal with individual religious traditions.

Potential authors were given the brief that books should not attempt a comprehensive survey or exposition of the main features of each religious tradition. The books were intended rather 'to take readers into important aspects of the faith in a way which will help them to glimpse a little of the faith which lies behind it'. A feature of the series was to be the inclusion of information and reflections from adherents to the traditions on topics such as worship and religious experience. This material was intended 'to form the basis for empathetic understanding and active learning . . .'. Pupils, whatever their cultural and religious background, would then be 'encouraged to make a thoughtful personal response'. Each book would consist of five chapters dealing with the topics 'A Glimpse of the Faith', 'Stories', 'Artefacts, Signs and Symbols', 'Worship' and 'Special Occasions'. Each chapter would be divided into five or six double page spreads, each spread being illustrated with two photographs. Spreads would be printed alternately in colour and black and white.

When I was approached as a potential author for the Hinduism book the editors and publishers were not aware of the Hindu Nurture in Coventry Project. When the Project's potential for providing material for the book was explained to them, however, enthusiasm was expressed about our involvement and Eleanor Nesbitt, the Project's Research Fellow, joined me as co-author. Subsequently some doubts were expressed by the publisher about the appropriateness of drawing on children as sources of information and insight, on the grounds that children 'are unlikely to offer very illuminating insights'. This gave us some cause for concern, especially since it was contrary to research evidence (Gates, 1976) and our own findings through ethnographic research, but in the end we were able to give our particular book its own distinctive shape and contents, which included substantial contributions from children.

Liberally interpreted, the specified chapter headings offered a very broad range of possibilities for including material from the Project. The technique adopted for considering material was to work through the field data index and slide collection, noting material that would fit potentially into the five chapter categories. The lists of possibilities under each heading were then scrutinized to see if any patterns or tendencies appeared that would provide ideas for shaping the material further. It was immediately noticeable that a significant amount of religious activity was based in the sphere of the home, rather than the temple or wider community, and we decided to ensure that this 'domestic' dimension was properly represented in the book. For example the practices of fasting and making vows – commonly engaged in by Hindu women in their daily lives – are mentioned rarely in children's literature on Hinduism. We were able to feature these in the chapter on Worship, showing an example of children's involvement with the ritual associated with the culmination of a fast. In this example young Gujarati girls become *goynis*, ritually embodying the purity and power of the goddess. It also became clear that the sectarian activity which had emerged in our research as a notable part of Coventry's Hindu life provided some excellent examples of faith and practice for the book. It was also apparent that families who showed allegiance to religious 'sects'[8] were not isolated from the rest of the community, but were deeply involved in the Hindu community life of their religio-ethnic group. We were able to reflect this form of pluralism in the children's book.

Particular families emerged as having been involved in a variety of relevant activities. In order to provide readers with a sense of continuity, we decided to concentrate on the children and parents in one Punjabi Hindu family, on a twelve-year-girl of Gujarati background and on a Gujarati Hindu community leader. Their personal reminiscences and reflections were to be punctuated with contributions from other children and adults. The Punjabi family was involved not only in the International Society for Krishna Consciousness (ISKCON), but also with the wider Hindu community. The father was secretary of a predominantly Punjabi Hindu temple and acting secretary of a national Hindu organization. The Gujarati girl was from a family committed to the Sathya Sai Baba organization. In listening to what they had to say, together with others having no particular allegiance to sects and movements, we were reflecting the changing Hindu scene in Britain (Knott, 1986b, 1989).

We then began to write draft material, linked where possible with Project slides that could be used to illustrate spreads. We also consulted the principal families in order to inform them about the proposed book and to seek their permission to be included in it. We were given warm encouragement to proceed as well as offers from the families to augment the material we already had on file. The additional interviews gained in this way, especially when focused on slides showing the people concerned taking part in rituals and ceremonies, were invaluable to us as source material. Our chosen subjects also directed us to key future events within their families and communities which provided yet more material relating to them. In this way the preparation of the book unexpectedly led to the collection of additional research material for the project. These events included a *mundan* or head shaving ceremony at the home of the Punjabi family, the laying of the foundation stone at a new Gujarati Hindu temple and the installation of new images at a mainly Punjabi Hindu temple. Appendix 1 indicates the final selection of material from the Project included in the book.

As with *Religions through Festivals: Hinduism*, (Jackson, 1989) we were concerned to balance data on Hindus in Britain with Indian material. In this respect we were able to employ material collected on recent visits to India. We then looked at connections between the British and the Indian material. For example, we juxtaposed a spread showing pilgrims bathing in the Ganges at Varanasi soon after dawn with another showing a British Gujarati girl on a pilgrimage to five Hindu temples in England. The connection between India and Britain was reinforced by using my slides of sunrise over the Ganges and of pilgrims bathing in the sacred river in order to stimulate reminiscences and a response about personal faith from a British Gujarati informant.

Bringing together the British and the Indian material also gave us fresh ideas for arranging the contents of some chapter. For example, the chapter on acts of worship has adjacent spreads showing domestic worship in Bombay and Madras and in Coventry. As well as obvious ritual connections, there is a further link made by the fact that the woman pictured praying at her home in Bombay is an aunt of one of the Gujarati children on our project. Further, the bringing together of visual material from British and Indian sources in the chapter on 'Symbols and Images' suggested a logical order for the spreads. Readers are taken from a symbol based in nature, fire, to graphic symbols, the written form of the 'Om' syllable and the swastika, then to an aniconic representation of deity, the linga, representing Shiva, to two dimensional religious pictures[9] and finally to three dimensional images, the last two spreads showing an image being carved in South India, and the installation of an image imported from India in a Coventry temple.

In the case of both books, members of the families read through sections to which they had contributed, occasionally suggesting alterations and making corrections. The manuscripts were regarded as complete only after the families had given their approval and a consultant from a local Hindu community had checked the complete text. We decided to address the matter of confidentiality by asking the families whether they preferred their own names to be used in the text or an appropriate pseudonym. In all cases permission was given to use actual names, though, initially, one child was concerned that the inclusion of her photograph and name might inflate her ego – something she thought would be morally bad for her. This was a another example of a question related to curriculum development eliciting further research data. Forenames only were used of children who did not appear with adult members of their families. Needless to say, without the support and encouragement of the families neither book could have appeared.

Conclusion

The experience of developing religious education curriculum material from specially commissioned ethnographic research was a fascinating and rewarding one, and we intend to extend the process into other faiths and communities. The most problematic part of the work was in finding appropriate publishing outlets for our material. Although neither the researchers nor the members of Hindu communities who appear in the books feel that the material was significantly distorted by being arranged to fit into a series of books and broadcasts that had been already planned, we consider that the potential of the research data has not been fully realized in curriculum terms. For our next project we are involving broadcasters and school publishers from the early stages of research design. The best compliment we have received is that some members of local Hindu communities plan to use the books with their own children. This was an unexpected development, as our materials were designed for use in religious education classes in maintained schools and it raises interesting questions about the relationship between religious nurture and religious education. It is also sufficient encouragement for us to move on to further research and curriculum development.

Appendix: 1 Contents of *Listening to Hindus* Indicating Material Drawn from the Hindu Nurture in Coventry Project

Chapter 1	*A Journey into Hinduism*
1 *The Variety of Hinduism*	British Hindu children saying what they think is important about their way of life.
2 *The Unity of Hinduism*	A Hindu living in Britain introduces some central ideas of the Hindu tradition.
3 *The Ganga at Varanasi*	A Coventry Gujarati Hindu talking about the spiritual significance of bathing in the Ganges especially at dawn.
4 *A Pilgrimage in England*	A British Gujarati Hindu girl talks about her visit to five temples in England in 1987.
5 *and 6 The Anand Family goes to Rathayatra*	A British Punjabi Hindu family attend a festival in London organized by ISKCON, the International Society for Krishna Consciousness. The father and two eldest children (13 and 11), describe the festival and their part in it and comment on and explain ISKCON's views on diet.

Chapter 2	*Stories*
1 *The Ganga comes down to Earth*	Includes a section on how British Hindu children learn stories – from relatives or in the temple; from 'comic' books; plays with actors or puppets; videos.
2 *and 3 The Image of Jagannath*	The story is linked to the festival of Rathayatra (Ch. 1 spreads 5 and 6).
4 *Krishna, The Naughty Child*	The story is linked to a British Punjabi Hindu family.
5 *Princess Meera*	The story is linked to a group of children who attended a summer camp organized by the Sathya Sai Baba organization. The children saw the story performed by puppets.

Chapter 3	Acts of Worship
1 *The Home Shrine*	The aunt of two British Gujarati children is shown performing puja at her home in Bombay.
2 *A Priest Visits a Home*	A brahmin priest conducts a puja in the home of a British Punjabi Hindu family.
3 *A Sathya Sai Baba Satsang*	A Gujarati Hindu girl described her visits to see Sathya Sai Baba in India and she and her cousin lead a devotional gathering (satsang) of followers of Sathya Sai Baba in Coventry. One of them describes the arti (offering of light) ceremony.
4 *Fasting and Food*	Two British Gujarati Hindu girls act as *goynis*, representing the purity and power of the goddess, during a ceremony following a period of fasting by the girls' aunt.
5 *Worship in the Temple*	Puja at a Hindu temple in Coventry plus information on Hindu temples in Britain and in India.

Chapter 4	Symbols and Images
1 *Fire*	A *havan* or *yagna* at the home of a British Punjabi Hindu family and a couple sitting near the sacred fire at a Gujarati Hindu wedding in England.
2 *Swastika and Om*	The swastika symbol at a Hindu temple in Coventry and the Om symbol made with rice and lentils at the home of a Coventry Gujarati Hindu home.
3 *Shiva*	A Shiva linga at a Gujarati Hindu temple in Coventry.
4 *Religious Pictures*	Pictures used in Gujarati Hindu homes in Britain.
5 and 6 *Murti Pratishtha*	The ceremony of installing new images at a mainly Punjabi Hindu temple in Coventry.

Chapter 5	Special Occasions
1 and 2 *Mundan*	A British Punjabi Hindu family have a life-cycle ritual (*samskara*) performed at home by a brahmin priest and a barber, involving the shaving of the head of the two-year-old-son.
3 and 4 *Raksha Bandhan*	The celebration of a Hindu festival at the home of a Coventry Punjabi Hindu family.
5 and 6 *Preparing for a New Temple (Bhumi Puja/Foundation Stone)*	The ceremony of 'worshipping the earth', showing the involvement of children, at the site of a new Hindu temple in Coventry, and the subsequent laying of the foundation stone some months later.

Notes

1 The term 'ethnography' is used by social anthropologists and other social scientists in several ways. This chapter employs two of the possible usages: sometimes the term indicates a set of methods and techniques used in qualitative research (e.g. participant observation and interviewing); sometimes it refers to qualitative accounts of the culture and social organization of particular groups of living people (as in 'an ethnography').

2 Those who assert that phenomenology when employed in RE inhibits students from engaging with questions of truth and falsity and leads to a relativistic view, make the unwarranted assumption that the application of phenomenological methods necessarily precludes the employment of other complementary approaches.

3 e.g. *A Journey to the Artic* and *The Netsilik Eskimos at the Inland Camps* (both published by Curriculum Development Associates, 1970) are books for children based on Knud Rasmussen's study in 1923, later published as *The Netsilik Eskimos*.

4 The first project (1984–5) – a study of the provision of formal teaching of the Hindu tradition in supplementary schools around England – is reported in Jackson (1985), Jackson and Nesbitt (1986) and Jackson (1987b). The third project – Punjabi Hindu Nurture in Coventry (1988–9) – involves research on the religious lives of children from two Hindu caste/sectarian Punjabi communities in Coventry. The second project – The Hindu Nurture in Coventry Project (1986–7) – is discussed in the present chapter. The first project was supported by the University of Warwick Research and Innovations fund. The second and third projects were funded thanks to the generosity of the Leverhulme Trust. All three projects were directed by Robert Jackson with Eleanor Nesbitt as Research Fellow.

5 The Sathya Sai Baba organization uses the term *Bal Vikas* for its educational ventures, a term literally meaning 'child blossoming'.

6 The following twenty minute programmes for BBC Education (Radio 4 VHF) drew on material from the Hindu Nurture in Coventry Project and feature members of families who contributed to the Project: *Hindus and Sikhs in Britain* (Radiovision); *Celebrating Holi*; *Celebrating Navratri*; *Celebrating Diwali* (all January and April 1987); *A Day in the Life of a Hindu Family* (November 1988).

7 Sometimes native English speakers stress the third 'a' assuming it also represents a long vowel sound. In fact the vowel sound in the first two syllables is long. The last two vowels are short.

8 The English word 'sect' (which implies a high degree of exclusiveness) is misleading, and yet is the nearest term in English to *sampradâya* which, in Indian languages, literally means 'handing on' or 'tradition' and connotes a succession of teachers and their followers who are located within the wider Indian tradition.

9 The history of these popular pictures also shows European–Indian links. The earliest oleographs were Catholic Christian, imported in to India from Germany. Before long pictures of Hindu subjects were being exported from Germany to India, then they were printed widely in India (Vitsaxis, 1977). Hindus in Britain buy pictures both imported from India and printed in Britain (usually from Indian originals) by firms such as Printrite in Coventry.

References

BALLARD, R. and BALLARD C. (1977) 'The Sikhs: The Development of South Asian Settlements in Britain' in WATSON, J. *Between Two Cultures*, Oxford, Blackwell.

BARTON, S. (1986) *The Bengali Muslims of Bradford*, Monograph series, Community Religions Project, University of Leeds.

BOWEN, D. (1981) 'The Hindu Community in Bradford' in BOWEN, D. (ed.) *Hinduism in England*, Bradford, Bradford College.

BOWEN, D. (1988) *The Sathya Sai Baba Community in Bradford*, Monograph series, Community Religions Project, University of Leeds.

BUSHNELL, H. (1967) *Christian Nurture*, New Haven, Yale University.

CANTWELL SMITH, W. (1978) *The Meaning and End of Religion*, London, SPCK.

CRE (1985) Ethnic Minorities in Britain: statistical information on the pattern of settlement, London, Commission for Racial Equality.

GATES, B. (1976) *Religion in the Developing World of Children and Young People*, PhD. thesis, University of Lancaster.

GATES, B. (1977) 'Religion in the Child's Own Core Curriculum', *Learning for Living*, Autumn.

GATES, B. (1982) 'Children Prospecting for Commitment' in JACKSON (1982a).

GRIMMITT, M. (1982) 'World Religions and Personal Development' in JACKSON (1982a).

GRIMMITT, M. (1987) *Religious Education and Human Development*, Great Wakering, McCrimmons.

HULL, J. (1984) *Studies in Religion and Education*, Lewes, Falmer Press.

JACKSON, R. (1976) 'Holi in North India and in an English City: Some Adaptations and Anomalies', *New Community*, 5, 3, 203–210.

JACKSON, R. (1981) 'The Shree Krishna Temple and the Gujarati Hindu Community in Coventry' in BOWEN D. (ed.) *Hinduism in England*, Bradford, Bradford College.

JACKSON, R. (ed.) (1982a) *Approaching World Religions*, London, John Murray.

JACKSON, R. (1982b) 'Commitment and the Teaching of World Religions' in JACKSON (1982a).

JACKSON, R. (1984) 'The Concerns of Religious Education and the Characterization of Hinduism', *British Journal of Religious Education*, 7, 2, 141–146.

JACKSON, R. (1985) 'Hinduism in Britain: Religious Nurture and Religious Education', *British Journal of Religious Education*, Spring, 68–75.

JACKSON, R. (1987a) 'Religious Education: A Middle Way' in A. BROWN (ed.), *The Shap Handbook on World Religions in Education*, London, Commission for Racial Equality.

JACKSON, R. (1987b) 'Changing Conceptions of Hinduism in Timetabled Religion' in BURGHART, R. (ed.), *Hinduism in Great Britain: The Perpetuation of Religion in an Alien Cultural Environment*, London, Tavistock.

JACKSON, R. (1989) *Religions Through Festivals: Hinduism*, London, Longman.

JACKSON, R. and KILLINGLEY, D. (1988) *Approaches to Hinduism*, London, John Murray.

JACKSON, R. and NESBITT, E. (1986) 'Sketches of Formal Hindu Nurture', *World Religions in Education*, The Journal of the Shap Working Party, 25–29.

JACKSON, R. and NESBITT, E. (1989a) *Listening to Hindus*, London, Unwin Hyman.

JACKSON, R. and NESBITT, E. (1989b) 'British Hindu Children and their Traditional Festivals' in WOOD, A. (ed.) *Religions in Education: The Shap Working Party 1969–1989*, London, British and Foreign Schools Society, available from The BFSS RE Centre, West London Institute of Higher Education, Borough Road, Isleworth, Middlesex.

KANITKAR, H. and JACKSON, R. (1982) *Hindus in Britain*, London, School of Oriental and African Studies.

KNOTT, K. (1986a) *Hinduism in Leeds*, Monograph series, Community Religions Project, University of Leeds.

KOTT, K. (1986b) 'Hinduism in Britain', *World Religions in Education*, The Journal of the Shap Working Party, 10–12.

KNOTT, K. (1989) 'Bound to Change? The Religions of South Asians in Britain', Unpublished Paper, Community Religions Project, University of Leeds.

NESBITT, E. and JACKSON, R. (1988) 'Growing Up in the Hindu Tradition: The Hindu Nurture in Coventry Project', *Resource*, 10, 2, Spring, 4–5.

SCHOOLS COUNCIL (1971) *Religious Education in Secondary Schools: Schools Council Working Paper No 36*, London, Evans/Methuen.

SHARMA, U. (1971) *Rampal and His Family*, London, Collins.

SWANN, M. (ed.) (1985) *Education for All: The Report of the Committee of Enquiry into the Education of Children from Ethnic Minority Groups*, London, HMSO.

VITSAXIS, V. (1977) *Hindu Epics, Myths and Legends in Popular Illustrations*, Delhi, Oxford University Press.

WAADENBURG, J. (1973) *Classical Approaches to the Study of Religion*, 2 Vols, The Hague, Mouton.

Chapter 12

Tailoring Irish Cultural Studies for Junior School Children

Tom Arkell

The Background

Multicultural Education

In the world of curriculum development a decade can often appear as both a long and a short stretch of time. During the 1970s, for example, many urban education authorities responded very successfully to the recent settlement of numerous 'coloured' immigrant families in their areas by pioneering innovative programmes of multicultural education. In general these were designed to promote racial harmony in schools by counteracting the virtually universal traditional stereotype of the British as a white protestant people. Such an approach to multicultural education, however, came to be regarded increasingly during the 1980s as little more than tokenism which neither challenged directly nor eradicated widespread endemic racial prejudice. And so within a decade or so the much more confident and assertive doctrine of anti-racism transformed the whole concept of multicultural education in many schools.

Unfortunately the achievements of this campaign for real multicultural education proved unwittingly divisive and contributed to some further polarization of the English education system. In areas where few migrants from the 'New' Commonwealth had settled, many teachers remained so unconvinced of the direct relevance of such innovations to their own pupils that they became no more than remote and semi-interested spectators of the multicultural scene. This relative detachment received superficial support from the demographic data. The census of 1981 showed only 5 per cent of the people living in Britain had been born outside the British Isles and less than half of these came from the New Commonwealth. Of the latter, 60 per cent had settled in the South-East of England and 12 per cent in the West Midlands. Altogether 630,000

British residents in 1981 had been born in the Indian sub-continent and 300,000 in the Caribbean.

The Irish in Britain

By contrast the Irish had migrated to Britain in relatively large numbers for well over a century from the 1830s to the 1960s, when a temporary economic revival in Ireland halted this diaspora for a time. The position of the Irish immigrants in Britain has always been rather ambivalent because, although all the Irish were technically internal migrants until the Irish Free State left the United Kingdom in 1922, most were regarded as belonging to an inferior race apart by their host community. Subsequently, and especially since 1949 when the newly-created Republic of Ireland finally left the British Commonwealth, the British government imposed virtually no restrictions on travel between the two countries and resolutely allowed all Irish citizens in Britain to enjoy the same privileges as British subjects. This policy reflected the myopia of most Britons who regarded the Irish as a homogeneous people and rarely distinguished between their 'fellow countrymen' from the North and the 'foreigners' from the Republic (Jackson, 1963).

The census enumerators were more discriminating and in 1981 recorded a total of over 600,000 Irish-born from the Republic living in Britain and nearly 250,000 from Northern Ireland. Half of those from the Republic had settled in the South-East, but only one-third from the North. In addition, about one-eighth of both groups were to be found in each of the West Midlands and the North-West and one-seventh of the Northern Irish in Scotland. These figures, however, do not reflect the full scale of Irish penetration into Britain because about another three million people living in Britain were of immediate Irish descent — that is either second or third generation Irish (O'Connor, 1972). In London, Birmingham, Manchester, Bradford and other towns where the Irish had settled in substantial numbers there were vigorous Irish communities whose presence was manifested most clearly by their social, cultural and sporting clubs and their many associations with the Catholic church. However, it would be wrong to suggest that all retained an acute sense of Irish identity because some had come to regard themselves, and been accepted, as overtly British and many more had developed a sense of dual identity (Lennon, *et al.*, 1988). Indeed, whatever their parentage, children who had been born, brought up and educated in Britain could rarely be regarded as Irish as those who had been reared in Ireland. From the 1960s the process of assimilation was helped by the sharp decline in the net migration rate from Ireland to Britain and by the simultaneous influx of 'coloured' immigrants, both of which trends encouraged many of the Irish in Britain to identify more closely with the British.

This relatively cosy situation was shaken in the early 1970s by the tragic series of events in Northern Ireland and the IRA's intermittent attempts to spread the violence to mainland Britain. The knowledge that a vocal minority of the Irish in Britain supported violence, or at least the threat of violence, as an acceptable alternative to traditional political methods triggered off a sharp revival of prejudice against the Irish, especially those who spoke with a strong Irish accent, among those Britons who felt that their own lives and safety were now at risk. Anyone who failed to disguise or deny their Irishness could expect to encounter suspicions of potential terrorism as well as the traditional English assumptions of racial superiority. And so this almost inevitable reaction generated a heightened sense of ethnic identity among many of recent Irish provenance. And yet in the later 1970s very few of the Irish in Britain regarded themselves as an ethnic minority similar to those from the New Commonwealth for whom schemes of multicultural education were being devised.

Ten years ago the introduction of any aspect of Irish studies to a school's curriculum was invariably an *ad hoc* development dependent on the personal enthusiasm of particular teachers and often took the form in junior schools of an extended St Patrick's day assembly. The idea that multicultural education in Britain was somewhat deficient without a specific Irish component was as foreign to the collective thinking of its exponents as the proposal that deliberately-planned Irish topics should be introduced to those Catholic schools where most children of Irish extraction were educated. Neither possibility was acceptable to the Roman Catholic hierarchy, which was acutely conscious of the fact that theirs was a worldwide international Christian church and so was very eager to avoid appearing as little more than an Irish ghetto religion in Britain.

Two EEC Projects

An EEC Directive

During the 1970s the hope was sometimes expressed that the simultaneous decisions of the United Kingdom and of the Republic of Ireland to join the EEC might help somehow to curtail the strife in Ulster. Such pious hopes were abortive, but one very minor consequence of their joining the EEC was the directive of 1977 on the *Education of the Children of Migrant*

Workers was applied to both countries. According to Article 3:

> Member States shall, in accordance with their national circumstances and legal systems, and in co-operation with States of origin, take appropriate measures to promote, in co-ordination with normal education, teaching of the mother tongue and culture of the country of origin for the children of compulsory school age dependent on migrant workers from another member state.

Irish children studying in British schools spoke English fluently and so had no special need to learn their mother tongue, but a strong case could be made for teaching them something about Irish culture. Therefore the University of Warwick applied to the EEC in 1979 for funds for a pilot project on Irish Cultural Studies to explore how effectively this directive might be applied in English primary schools. The application was made in conjunction with the Coventry LEA, which was already greatly experienced in multicultural education but had not so far included an Irish element within it, even though about one-fifth of all children in its schools had at least one Irish-born parent. The initiative was supported fully by the Department of Education in Dublin and by the DES on the understanding that to avoid polarization 'the teaching of Irish culture should not just be to an isolated group of Irish children, but should be regarded more widely in the context of inter-cultural education' and so be planned within the context of each school's whole curriculum.

The First Project

The first EEC-funded project on the development of Irish Cultural Studies in Coventry primary schools was approved in 1980 and launched in 1981. Its principal aim was to explore which Irish themes or topics appeared most suitable for teaching to 9 to 11-year-old children in England and how these might be integrated best into their schools' normal curriculum. It also examined critically the material that was available in both England and Ireland for teaching these themes and concluded that very few books could be used unaltered with this age range.

During the course of this year two teachers taught part-time on the project, working with the class-teachers of seven classes in three different Catholic primary schools and also making valuable contacts with various schools in Ireland. All the Coventry classes contained large proportions of 'Irish' children, but they were never taught separately from the non-Irish ones. Most of the work which they undertook successfully and very enthusiastically explored either their own family histories or the Irish cultural heritage: in particular music, dance, art, stories, drama and the achievements of the Celts. Attempts to cover later aspects of Irish history and migration and to introduce the children to contemporary Irish society and topography were much less successful. This was partly because most of the available material was far too detailed for them, but in addition many of these topics bore little relevance to the children's own experience of life and so were much more difficult to teach.

The report to the EEC on this first project (Arkell, 1982a) therefore argued the need for a successor that would concentrate on developing a well-balanced package of readily accessible child-centred teaching materials for all the themes that had been identified as being suitable for 9 to 11-year-olds and for the topic approach that was practised widely in English primary schools.

The Second Project

The second EEC project on the development of experimental materials on Irish Cultural Studies for 9 to 11-year-old children was funded for one year, but the work which began in 1983 needed several more years for its completion. It was aided by three further exchange visits between teachers in Coventry and Dublin, but its principal focus remained the production of a wide range of sample materials for use in British primary schools together with some guidance for interested teachers on alternative strategies for teaching various aspects of Irish studies. It was based initially on the experience of those teachers who had been involved in the preliminary project, but drew increasingly upon the expertise of other teachers and lecturers who were already well versed in curriculum development as well as from the closely-monitored experiences of other classroom teachers who entered the field of Irish studies as voluntary guinea-pigs. After these widespread trials, the prototype material was revised substantially and published (Arkell, 1988).

The format chosen was a reasonably flexible teaching pack which eventually contained fifteen booklets. It was not designed as a self-contained course on Irish studies, but rather as a resource or starter pack which assumed that teachers would make very different selections from it to use either on their own or with other additional materials, possibly in comparison with selected aspects of other cultures. However, it was conceived principally as a vehicle for those who wanted to undertake a fullscale Irish topic or project and on its own could last for half a term or more. From the start the emphasis was placed on eliciting an affective response from the pupils so that the material was made as visually attractive as possible. In addition, a variety of strategies was devised to avoid the straightforward presentation of factual information about Ireland and to give the pupils different insights into the nature of the Irish culture experience.

The material for the pack was chosen with the threefold aim of introducing children to aspects of Ireland today, to the richness and width of the Irish cultural heritage and to the extent and nature of Irish migration. By far the greatest challenge was posed by the need to present life in contemporary Ireland as appealing and intelligible to young children who had never been there, without resorting to those personal contacts enjoyed by many schools engaged in the pioneer projects. Ireland today is of course a modern industrial country like Britain and care had to be taken not to disguise this fact by overemphasizing those cultural factors from the past which help shape modern Irish people's sense of identity.

Limitations of space and time also precipitated difficult compromise decisions on the treatment given to the Irish language and Irish nationalism. Because the main emphasis was always placed on Ireland's cultural experience, the political dimension of Ireland's relationship with Britain was ignored almost entirely. This reflected in part the belief that appreciation of the Irish cultural heritage could be seriously distorted if it were presented as a predominantly political one generating conflict with Britain and in part the conviction that educationally the sounder sequence would be for the children to study the political and constitutional problems of Northern Ireland separately after they had been exposed to the main themes contained within this pack.

By the mid-1980s the climate had become much more favourable for the inclusion of an Irish dimension into the curriculum of most British junior schools. The clearcut anit-racist policies of many urban authorities now targeted all forms of racial prejudice, not just colour, and the Roman Catholic hierarchy and many rural authorities had also come to accept that the pupils in their schools should be educated deliberately to live in a diverse multicultural society (Cosgrave, 1984). At the same time the Irish community had at last developed various active pressure groups and organizations of its own. These included the bi-annual journal 'Irish Studies in Britain', annual conferences on 'Irish dimensions in British education' at Leicester, the Irish Commission for Culture and Education in London, the Irish Studies Unit, Polytechnic of North London, the Irish Education Group in Manchester and the Bradford Irish Music Association, and culminated in the formation of the British Association for Irish Studies and of the Institute of Irish Studies at Liverpool University.

Children's Attitudes

If two of the main purposes of teaching children about Ireland are to make them better informed and to influence some of their attitudes to the Irish, then it is important to determine the scope of their knowledge and attitudes before planning their programmes of study. And in this context it may also be relevant to uncover their perceptions of their own nationality.

A Sample Survey

For this purpose a class of thirty-one 9 to 10-year-old children in one Catholic school were asked to write what they knew about Ireland, what they thought about the Irish and what was their own nationality before their Irish topic began (Arkell, 1982b; Egan, 1977). Because the great majority was of Irish descent, it was not surprising to discover that for most of them Ireland was an attractive, rural country with kind and friendly people. Indeed, this idyllic picture was the limit of what 35 per cent (Category A1)* had to say. Almost all of this group used 'nice' to describe Ireland, although for two it was 'lovely' and one 'very peaceful and quiet'. Their comments on the Irish were more varied. According to two different girls, 'the Irish people are very friendly and caring' and 'everyone in Ireland is nice and they always stop to say hello.' In the words of another: 'I think Irish people are very good and kind. When they see you feeling sad, they will come and talk to you. You can tell them secrets and they can keep them.' Among the other adjectives applied to the Irish were polite, well-mannered, happy and helpful.

Six per cent (Category A2) presented a totally different view of Ireland and the Irish. 'The thing I mostly hate about Ireland is I always hear of lots of fighting going on there. The Irish people are always arguing and always want their own way.' 'In Ireland if they cannot get their own way they start a fight. The fighting started during the '60s. They were fighting because they hated each other.'

Twenty-six per cent (Category B) produced rather unsophisticated attempts to reconcile elements at least of these conflicting simplistic views. One boy started his panegyric of Ireland by saying that it is sometimes dangerous and a bit rough, but still nice, while a girl concluded hers: 'I think Irish people are very nice, but some are very bad and nasty at

---

*The essays were placed in categories of increasing sophistication from A, least sophistication to D, most sophisticated with gradations within some categories.

times.' Similar comments included: 'Some parts of Ireland are nice and other parts aren't.'

19 per cent (Category C) revealed more insight into the Irish situation, especially by placing the troubles firmly in Belfast or Northern Ireland. 'I think the Republic of Ireland is a nice country and kind people, but Northern Ireland is a violent country and not very nice because I heard that petrol bombs have been thrown at the police.' 'Ireland was beautiful before the troubles started during the sixties and are still going to this very day.' 'The Irish people are kind at times, but when they cause a little or should I say a big riot, you can get hurt badly. A place where there is fighting is on the Falls near Andersonstown where I stay when I am visiting Ireland.'

Finally, 13 per cent (Category D) displayed deeper knowledge of Irish history and/or geography. 'A long time ago all of Ireland used to belong to Great Britain but the Irish didn't like it so they had a war and the Irish won, but they only got back the Republic of Ireland.' Two others described the famine briefly and another revealed considerable knowledge of Dublin where his father had been born.

Like all children brought up in the 1970s and 1980s, these pupils had been exposed to, and influenced by, TV programmes showing violence and conflict in Northern Ireland. Their absorption and understanding of them appears to have depended partly on their own intelligence, but probably more upon the influence of their families and friends. In this sample, those in the least sophisticated categories (A1 and A2) came from a wide range of ability, but those revealing more knowledge and understanding (C and D) tended to be among the more able. The study also suggests the possibility of a significant difference in the attitudes and knowledge of girls, who formed 77 per cent of the least sophisticated group, and boys, who comprised 80 per cent of the more sophisticated one.

Although the placing of these children's compositions into the different categories entailed some arbitrary decisions and some may not have written all that they knew, this analysis does represent reliably the spectrum of views and knowledge about Ireland brought to school by these children. Although the sample was far too small and unrepresentative for any general conclusions to be drawn, because one would expect to find in most other schools less knowledge about Ireland and less sympathy for the Irish (Palmer and Ruddell, 1988), it does illustrate how varied may be the attitudes and knowledge which different classes bring to their multicultural studies. One would also anticipate that normally children in category A would require significantly different levels and approaches for their learning from those in C or D.

Ethnic Identity

Children's perceptions of their own ethnic identity may also be of equal relevance to the planning of their studies. In response to the question on their own nationality, one third of the same sample described themselves as Irish or partly Irish, although at least several of the 'English' revealed that they had Irish parents and/or relatives whom they visited regularly in Ireland. For some commentators the latter might be classified as incontestable examples of ethnic Judases who had been driven into denying their Irishness, but a closer examination of what the children wrote reveals that in reality the perceptions of some were much more complex. Not all claimed to be either English or Irish. Expressions such as 'I think my own country is England', 'I come from Ireland' and 'I belong to Scotland' might indicate almost as much ambivalence in their assessments of their own situations and identities as 'I am half English and half Irish' or 'I am half Irish and half English'.

Such responses reflect the fact that many people do not have a pure and unalloyed sense of national identity (O'Donovan, 1985). Often it is diluted by a strong sense of regional or sectional loyalty as well as by alternative ethnic or international leanings. In general the more simplistic expressions of national identity will probably spawn stereotypical views of national characteristics and so, along with basic ignorance, prove more fertile breeding grounds for racial intolerance and prejudice. Such thoughtless prejudices can emerge at a surprisingly early age and be reinforced by mindless and destructive repetition. When these reflect the attitudes and opinions of the children's parents, community and/or peers, they will become inevitably emotive and sensitive issues if schools decide that racial prejudice is a subject suitable for their overt attention. Teachers can of course tackle this evil on many different levels, ranging from simple attempts to dispel basic ignorance to head-on discussions of the relative morality and reasons for the views which people hold. Naturally there is no guarantee that the higher-profile approaches will be the most effective in influencing children's attitudes, in part because they invariably make heavier demands on the knowledge, skills, sensitivities and experience of the teachers involved. The concept of cultural diversity is so much more advanced than the simplistic notion of homogeneous nations that its development will require careful planning and its successful implementation is likely to have more of a long-term than a short-term impact on the children's fundamental attitudes and assumptions. Nonetheless, it is important that children with both straightforward and ambivalent senses of ethnic identity should come to appreciate that the latter is not abnormal.

Levels of Irish Studies

A somewhat impressionistic analysis of how over forty junior and middle school teachers introduced a substantial Irish dimension into the work of their classes during the mid-1980s suggests that these different approaches can be understood best if they are classified into three broad groups or levels, which are susceptible to further subdivision. Although the schools concerned covered a wide geographical spectrum and included substantial proportions with predominantly multi-ethnic and white 'Anglo-Saxon' pupils in addition to Catholic schools with their predictably larger numbers of 'Irish' children, few of these classes contained no child of relatively-recent Irish extraction.

1 The Basic Level

At the basic level teachers concentrated on informing their pupils about Ireland and the Irish in a variety of different ways. In classes with a substantial proportion of Irish children the most common approach to introducing an Irish dimension started with an exploration of their ethnic identity. Normally the most obvious entry point was via the children's own family histories and often entailed no more than plotting on a map or recording on a graph where their parents were born. In one Liverpool Catholic school 'the Heraldic Map of Ireland proved to be a real boon as the children soon realized they had Irish ancestry! Several art lessons were inspired by it, including one where children made their own Coat of Arms.' When the children were encouraged to pursue their own family trees, the number of places in Ireland with which some children acquired a vicarious sense of personal identity was increased further and sensitive handling by their teacher also ensured that this sense of personal involvement was shared by all the other pupils. In one north Warwickshire Catholic school such ancestral pursuits rewarded two fortunate pupils with the discovery that they were related to each other while a third confidently claimed kinship with the teacher. Invariably this approach involved many enthusiastic parents in their children's studies and led not just to offers of further assistance but on several occasions to rapidly burgeoning interest tables.

The teachers of classes with few or no Irish children obviously had to adopt different entry points. One very effective alternative proved to be planning a holiday visit to Ireland which used the Irish Tourist Board as the medium for giving an immediate sense of personal involvement and credibility to the Irish dimension. Very attractive brochures and posters introduced children to how the tourists travelled to Ireland and what they saw and did there and occasionally also unearthed photos, souvenirs and even reminiscences from those who had enjoyed an Irish holiday. This tourist's-eye view of Ireland normally encompassed its scenic splendours, seaside resorts, ports and airports as well as some of the best-known buildings, monuments, artefacts and ruins to be found in Dublin and elsewhere in Ireland and so introduced very positively important aspects of its non-industrial past and present.

For other teachers the starting point was their pupils' manifest ignorance of Irish geography in comparison to 'their awareness of the present troubles as presented by television.' It was not uncommon for children to point to Iceland or even Greenland when asked to indicate Ireland on a map so that other basic knowledge, such as the relative positions of Belfast and Dublin, were often welcome revelations to them. For example, one class of 9 to 10-year-olds 'really enjoyed the Wordsearch because they had heard of many of the places and were very enthusiastic about tracking them down in their printed maps and then in an atlas.' These children were also 'immediately fascinated by the division of Ireland' so that in this instance the geographical aspects dominated their work with cultural differences taking an obvious back seat. Other successful starting points included the cooking of Irish food, the making of Irish scrap books and the collecting of Irish 'memorabilia'.

The potential choice from this menu of Irish themes and topics was so great that no two teachers made identical selections. All chose varying aspects of Ireland's geography and many supplemented these with brief explorations of Celtic designs, Irish foods and products, Irish songs, Irish stories and/or heroes, while a few introduced Irish names, the Celts, St Patrick and the early Christians or an awareness of the great famine and Irish migration. The conclusions to these projects were as varied as their beginnings. Some ended with concerts or dramatic assemblies, while others concluded with a slide show about Ireland and once the pupils presented their own limericks to each other.

Most of these teachers tackled their work with considerable skill, dedication and imagination, but it was their limited objectives which ensured its classification at the basic level, which of course did not prevent many children from enjoying their Irish studies either. In general the children reported most favourably on those activities which excited their imaginations or required their active involvement. One boy of Asian origin, for example, 'enjoyed recording our songs and playing music to it. I also enjoyed making the potato cakes and I liked eating them.' For another 'the best thing was that you could bring in things from Ireland like postcards and money.' A girl concluded: 'Until I did the project I didn't know that I had so many things to do with Ireland at home. I like Ireland now.' Such responses echoed the relief of one teacher in another school, who had been 'quite apprehensive about embarking on a project on Ireland, taking into account the sensitive political nature of the subject. However, I was very pleased with the results and found the children's reactions very encouraging, e.g. no Irish jokes were heard throughout the term!'

A similar wariness influenced several other teachers to play for safety with rather limited approaches. In one 'monocultural' Dudley school, for example, the teacher of a class of 9 to 10-year-olds soon discovered that it contained two children of Irish parents who were 'extremely helpful with regard to up-to-date source information and objects for display', including maps, tourist booklets and a quantity of peat. However,

> both families did express concern about whether religion and politics were being included in the study and in how these were to be treated. And so she decided NOT to tackle religion, history or politics as she felt, as a non-Irish person, she was not competent to so do. Instead, she concentrated attention on Ireland's position in relation to the rest of the UK, its geography, stories and poems, songs and music.

Another teacher who reported that 'unfortunately there was no-one with Irish relatives' in her 9 to 10-year-old class 'did spend some time discussing the present troubles, but I must confess that I felt very wary of the subject and did not wish to get too involved.' Few pupils, of course, shared their teachers' sensibilities. An 11-year-old-boy, for example, declared that his topic had not been very interesting. 'We should have learned something about the terrorist activities in Ireland.' Nevertheless, such limited and cautious approaches to teaching about Ireland can have a strong impact on the children's attitudes, especially those in category A2. One of these, for example, pronounced at the end of her project that 'the Irish people are quite friendly I think.' Another concluded: 'I thought at first Ireland was full of violence, but it is not. It is calm and quiet and very nice.'

2 The Intermediate Level

The second or intermediate level of Irish studies was attained by teachers who explored the nature and consequences of Irish migration to Britain to develop the concepts of cultural diversity and pluralistic societies. Most made it additional to their basic study of Ireland, but a few tackled this level directly by undertaking such themes as movement or migration for their projects.

Such a dimension was essential for those schools with substantial proportions of Irish children because otherwise they would not appreciate that their own families were as concerned with these issues as those from other ethnic backgrounds. This was clearly the motivation of one Catholic school in Northampton.

> In view of the fact that a large percentage (up to 70%) of pupils is either first generation Irish or of recent Irish descent, it is judged that a good launching point for the appreciation of the multicultural society would be for the children first to understand their own roots or at least the roots of many of their peers.

In such classes many teachers adopted deliberate strategies to ensure that the non-Irish children became almost as interested in the Irish backgrounds of their friends as they were themselves, but the sensitive handling of some teachers did not end there. According to one from Bradford: 'The topic aroused a great deal of interest in all the children and many of the parents, who co-operated greatly in the work on "family trees". One "Indian" child and one "Greek" child were even encouraged and proud to do some work on their countries of origin, where previously they had been very reticent.' Other teachers identified isolated children in their classes with Polish, Italian or Jamaican backgrounds, which they were encouraged to research and report on to their peers. Another one extended the international coverage for her pupils by encouraging them to discover where their close relatives, such as uncles and aunts, were living.

In classes with few Irish children, some teachers made use of their backgrounds as an effective means of rousing the interest of the rest of the class, but others employed different manifestations of the Irish presence in Britain to demonstrate the relevance of the Irish dimension, for example, identifying Terry Wogan or other famous people as Irish. In one mainly Asian inner-city school in Coventry the teacher used the Victorian census returns to show that migrants from Ireland had once occupied their catchment area. In a similar inner-ring Birmingham school the teacher started by exposing the very negative perceptions of the Irish shared by her class, including one Pakistani child who 'thought that the word "Irish" was just a bad thing to call someone who is silly.' And so she started her project by inviting 'a few Irish people into my classroom to talk about themselves and their homeland. These were people whom the children know and respect and include our cook, a colleague and our local beat policeman' (Doyle, 1986). This phenomenon of cultural diversity among white people came as a blinding revelation to some children of Asian origin who had always assumed that it was confined exclusively to black and brown people.

The teaching-pack's booklet that described the experiences of Michael Davitt and his family as recent immigrants in Lancashire in the 1850s was used as an exercise in empathy by several teachers to explore the reasons for migration, to expose the consequent disorientation and isolation and to demonstrate how many Irish encountered in the past the sort of hostility experienced more recently by the Asian and Afro-Caribbean communities. It was generally a more effective trigger than discussions of the children's own experiences of moving to a new home or school. In one Coventry class of 85 per cent Asian parentage, the teacher used the Davitt account as a 'neutral' reference point to initiate a lengthy heartfelt discussion on the children's own experiences of migration. A similar approach with an exclusively 'white' class in Rugby turned into a rather different exercise. 'We finished the project by writing a letter home as an immigrant to France, telling our parents of the difficulties we encountered. Some of the "letters" were quite perceptive. Most commented on the need to speak the language, the different food and the lack of friends.'

Another teacher used the Davitt booklet as the starting point for a wide-ranging, but potentially less sensitive, discussion of those factors which are likely to divide an immigrant group from its host community: language, religion, personal and family names, food, clothes, songs, stories, history, games, links with their homeland, etc. Together they gave the pupils considerable insight into the demands placed upon the older adults who wanted to adjust or assimilate. They were also, of course, the main additional themes which teachers explored at this level in various different ways and combinations. Many teachers also exposed the existence of anti-Irish prejudice, most frequently in the form of Irish jokes, but at this intermediate level it was not studied in any meaningful way because those teachers who had begun to do so were operating at the advanced level.

3 The Advanced Level

(a) Racial prejudice

At the advanced level teachers confronted head-on important sensitive issues, usually in a direct attempt to alter children's attitudes. This approach was not advocated by the EEC project because of the very heavy demands it placed upon the teacher, its high risk of failure, its uncertain rewards and doubts in some instances of its appropriateness. Such apparent caution, however, was not accepted universally, especially by those involved in the implementation of deliberate anti-racist policies.

None of the few teachers who attempted to work at this level did so without considerable support and encouragement from their local multicultural education service. All tackled it as an integral part of work done at both the previous levels and not as isolated forays into anti-Irish racism, but they did attempt it in the relatively receptive environment of Catholic schools with mainly Irish children. In Bradford an adviser devised two Wordsearches on 'Ireland and the Irish' and 'England and the English', which together exposed various prejudices that were discussed at some length. They also enabled the teacher to introduce the idea of stereotypes and generalizations which precipitated a detailed examination of how the children might judge their relative accuracies. This exercise was concluded by the designing of posters to illustrate these problems of ethnic prejudice.

The same issues were tackled more thoroughly in two inner-city Catholic primary schools in Manchester. This work was designed by the city's Education Development Service as a prototype to help implement the LEA's policy of providing 'curriculum experience which meets the particular needs of ethnic minority children and offers an antidote to the racist practices of society for all children, by stressing the positive contribution of cultural diversity.' This initiative accepted the recommended sequence of proceeding from Ireland today to the Irish cultural heritage and the traumas of migration because 'the interweaving of expressive strands of Irishness throughout the work and the placing of the history *after* work on the present, came to be seen as the strengths of Irish Cultural Studies.' (Hankin, 1986). However, the pack's treatment of migration and prejudice was considered to be inadequate in Manchester so that additional material was introduced concerned directly with discrimination.

This Manchester approach incorporated simulation materials to provide a deeper understanding of why hardship drove people to emigrate and adapted ideas from world studies sources (*see* Hicks in this volume) to connect these impulses more overtly with the subsequent problems and resentment faced by all migrants. A further section was then composed to challenge stereotypes in the light of what the children had learned and 'where possible, to put the record straight.' It took anti-Irish jokes as its starting point to raise in whole-class discussions a number of controversial issues and to demonstrate that the denigration of the Irish through jokes and stereotypes went back over eight centuries. It then explored 'the effect of press coverage in larding images of violence onto those of dullness, the motivation behind terrorism and the assumptions behind "scientific racism".'

Since the children's attitudes were not assessed systematically both before and after their work, one can comment only generally upon its impact. Because few if any appear to have belonged to category A2 at the start, when many might have been classified as C or even D, opportunities for dramatic conversions were limited. Nevertheless, 'some change could reasonably be claimed as a result of this work.' The teachers reported on a new level of sophistication shown by the children in recognizing the propaganda aspect of newspaper 'information', on their perceptions of discrimination as a universal phenomenon that could be challenged and on the more explicit wording of their feelings. Furthermore, this project's impact was not just confined to the pupils who studied it because their enthusiasm aroused some interest in children from other classes, mainly in such cultural aspects as tin whistles and dancing. On the other hand, one sensitive teacher suspected that the intensity of her own commitment might have alienated some of her colleagues, especially some of the Irish-born who had been conspicuously unforthcoming with offers of help.

(b) Political conflict

The effect of the apprehension that many teachers felt about introducing a Northern Irish dimension has been discussed already and in one sense their desire for safety reflected the policy of the EEC project, which had argued that 'the Irish cultural heritage would be diminished and distorted if it were presented predominantly as a political one generating conflict with Britain.' It had therefore suggested that Northern Ireland's troubles should be raised only as relatively simple factual answers to whatever questions were posed by the children and that initially they should be given a more positive perception of the Irish cultural inheritance.

Not all teachers, however, shared these views. A teacher-adviser for the Wolverhampton Multi-cultural Education Service, for example, produced materials for use in local schools on the Norman settlement and Cromwell in Ireland because, although 'the current situation in Ireland is seen by many teachers as presenting almost insurmountable difficulties, it is my contention that a greater understanding of the background to the Irish "problem" can only prove beneficial to an appreciation of the "problem" and create a more harmonious situation.' And yet none of his materials covered the more recent historical developments nor the current situation.

The Manchester Educational Development Service argued similarly, but perhaps more coherently, that the Irish are prisoners of their history, that a sense of historical grievance was a central component of Irish identity and that Britain's imperial and colonialist past was a source of persistent racist attitudes. They therefore attempted to account for Ireland's domination by England from a non-Anglocentric viewpoint, including the traditional nationalist view that the great famine had mainly political rather than economic causes, but unfortunately 'in practice, reference to these later events in the classroom work as a way of making sense of the current state of affairs, was more tenuous than convincing. As the turn of events after Cromwell grows more complex and brutalized, so the connections that were made became more simplistic.' (Hankin, 1986). Perhaps this failure to explore adequately the current political scene stemmed from the Manchester initiative's attempt to open up too many fronts simultaneously in its Irish studies' campaign.

Of all the different approaches to teaching Irish studies that were reported, only one experienced and knowledgeable London teacher tackled the Northern Irish question in a direct child–centred fashion and as one aspect of a very wide-ranging project. 'After a great deal of discussion on many of the current issues affecting Ireland, the children attempted to empathize with different Irish people by writing accounts from different standpoints.' (Parkinson, 1986). These included days in the lives of a Belfast child, a Scottish soldier, a hunger striker and an Orangeman.

Clearly any such study of the current Northern Irish situation is attempting to operate at the very least at an advanced level, but vital though it is for British children to become better informed about the issues at stake and about the origins of this conflict, there are possible demarcation problems. Although these issues are clearly germane to the world of multicultural education, they are potentially even more an integral part of the children's political education and so should arguably be planned as such.

Conclusion

An increasing corpus of material and expertise is being built up to sustain the successful teaching of aspects of Irish studies in junior schools at both basic and intermediate levels, although there is still room for considerable further development. But teachers who want to tackle the more advanced levels of anti-Irish prejudice and political conflict will find fewer appropriate child-centred materials and much less guidance on alternative strategies on which they can draw. And so Irish studies at an advanced level in junior schools is currently not a viable proposition for any but the most talented, dedicated and knowledgeable teachers. Before it can happen a systematic appraisal appears to be needed of the experiences of those teachers who have attempted such advanced work as the preliminary stage for the development of appropriate materials and strategies, which should also be related to some assessment of the pupils' prior knowledge and attitudes.

Contrary to the precepts of some advocates of anti-racist education, it does seem evident that the steep and craggy peaks of Irish studies cannot be scaled properly without first establishing a base camp in the foothills and then consolidating the intermediate slopes. Alternative attempts to tackle anti-Irish prejudice and political conflict directly would appear to resemble much more attempts to drop climbers from a helicopter on to those slopes nearest to the mountain-top. Even if the climbers reached it successfully from there, they would acquire only a very limited perception of the mountain that they had conquered. By contrast, many of those who walked on the lower slopes without a sense of stress or danger may have absorbed a much clearer view of the mountain range, including its snow-covered peaks.

Note

Various letters and informal reports submitted by individual teachers have been the source for most of the quotations in this chapter.

References

ARKELL, T. (1982a) 'Report to EEC on the pilot project in 1981 on the development of Irish Cultural Studies', *Compass*, 3, 1, 1–7.

ARKELL, T. (1982b) 'Some reflections on the teaching of politically sensitive Irish history to English children', DES Conference: *The teaching of politically sensitive issues with particular reference to Irish history*, Bournemouth.

ARKELL, T. (1984) 'Introducing Irish Cultural Studies to the English primary school', *Irish Educational Studies*, 4, 2, 119–132.

ARKELL, T. (ed.) (1988) *Irish Cultural Studies: a teaching pack*, Stoke, Trentham Books.

COSGRAVE, A. (ed.) (1984) *Learning from Diversity: a challenge for Catholic education: Report of the Working Party on Education in a Multicultural Society*, London, Catholic Media Office.

DOYLE, M. (1986) 'A primary school "Irish project"', *Multicultural Education Review*, 6, 18–20.

EGAN, O. (1977) 'Affective development in adolescent conceptions of Ireland', *Irish Journal of Education*, 11, 2, 61–73.

HANKIN, L. (1986) *The Irish Dimension in the Education of Manchester Schoolchildren*, MEd dissertation, University of Manchester.

JACKSON, J. (1963) *The Irish in Britain*, London, Routledge and Kegan Paul.

LENNON, M. *et al.* (eds) (1988) *Across the Water: Irish women's lives in Britain*, London, Virago.

O'CONNOR, K. (1972) *The Irish in Britain*, London, Sidgwick and Jackson.

O'DONOVAN, I. (1985) 'An interactive model of immigrant adjustment applied to the Irish in Britain', in DANAHER, N. (ed.) *Irish Dimensions in British Education: Report on 2nd National Conference*, Leicester, Soar Valley College, 13–16.

PALMER, C. and RUDDELL, D. (1988) 'The Irish Dimension: Essential concern or red herring?', *Multicultural Education Review*, 8, 11–17.

PARKINSON, A. (1986) *Ireland in the Primary Classroom*, Report, Henry Fawcett Junior Mixed School, Kennington, London.

Part Five
Assessment

Chapter 13

Process, Content and Assessment in Primary Humanities

Alan Blyth

Introduction

Assessment is a powerful incentive to clear thinking about curriculum. It obliges teachers and administrators to ask just what they regard as essential and what they consider peripheral, in primary humanities as elsewhere in the curriculum. This chapter will set out some general principles of assessment in primary humanities appropriate to an enabling curriculum (Blyth, 1984), so that emphasis will be placed first on aspects of children's development and then, secondarily, on the content of what is learned. At the end, a few observations will be hazarded about the way in which these proposals might be accommodated within the framework of a national curriculum.

The Basis of Assessment

Reasons for Assessing Primary Humanities

The most immediate reason why assessment should be undertaken is that it will be compulsory. Legal obligation concentrates the mind wonderfully, especially when it becomes evident that protest is pointless; but it leaves the justification of human action at a rather pedestrian level. To find more adequate reasons for assessment, reasons which can clothe legal duty and a sense of public obligation with more thoughtful support, it is necessary to look for some argument that the need for assessment is essential to the process of education itself. In fact, there are two such arguments.

The first of these is a matter of professional conscience. It might be possible to teach on the assumption that educational pearls should be broadcast without much concern about whether anybody picked them up, or about what was done with the pearls after they had been picked up; that, after all, is what happens in the case of some public lectures. But in the case of primary education, somebody is paying and expects accountability. Despite contrary myths, few primary teachers would expect to remain unconcerned about their pupils' response, and many are very vigilant about individual progress; their consciences would not allow them to do otherwise. Their concern is not so much about whether pupil assessment is important, but about how to do it and how to find time and opportunity to do it.

The second reason why assessment is necessary to education is rather different in nature. It is related to children's growing capacity for self-awareness, which is itself usually regarded as an important aspect of personal/social education. One way of imparting fine tuning to this growing capacity is by considering, as children do, the opinions that teachers, parents, peers, and other adults in the community hold about them. Within this set of 'significant others', teachers hold a special position as the official representatives of public notions of standards of behaviour and achievement, and as such contribute uniquely to the formation of children's self-portraits, even when those self-portraits involve the rejection of conventional values.

Both of these justifications of assessment relate to the curriculum as a whole. It is, however, quite common practice to maintain that global cross-curricular assessment is all that is needed, or practicable, or perhaps more frequently that specific detailed assessment should be confined to literacy and numeracy, Alexander's traditional Curriculum I, for example, (Alexander, 1984), now perhaps with the addition of science, and with a few other spasmodic observations. In such a view, humanities occupies no recognizable place. Even when specific attention is given to some other aspects of curriculum such as art, music or P.E., humanities may still be omitted or concealed under a heading such as topic work. The reasons for this relative ignoring of primary humanities in assessment programmes is partly explicable in that humanities shares so much with every other aspect of curriculum that its independent claims can be virtually overlooked, as was the case when no less a body than the Assessment of Performance Unit drew up its list of six areas of experience (Gipps and Goldstein, 1983; Blyth, 1987). So it is necessary to re-assert the claims of humanities to represent ways of understanding that, however much they may have in common with other approaches, exist in their own right and cannot be subsumed under other convenient umbrellas. For learning about human society, past and present, as it is found on the face of the earth is not the same as language or science, mathematics or technology, the arts, physical development, or even moral and religious education, and is just as important to a full primary education. If the place of humanities in the primary curriculum is to be assured, its place in primary assessment should also be given particular scrutiny.

There is a different point of view on this issue which, while equally exercised to prevent the partition of humanities among other concerns, believes that it is separate subjects in the humanities sphere, particularly history and geography, that should be the focus of assessment. In this view, the designation 'humanities' is itself nebulous and potentially insidious, and the possibility of assessment across the whole humanities doubtful and indeed little improvement on cross-curricular assessment itself. An adaptation of this view, less sceptical about the integrity of humanities but emerging on grounds of realism, is that, if necessary, assessment should be enacted on a subject basis, to secure something on behalf of humanities, on the grounds that half a loaf of assessment within humanities would be better than none at all. This point of view, especially in this modified, pragmatic, version, is one that deserves sympathetic understanding, provided that it is recognized that a strong case can be made for a more thorough-going assessment policy for humanities as a whole, one that could prevail if assessment as a whole is based on professional insight and experience rather than solely in response to legal requirements and political pressures.

Such a policy is necessarily related to a theory of curriculum. Where this is based on a radical, unstructured, child-centred approach, assessment in humanities could be a contradiction of the basic rationale of curriculum. Where it is based on a genuine belief that the forms of understanding represented within humanities can be expressed in the primary curriculum only through the medium of subject studies, then assessment would follow suit, as has just been indicated. The theory on which the present chapter is based, that of an enabling curriculum, shares something with each of these views but also differs from both of them. It is necessary next to indicate the place of humanities within an enabling curriculum.

Humanities in an Enabling Curriculum: the Primacy of Process

The essence of an enabling curriculum is that it is grounded in children's development and experience, and that teachers intervene in the interaction between development and experience in order to extend children's potential, and to take some, though not paramount, notice of the proclaimed needs of society. In effecting that intervention, teachers are necessarily guided by the organized forms of understanding that we term, in the school context, 'subjects', and at a more scholarly level, 'disciplines', for these are the cumulative though adaptable tools developed by men and women through the ages, and particularly in recent times, for the understanding and modification of our world. In a curriculum conceived on this basis, the emphasis in children's educational experience moves, as they grow from the nursery and infant years towards upper primary education, from the subjective to the relatively objective. Curriculum, initially conceived in terms of movement, expression, communication, exploration and behaviour, comes to be designated through broadly objective formulations such as P.E., the expressive arts, the world of nature, language, number, moral and religious education, and humanities. Gradually, these broad areas of curricular experience become differentiated into something more akin to subjects, until in secondary education subjects reach a central significance, though their inter-relationship should never be forgotten. In such a curriculum, at the primary level, the main emphasis must be on developmental processes; that is, on the acquisition and extension of skills, concepts, attitudes, and what will be described later as task procedures, necessary for purposive introduction to the different ways of understanding that subjects represent. For children in primary education, it is more important to think as historians think than to know what historians know. Thus, almost by definition, humanities holds a firm place in an enabling curriculum, for the thinking that historians do, and geographers and economists and sociologists, anthropologists and psychologists and political scientists too, represents when adapted to children's thinking and experience a part of their entitlement which nobody else can give.

The way in which humanities can figure in this kind of primary curriculum may be illustrated from two examples; one, of a six-year-old class following a topic on weather, and the other, of a third-year junior class considering road-making. Incidentally, both topics abut on the 'programme of study' now suggested for primary science in the National Curriculum (DES and Welsh Office, 1988): a relevant, though not a decisive, justification for their inclusion. How they may relate to the programmes yet to be devised for history and geography remains to be seen; this is an issue touched upon at the end of this chapter.

The teacher of the six-year-olds chose weather partly from custom and partly through making a virtue of the necessity of coping with wet playtimes and soggy clothing. Following a general awakening of interest in the topic, she detailed some children to devise a big chart with suitable symbols to show a weekly record of the observations, and everybody to paint different kinds of weather, to hear and write stories about weather in different places and times, to notice how kinds of weather such as south-west winds and mild, rainy days go together, to make up poems and songs and a dance about weather, then perhaps a rain-making ceremony and so the work might develop imaginatively, with scant concern for subjects and their boundaries as such, but with the central concerns of humanities in there with the rest, and with an emphasis on enabling and fostering different kinds of understanding and experience.

Meanwhile the nine-year-old road-makers have moved further towards differentiation of those forms of understanding and experience. Their teacher has aroused their interest by means of a visit to a road-widening site, and has then spun a topic web, selecting from it the aspects that seemed appropriate for her class and that appeared to evoke a response when the children gathered round to discuss it. Some have used library resources to find a little about how the first roads were made, and why; what surfaces Roman road-builders used; how medieval communities maintained their roads; and how modern road construction has developed; always with an emphasis on real people and how they lived in their own times. Others have looked at roads in cities and forests and deserts and across mountains, in affluent lands and in those with scant resources, again with an eye to the people who make and use the roads. Still others have followed up the road-widening operation to consider the planning of a by-pass, what it might cost, how the money could be raised, who might build it, and what impact it might make on local communities. Thus, although technology figures prominently in this work, and other aspects of curriculum continue to be involved, the human perspectives of history, geography, economics and sociology are more clearly brought to bear on the topic now than was the case among the six-year-olds, and attention is paid to their systematic and progressive development from year to year. Moreover, as part of their enablement, these children are becoming more able to handle ideas for themselves, and to see themselves doing so, thus learning a kind of metacognitive self-awareness that constitutes an essential step towards realistic self-assessment.

Humanities in an Enabling Curriculum: the Place of Content

It is sometimes believed, by both supporters and opponents of an enabling approach to curriculum, that in such a curriculum no notice will be taken of the actual content of what is taught and learned. Therefore some definition of the relation between process and content must be attempted, as Harlen (1985) did in the case of primary science. Incidentally, her analysis illuminates some of the epistemological differences between science and humanities and therefore some indication of the need for each to be separately represented in the primary curriculum.

The first kind of importance of content is as the material on which aspects of process such as skills and concepts are developed. In craft, design and technology it is impossible to learn to handle tools without something to work on; and the same is true of humanities. Moreover, the more attention is focused on the thorough understanding of content, the more effectively skills and concepts are likely to be acquired. In the examples of weather and road-making already cited, attention would be focused on knowing what the weather actually was on Tuesday morning, in order to practise the skill of observation and expression, and also on the detail of an actual narrative of road-building, so that the problems could be understood. In neither instance would there be a case for superficiality or carelessness in learning content; yet when compared with all the possible content that could be learned, this amount is trivial and, in any terms except those of process development, arbitrary.

It is, therefore, necessary to consider whether there might also be some kinds of content that require admission to primary humanities in their own right, in addition to any value that they may have as vehicles for process development. One claimant for inclusion in such a list would be the locality of a school, its physical characteristics, its human past, and the multifarious lives of the people in the community, for this topic must have significance for all children. Other possibilities for inclusion are family life and community health, the latter in conjunction with aspects of primary science. But in addition to these aspects of content that occupy, as it were, the educational foreground, there is a case for building up, progressively, what might be termed the backcloth of humanities. This would comprise awareness of the major epochs of Western history, progressively set in a still wider context, so that terms such as Iron Age and Roman and Elizabethan would come into play, related to time-charts used regularly. It would also, simultaneously, include reference to the major continents and oceans and to place-location in relation to them, again with regular use of globe and atlas. In this way the 'shape' of human society in place and time would gradually become established. This is as far as systematic knowledge of the past and present of human society should be expected to go during primary education, in a curriculum that gives priority to process. More systematic study of sequential content in history and of substantive geography would follow in secondary schools. But the other aspects of content already mentioned should figure in any strategy of assessment at the primary stage.

Procedures for Assessment

There is a range of procedures suitable for assessment of process and content in an enabling curriculum. Since it is necessary to emphasize children's acquired capacities and understandings rather than their factual knowledge, emphasis should be laid on the monitoring of normal classroom and outdoor activities rather than on formal testing. Therefore everyday observation, which is bound to loom large in nursery and infant education, remains important at every age-level. Such observation should however be systematic, not just casual or random, and could well be designated *appraisal*, the term devised by Tough for a slightly different purpose (Tough, 1979) leaving *assessment* as the designation for something more formal and additional to the daily round. Appraisal can consist of systematically watching children at work, or of making purposive comments on their topic books or artwork, or of initiating discussions with small groups, perhaps with the use of audio-tapes which can be briefly analyzed afterwards. To use the now familiar terminology (e.g. Shipman, 1983), appraisal is almost certain to be more diagnostic and formative than summative in character, more concerned with locating children's difficulties and with estimating their potential than with recording their specific achievements, however important those may be. Appraisal is also more likely to be criterion-referenced (concerned with the capacity to undertake a task successfully) than norm-referenced (comparing a child's performance on a task with that of other children in the class or the nation). It may also be self-referenced, that is, based on comparison with the child's own previous achievements, which is itself a useful means of promoting self-assessment. The whole purpose behind this diagnostic, formative, criterion-referenced approach, with its emphasis on appraisal rather than assessment, is to develop individual excellence; ironically, that is also the aim of those who advocate an opposite style of assessment.

There is also some place for summative assessment of a more formal nature, especially at the culmination of a topic, to find out just how much each individual has gained from what has been going on. Pencil-and-paper testing of an amusing and provocative kind has its value with older and verbally capable children, and has the advantage that every child is exposed to assessment as inescapably as a horn-player in an orchestra. Much more fruitful information, at all age-levels and ranges of capacity, can be derived from small-group discussions, perhaps taped, along the lines already indicated. It is however imperative that these should be planned in such a way as to ensure that individuals are still suitably exposed, and that each contributes significantly to the discussion, rather than leaving the more articulate, bright-eyed ones to cover for them in assessment — as indeed they may well have done in the work itself, which makes exposure in assessment all the more necessary. Such discussions may have to be conducted in corners while the rest of the class is engaged in other work, not necessarily in humanities: other parts of the curriculum would receive reciprocal treatment. Recently, suggestions have been made for other forms of systematic summative assessment, such as Duncan and Dunn's proposed 'assessment activities' (Duncan and Dunn, 1988), in which it is the children being assessed who are temporarily removed from the teacher's field of action while they carry out tasks designed to show how much of the work they have mastered, after which they present the outcome to the teacher. Such activities do, like pencil-and-paper tests, make considerable demands on younger and less able children, but they have the advantage of directly promoting self-assessment. Their relevance to the National Curriculum will be mentioned later.

A Model of Learning

In order to apply assessment procedures meaningfully, it is necessary to postulate a model of learning. The one used here is a very simple one, though similar to what many teachers' groups and LEAs use. It envisages human learning as an irregular and spasmodic progression from complete ignorance or incapacity to a point of mastery at which learning has become totally internalized and can be mobilized and applied for other purposes. One or more stages may intervene between these two extremes. For example, in the case of a specific skill such as learning to ride a bicycle, the starting stage would be: Falls off every time; the final stage might be: Takes part in sponsored events as though born in the saddle. The intervening stages could be sketched in by anybody who has learned, or has watched others learn, how to ride a cycle. The same principle could be applied to learning in primary humanities. Suppose a class is looking at how the city of Sydney celebrated the (white) bicentennial. One child asks whether the people who founded New South Wales met dinosaurs there, and is not quite sure if there is any difference between Australia and Austria. Another, unprompted, and with no intention of appearing priggish, refers easily to the Harbour Bridge and Bondi Beach and points out that the United States had become independent not long before the first landings at Botany Bay. One of the two has quite a lot of learning to do; so, in fact, has the other. In this model of learning, it becomes possible to envisage the stages in skills and concepts through which each is likely to pass as that learning takes place, though nobody can be quite sure how, when, or indeed whether that learning will take place. Occasionally, most of it happens in a short spurt in response to some surge of interest or encouragement or necessity.

In this chapter, emphasis will be laid on the nature of assessment in primary humanities, in the light of the foregoing considerations. Space does not permit more than brief references to actual tests or other procedures; I hope to be able to amplify these references with examples in a further publication (Blyth, 1989). The following suggestions embody the principles on which more detailed suggestions can be grounded.

Assessment of Process

(a) Skills

Attempts have often been made, for example by local teachers' groups, to list the actual skills necessary in an enabling curriculum, and there is quite a high measure of agreement about what they are. First, there are clearly a few notational and representational skills that must be taught and assessed because they constitute the basic grammar of humanities. These include the use of maps and the globe, the habitual dating of events in relation to the conventional time-scale, the presentation of social data in graphical form, skills of data-collection and referencing, including accessing databanks, and communication skills. Study skills, information skills (Wray, 1985), and those involved in geographical observation and recording and in social and economic data collection through such procedures as questionnaire construction and interviewing, are more demanding and develop later. As for higher-order thinking skills, including the formulation and testing of hypotheses and generalizations in the fields of human society, the making of judgments on partial evidence, and the toleration of ambiguity, they necessarily depend both on language development and on a kind of personal maturity and stability.

Some at least of these skills are open to formal testing; all can figure in appraisal. In general it can be said that the notational and representational skills are the easiest to assess, and that the more sophisticated skills must depend more on the outcome of regular monitoring of children's work, supplemented by incidental questioning and discussion, closely matching, in my experience, the way in which the learning and teaching is conducted. There is certainly no place for the view that the learning, and assessment, of process skills in primary humanities is a trivial or inconsequential matter.

(b) Concepts

Concepts are more difficult to classify, or even to define. They include categorical concepts such as place and time, and methodological concepts including similarity/difference, continuity/change, and the relation between causes and outcomes. These general concepts are necessary to humanities, but are relevant to this curricular area in distinctive ways. The same is true of the major substantive ideas that facilitate understanding in humanities as a whole, such as the four selected by the Schools Council Project *Place, time and society 8–13* (Blyth *et al.* 1976) – communication, power, values and beliefs in society, and conflict/consensus – and others such as interdependence and hierarchy. These are not intended to constitute actual content, for they are the kinds of general key concepts that individuals build up over a long period of time, but children can be pointed towards these ideas if teachers, who have mastered them, use them in the selection and organization of the content that they offer. At a more modest level, however, there are specific concepts such as price, location, empire, tribe, and desert which can and should figure centrally in topics in primary humanities at different age-levels. Children's understanding of these specific concepts can be appraised by how they are regularly used without direct prompting. This can be more formally assessed through questioning, sentence-completion or absurdities tests, all of which require a grasp of the concept for their successful performance. Some indication of how such procedures could be applied can be derived from devices such as the Gunning/Wilson 'concept ladder' (Gunning, Gunning and Wilson, 1981) with its intimations of how concept development can take place. I have elsewhere given some indication of how these procedures might be worked out in the field of primary industry education. (Blyth, 1988)

(c) Attitudes

The assessment of attitudes presents still more difficulties, so much so that LEAs and others, while emphasizing the importance of including attitude modification among the aims of primary humanities, avoid trying to assess the impact of curriculum on attitudes. Even the Task Group on Assessment and Testing, whose main Report (TGAT, 1988) has set the pattern for the national assessment programme (see pp. 230–32) fought shy of prescribing attitude assessment.

One reason for this reticence is that attitudes are themselves so controversial. These are matters on which adult opinion is either sharply divided or numbed by complexity. Teachers themselves may hold strong views, yet try to offset those views by attempting to introduce 'balance' and in the process offending everybody, not least because they may seem to imply that every issue can be reduced to a compromise between right and wrong. So it is small wonder if a teacher, faced with such dilemmas, declines to compound her difficulties by attempting to appraise or assess children's responses.

Even if she did, the children's responses might be a poor indication of what their attitudes really were. For one thing, their views could well be based on an amalgam of adult opinions, themselves far from uniform, with their own experiences of primitive playground justice divorced from the subtleties of what Furth has categorized as 'the world of grown-ups' (Furth, 1980). For another, they might not know their own attitudes, since these can be maintained at a pre-conscious level. Again, being partly aware of the sensitivity of these issues, they may regard the expression of attitudes in school almost automatically as a matter for tactical negotiation, one on which it seems prudent today to give soulful endorsement to what they think are the teacher's preferred views, while tomorrow they will tease her by pretending to hold the very views that they think she detests. The relationship of such tactical moves to their real attitudes must remain problematical; and those real attitudes, if indeed they exist and are genuinely expressed, may still not bear a close relationship to their actual behaviour, as those experienced in moral and religious education well know.

Yet there are other, more specific, attitudes that are more open to appraisal and assessment. One of these is the readiness to make serious studies in humanities rather than to accept other people's views without scrutiny; this 'task attitude' is open to systematic observation and may, incidentally, pave the way for attitude change of a more fundamental kind. A discussion on the theme of 'How could we set about learning more about . . . ?' can give some indication of the success with which task attitudes are being developed. As will be seen, that development is closely related also to the evolution of task procedures. The development of empathy, (*see* Little, Chapter 3) with its blend of cognitive and affective elements, is another element open to fairly reliable appraisal. It is possible to detect the degree of accurate imagination with which children can take the role of an improving landlord in a simulation located in the days of enclosure, or of a miner on the Rand today, sensitive though these roles inevitably are. Finally, attitudes can be modified, and their modification appraised, as a result of some particular curricular experience that may help to convince them that, for example, not all factories are dirty or noisy, nor all bureaucrats high-handed and hard-hearted.

(d) Task Procedures

By comparison, task procedures are relatively open to observation and even to formal assessment. Duncan and Dunn (1988), in the work already mentioned, emphasize the value of encouraging children to deploy skills and concepts in their own way, which is necessarily linked with the task attitudes already mentioned and is an important component in the development of self-assessment. Task procedures require some prior mastery of skills and concepts, and so figure in the upper primary years rather than before. They can best be assessed by seeing how children respond to challenges to plan, individually or in pairs or groups, such imaginary but real-world ventures as a journey to Los Angeles, a camping holiday in Sweden, a study of a historical building in the vicinity, or the submission of a serious proposal for the development of a patch of waste land beyond the schools' perimeter fence. All of these require the deployment of a range of skills and understanding which, taken in combination, reveal tellingly the extent to which understanding in humanities has developed. Of some ten-year-olds it could be said that their grasp of task procedures, in humanities and elsewhere, is impressive. Sadly, this is often overlooked when they proceed to secondary education and it is hoped that the growing concern about continuity between phases in the educational system will help to remedy this unintended indifference. It could well be that the emphasis on profiling and individual course work for GCSE will hasten this change, since secondary teachers may find it very useful to know how far pupils from primary schools are already consciously able to show self-directed initiative of the kind that task procedures embody.

(e) The Importance of Transfer

In any learning of skills, concepts, attitudes and task procedures, there is a sequence that corresponds to the model of learning previously outlined. The first step beyond total ignorance or incapacity is to learn something, however elementary, diligently and then to be able to recall or replicate it. Thus in any piece of assessment there will be some instances of simple recall, using skills and concepts as they were used in the original work itself. Questions after a visit to a canal are about that canal. But there comes a stage at which the learning to be assessed moves beyond simple recall. The next step towards mastery consists of using the skill or concept or procedure in a similar but not identical situation. For example, the issues encountered in visiting a fruit farm might tap skills such as observation and sketching and concepts including that of frost drainage. Subsequently, assessment would probe children's capacity to apply that concept to other farms, and then more widely to the nature of physical controls in agriculture and elsewhere. Mastery would be reached when such considerations could be summoned up effortlessly on the screen of organized memory when some agricultural issue is discussed. Probably mastery of that kind would, or should, be an end-product of secondary rather than of primary education; but an enabling curriculum in primary education can be designed in such a way as to move children some way towards effective transfer, and any programme of appraisal and assessment should be designed in such a way as to take special note of the ability to effect transfer.

Assessment of Content

Just as content occupies a minor but significant part in humanities in an enabling curriculum, so it should have a minor but established place in assessment. Traditionally, content has been assessed by recalling factual material through summative testing, and that is quite defensible provided that it is applied to suitable subject-matter. It is through assessment of this nature that learning of content is reinforced. This applies both to the closely articulated content involved in particular schemes of work, and to information about the relation of particular events to the place-time matrix that is intended to become part of children's background knowledge. It also concerns knowledge of the locality, a field in which it is possible not only to make systematic appraisals at various age-levels, but also to devise exciting and amusing assessment procedures for use at various age-levels, based on verbal, visual and computer-based stimulus material. Indeed, children can devise their own materials to test each other, thus further developing a capacity for self- and mutual assessment. It is then the teacher's function to ensure that, in the spirit of an enabling curriculum, knowledge of local content does not deteriorate into parish-pump or antiquarian interests or into mere quiz-making, but retains elements that can be built on as a basis for comparisons in place, time and society.

Of course, assessment of content soon leads to process considerations too. Questions in the form of 'Why, do you think, . . . ?' and 'What is the most likely reason for . . . ?' will soon be encountered, and these involve the practice of higher-order thinking skills. Similarly, it is impossible to verify understanding of particular events in place and time without practising the categorical and perhaps other skills involved in locating them in the record. Even apparently factual questions may require more interpretation than at first sight appears necessary: it is not possible to answer the question 'Which is the nearest town to X?' without first deciding what counts as a town, and why.

Individual Children: Baselining and Record Keeping

Assessment remains patchy and of limited value unless it forms part of a programme of record keeping that follows the fortunes of individual children in humanities and other work throughout primary education. Even within a year, the memory of any teacher, however sensitive or devoted, becomes less reliable as new events flood in, so that some regular written record becomes essential.

Most public systems of record keeping have little place for humanities, so that it becomes necessary to devise a system. Often, attempts to do so are based on something like the model of learning discussed in the present chapter, involving a matrix in which children's movement towards mastery of specified skills and concepts (usually those) is tracked by various devices (e.g. Cooper, 1976). This approach has much to commend it, but there are two drawbacks. First, the combination of effort and monotony involved may deter teachers from persevering with it. Second, it assumes that the skills and concepts can be determined in advance. It is, however, possible to devise another approach, within the framework of an enabling curriculum and using the same model of learning, which avoids those drawbacks and also allows more adequately for individual differences in amount and rate of learning. For its effective use it requires the adoption of a procedure that may be termed *baselining*.

Baselining is simply a strategy of discovering where individual children are at, before embarking on a scheme of work. In the case of the Sydney bicentennial discussed previously, it would be pointless to proceed to any kind of assessment or record keeping without taking note of the huge gap in knowledge and understanding between the two children in the example. The teaching strategy envisaged by the teacher would itself require this; her assessment strategy would render it all the more essential. In practice, the need is to set before each child a challenge that is realistically within his or her grasp, even though, as in a handicap race, the course run by one child is quite different from the one followed by another. Where the journey towards mastery of an essential idea has only just begun, the emphasis would be on recall at first and then on a little transfer; where mastery already exists, it should be used in a new challenge. Everybody's baseline is different; everybody still moves forward rather than stagnating or trying what is temporarily impossible. That does not mean that children must work on their own, as was long ago the practice in the Dalton Plan; rather, there is a challenge to a teacher to use widely varying skills and attainments in mutual assistance towards the common class goal. Appraisal and assessment are then designed to monitor each child's movement towards his or her next step, and their contribution to the work as a whole, rather than to concentrate on common pieces of learning with norm–referenced overtones.

If this baselining strategy is used, then record keeping can take it quite simply into account. Before a piece of work is begun, a teacher would make a very simple forecast of how each child in a class — it must be *each* child — would be expected to develop as a result of the topic concerned. This is not the same as laying down precise or predetermined objectives; indeed, one of the outcomes sought might be an opportunity to exercise judgment in altering the scheme of work as it proceeded. Then the necessary record keeping would simply take the form of noting whether each child had developed as expected. To save effort, there would be no need to record instances in which expectations were reasonably fulfilled. But where an individual fell short of expectations, or exceeded them, or developed in quite unexpected ways such as the emergence of new interests or enthusiasms or aversions, would be recorded. The procedure might indeed be called *deviation recording*. At the end of a term, such comments might be consolidated into a record of positive achievement: negative observations should not be included, and indeed would add little of importance. At the end of a year, when records are handed on to another teacher or another school, the consolidation of comments on humanities should certainly take place, and should be taken into account by the new 'management'. This strategy, based on the notions of baselining and deviation, would provide the essential minimum of record keeping required, and should not prove onerous. Adapted for use in other aspects of curriculum, it could become a habitual part of a teacher's professional life.

Of course it could be extended into something more sophisticated, but the first step would be to establish record keeping at this unambitious level. To do even that would involve a sustained initiative to ensure inclusion of an element on assessment and record keeping in programmes of initial and inservice teacher education and staff development, for these, too, are skills to be learned, and teachers themselves need encouragement to move along their own curve from incapacity to mastery.

Adjustment to the National Curriculum

The whole future of curriculum and assessment in primary humanities must now be considered in the light of the proposals enshrined in the Education Reform Act, 1988, and of the Circulars and Memoranda which will follow. The language in which public policy on these matters has hitherto been couched suggests a reversal of the priorities expressed in this chapter, for the emphasis is apparently on content rather than process and on summative rather than formative assessment. However, the main framework of the National Curriculum itself need not be in conflict with the principles of an enabling curriculum; indeed, an agreed set of skills and concepts could represent a common path for schools across the country, though any attempt to impose common content could raise more difficulties. At least it appears that humanities is likely to be represented in the primary curriculum, through history and geography as foundation, although not core, subjects, and through the attention to be paid to multicultural issues and to economic awareness.

A little more can be said about prospects for assessment, and that little is encouraging, now that it seems that the proposals made by the Task Group on Assessment and Testing (TGAT, 1988) are likely to be substantially implemented. Their Report is, by common consent, an ingenious blend of flexibility in assessment with the requirements of national accountability. The basic strategy recommended in the Report is the development of a series of profile components that will be centred on the three core subjects of language, mathematics and science (perhaps with technology) but will range more widely, and may merge and diverge between age-levels. To comply with the statutory requirement for assessment at seven and eleven as well as at fourteen and sixteen, a bank of standard assessment tasks, somewhat akin to Duncan and Dunn's 'assessment activities' previously mentioned (Duncan and Dunn, 1988), is to be compiled in order to monitor progression through the profile components, with a limited range at seven and a little more at eleven. Progress within profile components is to be expressed in terms of ten levels of achievement, to be considered primarily as criterion-referenced landmarks for children rather than as norm-referenced data for comparisons between pupils and schools. In addition to all of this, a substantial component in the total assessment programme will consist of teachers' own appraisals, moderated across schools in an area by LEA advisers working under the aegis of HMI. There have, of course, been substantial criticisms of these proposals, but much is hoped from them.

In those proposals, little is actually said about primary humanities. In general terms that is unimportant, for they allow, within teacher-led appraisal, for the continuance of practice along the lines advocated in this chapter. In practice, the position may prove more worrying, for three reasons.

The first might be termed the 'plaster' reason. Breakneck priority is being given to establishing curriculum and assessment in the core subjects, so that the styles and modes of assessment proper to language, mathematics and science (when these are eventually agreed, are likely to set like plaster, providing a template to which assessment in other forms of understanding must conform. The priority of core subjects in the establishment of profile components may accentuate this tendency. The second reason may derive from the first, for it might well happen that one consequence of the need for haste and economy would be the almost perfunctory inclusion of some material with a historical or geographical or social flavour within the core components, after which the assumption would be allowed to take root that humanities had now been catered for. This, the 'incorporation' danger, with its echoes of the earlier APU strategy, constitutes the second reason for anxiety, all the more so because it seems likely that the APU itself may again be called upon to take part in the strategy that is taking shape. The final danger could be designated the 'exhaustion' reason, through which teachers simply feel unable to do anything about assessment in humanities when they have to undertake so much else. This is not intended as a criticism of the TGAT Report, but it is meant to indict the combination of manipulation and haste with which these matters appear to be conducted.

So this is a time when the future of assessment of process and content in primary humanities is uncertain and the prospect not entirely reassuring. It is also a time when all concerned need to co-operate to ensure the design of procedures that are practicable, meaningful, compatible not only with their own curricular principles but also with the requirements of the national programme that will come into being. This will not be easy. It will depend on an effort of mutual support by teachers, advisers, and staffs from institutions of higher education, themselves beleaguered by financial and administrative pressures. I am endeavouring to play some part in this process through chapters such as this and through a forthcoming book intended to make fuller and more specific suggestions (Blyth, 1989). It is possible that these co-operative efforts could be linked in practice with the local cross-moderation of teachers' appraisals advocated by the TGAT Report itself. It will require time to develop, much more time than is likely to be made available for humanities in the inservice programmes that are being designed at present. Yet the goodwill is undoubtedly there, and a co-operative effort, developed collaboratively in concert with other parts of the national curriculum, may prove able to preserve the essence of an enabling approach to humanities within the requirements of the national curriculum. That is not certain to happen; but there is a good chance that it may.

References

ALEXANDER, R.J. (1984) *Primary Teaching*, London, Holt, Rinehart and Winston.

BLYTH, W.A.L. *et al.* (1976) *Place, Time and Society 8–13: Curriculum Planning in History, Geography and Social Science*, Glasgow and Bristol, Collins/ESL Bristol.

BLYTH, W.A.L. (1984) *Development, Experience and Curriculum in Primary Education*, London, Croom Helm.

BLYTH, W.A.L. (1987) 'Towards assessment in primary humanities', *Journal of Education Policy*, 2, 4, 353–360.

BLYTH, W.A.L. (1988) 'Appraising and assessing young children's understanding of industry' in SMITH, D. (ed.) *Industry in the Primary School Curriculum*, Lewes, Falmer Press.

BLYTH, W.A.L. (1989) *Making the Grade: Assessing Humanities in Primary Schools*, Milton Keynes, Open University Enterprises.

COOPER, K.R. (1976) *Evaluation, Assessment and Record Keeping in History, Geography and Social Science*, Glasgow and Bristol, Collins/ESL Bristol.

DEPARTMENT OF EDUCATION AND SCIENCE AND WELSH OFFICE (1988) *Science for Ages 5 to 16: Proposals of the Secretary of State for Education and Science and the Secretary of State for Wales*, London, DES.

DUNCAN, A. and DUNN, W. (1988) *What Primary Teachers Should Know about Assessment*, London, Hodder and Stoughton.

FURTH, H. (1980) *The World of Grown-ups*, New York, Elsevier.

GIPPS, C. and GOLDSTEIN, H. (1983) *Monitoring Children: an Evaluation of the Assessment of Performance Unit*, London, Heinemann Educational.

GUNNING, D., GUNNING, S. and WILSON, J. (1981) *Topic Teaching in the Primary School*, London, Croom Helm.

HARLEN, W. (1985) 'The question of content' in *Teaching and Learning Primary Science*, London, Harper and Row.

SHIPMAN, M. (1983) *Assessment in Primary and Middle Schools*, London, Croom Helm.

TASK GROUP ON ASSESSMENT AND TESTING (TGAT) (1988) *First Report*, London, DES and Welsh Office.

TOUGH, JOAN, (1979) *Talk for Teaching and Learning: Schools Council Communication Skills Project 7–13*, London, Ward Lock Educational.

WRAY, D. (1985) *Teaching Information Skills through Project Work*, London, Hodder and Stoughton.

Notes on Contributors

TOM ARKELL is a Senior Lecturer in Arts Education, University of Warwick. He edited the teaching pack *Irish Cultural Studies*, Trentham (1988) and is a member of the editorial board of *Local Population Studies*. His recent articles include 'The incidence of poverty in England in the later seventeenth century' (1987), 'History's role in the school curriculum' (1988) and 'Analyzing Victorian census data on computer' (1989).

ALAN BLYTH is Emeritus Professor of Education and Honorary Senior Fellow in the University of Liverpool. He has been extensively involved in the study of primary education and in primary teacher education, and is at present completing a study of assessment in primary humanities. He is author of *Development, Experience and Curriculum in Primary Education*, (1984), Croom Helm.

JIM CAMPBELL is Reader in Education, University of Warwick; he is author of *Developing the Primary School Curriculum*, Holt Rinehart and Winston (1985); *The Routledge Compendium of Primary Education*, Routledge (1988) and editor of the journal *Education 3–13*.

SARAH CAMPBELL is a primary school teacher and was the Mary Glasgow Teacher Fellow at Bath University.

DAVID HICKS is Director of the Global Futures Project at the Institute of Education, London University. From 1980–89 he was national Co-ordinator for the *World Studies 8–13* project. His publications include *World Studies 8–13: A Teacher's Handbook*, Oliver and Boyd (1985); *Education for Peace: Issues, Principles and Practice in the Classroom*, Routledge (1988); and *Making Global Connections: A World Studies Workbook*, Oliver and Boyd, (1989).

ROBERT JACKSON is Senior Lecturer in Arts Education, University of Warwick. He edited *Approaching World Religions*, John Murray (1982); he is co-author (with Dermot Killingley) of *Approaches to Hinduism*, John Murray (1988), author of *Religions through Festivals: Hinduism*, Longman (1989) and co-author (with Eleanor Nesbitt) of *Listening to Hindus*, Unwin

Hyman (1989). He is editor of the journal *Resource*.

VIVIENNE LITTLE is Lecturer in Education, University of Warwick. She is author of 'What is Imagination?' in *Teaching History*, No. 36, Autumn 1983, and with T. John, of *Historical Fiction in the Classroom* (1986) Historical Association. She is co-editor of the journal *Early Years*.

BILL MARSDEN is Reader in Education at the University of Liverpool. He is author of *Evaluation the Geography Curriculum*, Oliver and Boyd (1976); *Unequal Educational Provision in England and Wales: the Nineteenth-Century Roots*, The Woburn Press (1987); and *Educating the Respectable: a Study of Fleet Road Board School, Hampstead, 1879–1903*, The Woburn Press (in press)

SALLIE PURKISS is Senior Lecturer in History at Homerton College, Cambridge and co-editor of the journal *Teaching History*.

ALISTAIR ROSS is Principal Lecturer and Director of the Centre for Primary Schools and Industry at the Polytechnic of North London. He edited *Economic and Industrial Awareness in Primary Education* (1989) NCC, and is editor of the journal *Primary Teaching Studies*.

CAROLYN STEEDMAN is Senior Lecturer in Arts Education, University of Warwick, and also teaches on the MA in Interdisciplinary Women's Studies. She is author of *Landscape for a Good Woman*, Virago (1986), Rutgers University Press (1987), and *The Radical Soldier's Tale*, Routledge (1988). She is an editor of *History Workshop Journal*.

DAVID SYLVESTER is one of Her Majesty's Inspectors of Schools. Previously he was Director of the Schools Council History Project.

ANDRE WAGSTAFF is Primary Co-ordinator at the National Council for Educational Technology. He contributed towards *Emerging Issues in Primary Education*, Falmer Press, 1988.

Index